Assistance Benefits in Brazil

Marco Aurélio Serau Junior
José Ricardo Caetano Costa
Editors

Assistance Benefits in Brazil

Changes and Challenges to the Exercise of a Constitutional Right

Springer

Editors
Marco Aurélio Serau Junior
Tribunal Regional Federal, 3a. região
São Paulo, São Paulo, Brazil

José Ricardo Caetano Costa
Isquierdo e Costa Advogados Associados
Pelotas, Rio Grande do Sul, Brazil

ISBN 978-3-319-27044-9 ISBN 978-3-319-27046-3 (eBook)
DOI 10.1007/978-3-319-27046-3

Library of Congress Control Number: 2016931620

Springer Cham Heidelberg New York Dordrecht London

Printed on acid-free paper

Springer International Publishing AG Switzerland is part of Springer Science+Business Media (www.springer.com)

This book is dedicated to our families and all the people in the world who need social assistance. (Serau Jr. & Costa)

Foreword

Thanks to the initiative and the efficient organization of professors Marco Aurélio Serau Junior and José Ricardo Caetano Costa, the chapters collected here will fill a wide gap in the Brazilian legal literature.

On the one hand, there are many works dedicated to capital issues of social security—some of them inclusively authored by distinguished jurists and also present in this collection. On the other hand, it seems that the problems of social assistance for some reason do not give rise to the same concern.

Many factors can explain the negligence with which the jurists view social assistance. In my opinion, this attitude derives from the conceptual gap underlying the decision of the member of the constitutional convention to bring together, under the sole coverage of Social Security (in the broad sense), and Social Assistance and Social Security in the strict sense.

The binomial, under the doctrine that prevails in Western countries, conceptually includes a mutual exclusion. A typical Social Security system would neither include the creation of contributory benefits, nor their existence funded by the collection mechanisms established in the form of compulsory savings, which are typical elements of Social Security systems. According to the solution devised by the members of the Constitutional Convention in 1988, Social Security in the broad sense would not be a system covering contingencies universally and qualitatively different from Social Security in the strict sense, but otherwise, the result of Social Security in the strict sense and Social Assistance considered as a whole.

The solution provided in the wording of the 1988 Brazilian Constitution bucked the conceptual outlines and distinctions that were established in the twentieth Century based on the paradigmatic experiences of other countries. Until then, Social Security (or even social safety) meant a system that covered contingencies, or, more specifically, their social effects, which are indiscriminately extended to all people, whether they are taxpayers or not, who are in need. And, according to the summary of the *Beveridge Report*: a promotional and protective system aimed at the mitigation of needs. In turn, Social Security in the strict sense meant a system that covered the contingency effects, and resulted from the legal enforcement of contributions and benefits, based on the delimitation of the subjective group of beneficiaries according to their status as taxpayers or their dependents.

The purpose of the 1988 Brazilian Constitution was to establish a solution comprising a commitment between two social protection models, as provided for in the introduction of Section 194 of the Constitution, ended up producing, as one could clearly predict, a weakening of the rules on the coverage intended to non-taxpayers, that is: the poorest. Therefore, Social Security and Social Assistance have models that not only are different but also devoted to different groups of recipients.

Therefore, Social Assistance was reborn in 1988 as a kind of poor man's social protection,[1] but with a noble purpose because it brings together assistance rights provided with the status of fundamental rights.

Two decades after Act Number 8472/93 came into force, the ongoing discussions seem to properly reflect the enhancement of the Social Assistance *agenda*, at the interface between the public policies for social promotion and fundamental rights.

If, on the one hand, subjects such as the constitutional limits on the household compensation criterion for the objective measuring of the misery status have emerged, on the other hand, the reasonable effectiveness of promotional policies has given rise, in the axis of methodological concerns, to the problem of the "reversal strategies" in relation to beneficiaries of Social Assistance programs.

From a legal standpoint, particularly that of the fundamental rights, the chapters collected here, conceived based on different points of observation, provide for the major issues that emerged from the tensions between the regime of Act 8472/93 and the scope of the constitutional protection of the doctrines of Section 203 of the Constitution; particularly what is provided for in its paragraph "V".

Its organizers state in the introduction: "A work like this is doomed to incompleteness". However, I would say it a little differently: the incompleteness does not refer to the work but to the challenges of Social Assistance, which are quite enormous in a country like Brazil, marked by social exclusion and a sharp inequality in the distribution of wealth.

In this text, the reader will be able to see the findings of the research carried out by several scholars as well as their reflections, all of which are duly backed up by studies that deal with topics ranging from the major problems of the general theory of Social Security and Social Assistance to criminal projections of the administrative advocacy on assistance claims, as well as chapters on the granting conditions, procedural aspects, financing, and funding.

[1] Just after the promulgation of the 1988 Constitution, the disorders resulting from this unorthodox choice—a typical choice of those who neither want to opt nor support the political cost of the option—gradually gained increased visibility. I could notice factors that indicated this insight at the beginning of the debate generated by the discussion raised by the rural worker integration process in "Cenários e Perspectivas dos Direitos Sociais para o Campo—A Inserção do Trabalhador Rural naSeguridade", *in* Os Direitos Sociais e a Constituição de 1988, Rio de Janeiro: Forense, 1993; pp. 69–130. I also noticed that many of these disorders would later be the background for the discussions in the STF at ADI 1232-1/DF about the constitutionality of Section 20, 3rd Paragraph of Act No. 8742/93.

The timeliness and depth of this material, written with elegance and clarity and strengthened by the authors' renowned practical experience with the Social Security agenda, allows us to conclude that this is a must-read book for all stakeholders of the Social Assistance field, i.e., its managers and servers, lawyers, members of the public prosecutors, judges, and university professors.

Reading of this textbook is also recommended for those who, either as researchers or as citizens, are interested in current Social Assistance issues, which are reviewed not only from the standpoint of the Social Security law, but also from that in which Social Security and Social Assistance show the magnitude of the fundamental rights.

Antonio Rodrigues de Freitas Jr.
Associate Professor, Labour Law and Social Security Department
USP School of Law, Largo de São Francisco,
São Paulo, Brazil
Winter 2015

Preface

In the area of social protection, welfare policies are those that are mostly perceived as founded on an authentic human rights.

They consist of non-contributory actions and benefits, welfare rights carry the stigma of being considered minor rights when compared with other Social Security rights, and even weaker when compared with human and fundamental rights of the first dimension (rights of freedom, such as freedom of expression or the right to property).

Two steps are important to show the recognition, protection, and realization of welfare rights.

The first step is the recognition of its rules imposing constitutional dignity.

The right to Social Assistance is enshrined constitutionally, and in 1988, the Constitution shaped Social Security as our model of social protection. If managed-evolve, in terms of social protection, relative to the model of social security prevailing until then.

The Social Security model expressed political thought that social protection should be given based on the merit of each individual. From this perspective, it would be fair to offer social protection only to those who cooperate with social development and contribute to a common fund in the event of certain eventualities. For this reason, people protected by this social protection system were fundamentally formal workers and their families.

The adoption of such a social protection technique did not stop, it recognized the use of either welfare policy protection to poor people, but were not understood as a enforceable right by its recipients. Previously, they could be discerned as a result of favorable socioeconomic contingencies that made possible the provision of minimum benefits for the qualification and social integration of those excluded from social, cultural, and economic participation. They met such benefits, as if in a broad scope of discretion of the political agents, corresponding to a boon, a favor almost undeserved, a more or less arbitrary gift.

Perhaps it can be stated that the care activities found themselves rooted less in solidarity, and more in compassion and benevolence. This is because the so-called Bismarckian model was founded on a weak notion of solidarity as simply organizing the payment of premiums by employees for a certain period of time so that they were guaranteed the right to a benefit upon the occurrence of protected social risks. He played with the aversion to risk.

These individuals merit consideration, found at the base of solidarity (weak) social insurance, not taking into account, however, their differences of race, gender, social class, or even the ability to work or their environmental factors.

The 1988 Constitution has merit in breaking with this security-logic that, by offering coverage only to those who, starting, presented themselves in a position to enter the labor market and contribute to the formation of the common fund (reduced field protection), had very low potential for redistribution of income and wealth and social inclusion.

It is precisely from the Constitution that the right to Social Assistance manages to achieve fundamental constitutional dignity, as repeatedly recognized by the Supreme Court. The fundamental nature of the right to Social Assistance now binds all state activity, which is not given, therefore not offering sufficient protection (Rcl 4374, Rel. Min. Gilmar Mendes, Full Court, j. 04.18.2013, DJE 04/09/2013).

However, there is a second important step toward the realization of this fundamental social right. It is the understanding that, while the right to social protection and, in particular, protection of human life against social contingencies that challenge a person's dignified existence, has two authentic assumptions of effectiveness.

On the one hand, one must understand that the welfare policy has important preventive aspects. As includes the right to health, welfare objective focuses on the idea of preventing the harmful effects of social exclusion. One should not expect that the person or family group, step by step, day by day, migrate from the periphery to a state of absolute absence of conditions for social participation. In other words, one should not condition the welfare protection of evidence that has finally installed the economic need of the family group.[1] Precisely in view of the preventive dimension of Social Assistance and the trend of vulnerable people have also decreased their production and high capacity spectrum of needs—as is the case in the elderly, for example—protection must be given before a state of human degradation. This corresponds to the essence of the idea of protection: to prevent the occurrence of damage as much as possible; mitigate its effects to the fullest as much as possible, as if they had never existed.

On the other hand, the welfare policy has material equality as a real constitutive element. The goal of Social Assistance, while social policy, is to eradicate poverty, reduce social inequalities, provide conditions so that the individual has ensured their physical existence and, moreover, gather resources to develop their personality and to participate socially. Improving the socioeconomic condition is inherent to welfare policy. The purpose is not only to provide its recipients to conserve the state

[1] And here the term "economic need" is purposely invoked to contrast with the notion that it is not confused with and is much more restrictive, namely, the "misery". Indeed, the constitutional guideline is to care protection to the needy (Constitution, article 203). This means that one should not require proof of misery for the granting of this social protection.

of affairs, maintaining poverty, perpetuating the state of semi-exclusion or the provision of necessary resources exclusively to their food. Being a selective policy, its potential redistribution of wealth and income cannot be underestimated.

These assumptions for understanding Social Assistance are just a few among the many issues that deserve to be reflected on seriously by the legal community.

In this context, it is unnecessary to express the importance of the collective effort undertaken by important arbiters of political and legal assistance issues.

It is a heavy undertaking and it was written by lawyers, who, with contributions from individuals with different perspectives, were guided by the compenetration for the need to make effective the fundamental constitutional objective of "social justice" and the amalgam which for much time represented the estimated Teachers Marco Aurélio Serau Junior and José Ricardo Caetano Costa, his coordinators.

José Antonio Savaris
Federal Judge
Author of many books of social security
University of Sao Paulo
Sao Paulo, Brazil

Contents

Contributors

Editors

Marco Aurelio Serau Junior Master's Degree and Doctor in Human Rights (USP). Specialist in Constitutional Rights (ESDC) and in Human Rights (USP). University Professor and Professor in several graduate programs. Author of several legal papers published in Brazil and abroad, and author of the following works, among others: *Curso de Processo Judicial Previdenciário*; *Recursos Especiais Repetitivos no STJ*; *Seguridade Social como direito fundamental material* and *Economia e Seguridade Social—análise econômica do Direito*: *Seguridade Social.*

José Ricardo Caetano Costa Master's Degree in Social Development (UCPel). Master's Degree in Public Law (UNISINOS), and Doctor in Social Service (PUCRS). Post-doctorate in Environmental Education (PPGEA/FURG). Coordinator and Researcher of the *Centro de Estudos e Pesquisas em Seguridade Social*—CEPESS. Researcher of the CEJE—*Centro de Estudos Jurídico-Econômicos* (FURG). Member of the Social Security Committee of OAB/RS. Professor of Social Security Law (FADIR/FURG) and Invited Professor of the Master in Law and Social Justice Program (FADIR/FURG). Social Security Lawyer.

Authors

Alexandre Schumacher Triches Master in Social Security Law at Pontifical Catholic University of São Paulo—PUC-SP. Post Graduate in Public Law at Pontifical Catholic University of Rio Grande do Sul—PUC-RS. Lawyer, researcher and teacher. Author of works in the Social Security Law.

Ana Maria Correa Isquierdo Holds a graduate degree in Family and Successions Law (ULBRA/RS), a graduate degree in Labor and Social Security Law (FACULDADES ATLÂNTICO SUL/PELOTAS), Social Security Lawyer.

Bruno Takahashi Master of Laws (University of Sao Paulo). Federal Judge.

Camila Bibiana Freitas Baraldi Master in Law in the area of International Relations at the Federal University of Santa Catarina (PPGD/UFSC), and PhD at the Institute of International Relations at the University of São Paulo (IRI/USP).

Fabio Luiz dos Passos Master of Legal Science; Master in environmental law and sustainability. Expert in labor law and social security specialist in Civil Procedure. General Secretary of the Brazilian Institute of Social Security Law (2012–2014). Professor of social security law. Lawyer.

Flávio Roberto Batista Professor at the Department of Labor and Social Security Law of the University of São Paulo.

José Carlos Francisco Professor of School of Law of University Mackenzie/SP, Director of Centro de Estudos da Associação dos Juízes Federais de São Paulo e Mato Grosso do Sul—AJUFESP (Center of Studies of the Association of Federal Judges of São Paulo and Mato Grosso do Sul), Director of Instituto Brasileiro de Estudos Constitucionais—IBEC (Brazilian Institute of Constitutional Studies), Masters and Doctor in Constitutional Law at University of São Paulo—USP, Postdoctor at Université de Paris 1 (Panthéon-Sorbonne), and Federal Judge of the 3rd Region.

Karina Carla Lopes Garcia State Attorney. Teacher. Author of many articles in Federal Procedure Law.

Miguel Horvath Júnior Federal Attorney, Professor *of the Stricto* Sensu Post-Graduation Program at PUC/SP. Author of Social Security Law (Direito Previdenciário). Ed. Quartier Latin 10 ed. 2014 among others.

Sérgio Henrique Salvador Specialist in Social Security Law by EPD/SP and Civil Procedure at PUC/SP. Ex-President of the Social Security Affairs Commission of the 23rd Subsection of the OAB/MG. Professor in IBEP/SP and of the Law Course at FEPI—Centro Universitário de Itajubá. Writer. Partner, Law Office specializing in Labor & Social Security Law. Writer. Lawyer in Minas Gerais.

Silvio Marques Garcia State Attorney. Master in Social Security Law at UNESP (University of State of Sao Paulo). Teacher and author of papers.

Táli Pires de Almeida Master in Latin American Integration at the University of São Paulo (PROLAM/USP).

Tatiana Chang Waldman Master and PhD student in the area of Human Rights at the Law School of the University of São Paulo (FD/USP).

Theodoro Vicente Agostinho Master in Social Security Law at PUC/SP. Specialist in Social Security Law by EPD/SP. Member of the Social Security Commission of the OAB/SP. Coordinator and Professor of the Graduate Program in Social Security Law at Complexo Jurídico Damásio de Jesus. Writer. Professor IBEP/SP. Lawyer in São Paulo.

Wagner Balera Lawyer. Master, PhD and Associate Professor at the Catholic University of Sao Paulo. Professor of Human Rights at the Catholic University of Sao Paulo. Coordinator of the Chair "Sergio Vieira de Mello"—International law on refugees (Convention of the Pontifical Catholic University of São Paulo with the United Nations High Commissioner for Refugees—UNHCR). Coordinator of the Journal of Human Rights. Member of the Editorial Board of *Revista Forense*, and "*Revista da Previdência Social*".

Chapter 1
An Introduction to Brazil's Social Security System

Marco Aurélio Serau Junior and José Ricardo Caetano Costa

Abstract Brazil's Social Security System, as shaped by the Federal Constitution, is a complex public policy of social protection. As stipulated in article 194 of the Federal Constitution, the Social Security System is an integrated set of actions initiated by public authorities and society to ensure the rights to health, social assistance (both non-contributory benefits), and social security in the strictest sense (contributory benefits). This chapter explains the three structural elements or parts of Brazil's Social Security System, the principles, and the most important characteristics of each subsystem. The chapter also details some options of the legal terms used in this translation, demonstrating that there is no precise correspondence, because the Brazilian legal system is unique in its social protection scheme.

Keywords Social security • Constitutional structure • Social assistance • Principles

1.1 Constitutional Structure of Brazil's Social Security System

Brazil's Social Security System, as shaped by the Federal Constitution, is a complex public policy of social protection. In the constitutional architecture, as stipulated in article 194 of the Federal Constitution, the Social Security System is an integrated set of actions initiated by public authorities and society to ensure the rights to health, social assistance, and social security in the strictest sense (contributory benefits). Therefore, the Social Security System is comprised of three subsystems: Health, Social Assistance, and Social Security in the strictest sense, with three structural elements or parts.

M.A. Serau Junior (✉)
Tribunal Regional Federal, 3a. região, São Paulo, São Paulo, Brazil
e-mail: maseraujunior@hotmail.com

J.R. Caetano Costa
Isquierdo e Costa Advogados Associados, Pelotas, Rio Grande do Sul, Brazil
e-mail: jrcc.pel@gmail.com

M.A. Serau Junior, J.R. Caetano Costa (eds.), *Assistance Benefits in Brazil*,
DOI 10.1007/978-3-319-27046-3_1

The subsystem of Health, provided in articles 196–200 (Federal Constitution), regarding the enforcement of the fundamental right to health, connected to its good physical and psychological conditions. It is the right of all, and the duty of the state, also providing its provision to the private sector.

Unlike Social Security, Social Assistance provides benefits and services regardless of the contributions of citizens/beneficiaries.

Social Assistance, referred to in articles 203 and 204 (Federal Constitution), provides its provision by the State and also to the private sector, is a set of actions whose objectives are (article 203):

> I - the protection of the family, maternity, childhood, adolescence and old age;
> II - the protection of poor children and teenagers;
> III - to promote integration into the labor market;
> IV - the professional qualification and rehabilitation of persons with disabilities and promoting their integration into community life;
> V - ensuring a minimum wage of monthly benefit to the handicapped and the elderly who prove to not have means to provide for their own support or by having it provided by family, under the law.

The benefit provided in article 203, V, of the Federal Constitution is the topic for several chapters in this book.

Social Security, in the global sense, obeys seven principles contained in article 194 of the Federal Constitution:

- **Universality of protection and attendance:** It is a consequence of being a citizen: anyone, in abstract, is excluded to the right of social protection, and no event is excluded, *a priori*, of the possibility to generate social protection. Obviously, it is impossible to generate social protection to all situations in a society. Therefore, this principle is softened by other principles.
- **Equality and equivalence to the benefits destined to the urban and rural population:** Until a few years ago, Brazil was a rural country. For a long time, rural workers were excluded from social protection. This principle seeks to correct this historic distortion, ensuring equal legal treatment between the urban and rural populations. It happens because every benefit attributed to the urban population should also be applied to the rural population. The principle also states that to observe the harsh realities of life and work in the countryside (informality and precariousness). To grant social benefits, rural workers do not need to contribute directly to the system, having just to prove its right to retirement.
- **Selectivity and distribution for the provision of benefits and services:** budgetary impossibility to address all social contingencies determines the adoption of the criterion of *selectivity* by choosing the topics and hypotheses that will be covered by Social Security. It is not a random choice, but through the additional *distributivity* criterion, i.e., one chooses the events through which it reaches the larger and more effective number of people/social situations.
- **Benefit amount of irreducibility:** the principle guarantees the irreducibility value of the benefits provided by Social Security. As the Supreme Court, the constitutional guarantee comes down to the nominal value by applying adjustment indices provided by law; it is not the maintenance of the benefits of purchasing power.

- **Equity in the form of participation in funding:** financing contributions to Social Security are the responsibility of society as a whole (article 195, Federal Constitution). However, it shall be established as the economic capacity for each group: individuals or legal entities; workers or employers; rural workers (informal work) or urban workers (formal work).
- **Diversity in the funding base:** Social Security was created by Otto von Bismarck in 1889 in Germany, seeking to deal with conflicts between employers and employees. Initially, the entire cost of pensions was coming from contributions levied on wages paid by employers and employees. Therefore, rising costs of this public policy required the increase of the resources allocated for its operation. Thus, this principle states that other sources of funding should be sought, not only related to payroll (i.e., lotteries taxes or profit and revenues of legal entities).
- **Democratic and decentralized character of the administration of Social Security:** because of republican and democratic principles, modern administrative actions require citizen participation, controlling, supervising, and legitimizing their conduct. This principle requires the administration of Social Security in the Councils and organs of administrative decision, claiming the participation of workers, employers, retirees, and the government.

1.2 Social Security System in the Strictest Sense

The Social Security System in the strictest sense ("*Previdência Social*") also integrates the Social Security System in a global sense. It is a contributory public policy: the benefits are conditioned on the participation of citizens who must make contributions to the system.

The government seeks to ensure, through the payment of monthly cash benefits, the following events: death, old age, disabling condition, disease, maternity, involuntary unemployment, as well as others.

From the Federal Constitution of 1988, pension rights were sedimented, ceasing inequality between rural and urban workers, guaranteeing not to lower benefits to the minimum wage and the annual adjustment of expected benefits, preserving the purchasing power, among other rights.

The Social Security *in strict sense*, in turn, is divided into three subsectors:

- *General System of Social Security in strict sense* ("Regime Geral de Previdência Social—RGPS"): designated to the most citizens who do not work for the government or those who voluntarily contribute to Social Security or public employees who do not have *RPPS* (article 201, Federal Constitution).
- *Specific systems of Social Security in strict sense* ("Regimes Próprios de Previdência Social—RPPS"): designated to public employees by paying contributions (article 40, Federal Constitution);
- *Supplementary Pension* or *Pension funds*: guarantee a higher income to the insured than the maximum ceiling provided for the value of Social Security benefits (article 40, Federal Constitution; Lei Complementar n° 108 and 109, both of 2001).

Finally, there is a specific retirement scheme for the military, according to article 142, X, of the Federal Constitution, regulated by specific legislation and endowed with well-diversified characteristics of the rules applicable to civil employees (lower career time and differentiation of the amounts paid).

1.3 Social Assistance

Social Assistance in Brazil has always been linked to a conception of charity and assistance rather than a fundamental right, but as a legacy of the European "Poor Laws." The birthplace of aid to the poor in Brazil was first linked historically with religious philanthropy and public institutions with private management, such as the LBA—Brazilian Legion of Assistance.

Until 1920, the Brazilian State did not intervene in labor relations and did not propitiate social rights such as pension or welfare rights. However, from 1930, with President Getulio Vargas, the state conflicted with the liberal oligarchy, pointing out new perspectives (Mendonça 2009). The inverse of the *marshallian perspective*,[1] the granting of the social rights, in Brazil, it led to political rights, in a process known as "regulated citizenship" and was supervised by the state.

There was some progress in terms of promotion of social rights to the Organic Law of Social Welfare (Law 3807 of 1960) through the unification of six of them, then Retirement Institutes existed for certain occupational groups (such as rail and commerce), but continued to exclude agricultural workers, domestic workers, and unregistered workers (Costa 2010).

Social Security rights were granted to workers formally recognized professionally. But, for the other workers (not formally professionally recognized), the condition was different: "to those excluded from the process, was reserved only space of philanthropy and charity to help them survive the misery" (Mendonça 2009).

Social Assistance, however, had another turn after the promulgation of the Constitution of 1988 long clash result of social forces that conceived. Social Security and Health and Social Security now understood as a fundamental right (Serau Jr 2011).

It is therefore a significant step toward designing social welfare rights as rights that citizens even devoid of the social minimum have the prerogative to have a specific minimum wage, guaranteeing them a modicum of dignity.

In this sense, the first article of the *Organic Social Assistance Law* (Law 8742 of 1993) summarizes how the institution of Social Welfare in Brazil should be understood: "Social assistance, citizen's right and duty of the state is social security policy non-contributory, which provides the minimum social, accomplished through an integrated set of public and private initiative actions, to ensure the meeting of basic needs".

[1] Regarding T.S. Marshall, author of "Citizenship status and social class".

Since 2004, the National Plan for Social Assistance (PNAS), the Unified Social Assistance System (SUAS; from the Portuguese expression: "Sistema Único de Assistência Social") was established, through which the programs, services, projects and benefits now focus attention on families and their respective needs. SUAS establishes a form of shared management, with the co-financing of the welfare policy of all levels of government (Federal, State and Municipal), for purposes of the consecration of citizenship rights and social inclusion (PNAS 2004).

The assistance benefit provided in article 203, section V, of the Federal Constitution of 1988 must be understood in this context. The contributions that follow in this book are important to point out its main challenges and controversies.

1.4 Notes on This Translation

This book was originally published in Brazil, under the title "*Benefício Assistencial (Lei 8.472/93)—Temas Polêmicos*". This version is an adaptation on that particular work.

There is no perfect translation into English for the benefits stipulated in article 203, V, of the Federal Constitution, which is the basis and subject of this book. The same benefits do not exist in others social security systems, particularly in English-speaking countries.

Therefore, in this book you can see many translations used in reference to this benefit. The Brazilian authorities and the World Bank prefer the expression "Continuous Payment Benefit" or the abbreviation CPB—moreover, next expression that used in Portuguese: "BPC" or "Benefício de Prestação Continuada." However, in this book the contributors use others expressions, all valid, such as "Welfare Benefits" or "Social Assistance benefits," among others.

References

Costa JRC (2010) Previdência: os direitos sociais previdenciários no cenário neoliberal. Juruá, Curitiba

Mendonça, AMÁ (2009) Estado e Direitos Sociais no Brasil: entre a modernidade e o retrocesso. Editora da UFAL, Maceió

Serau Jr MA (2011) Seguridade social como direito fundamental material, 2ª edição. Juruá, Curitiba

Part I
General Theory

Chapter 2
The Social Limbo Protection Between Support and Security

Fabio Luiz dos Passos

Abstract It is possible to realize the existence of a social protection gap between the catchment areas of social security and social assistance; a 'limbo' in which the citizen is unaided by the State, and an interpretation of the scope of detached welfare of economic and social realities experienced by (and in the) Brazilian State in this early twenty-first century, and yet grounded in the restrictive legal interpretation and limited state capacity characteristic of protection from the beginning of the 1990s. Social inequality is a key factor in maintaining poverty levels and legitimizes the adoption of socially exclusionary practices that gets benefits from the social exclusion reality in order to further aggravate the very social inequality as to conform the excluded population a mindset that allows the distinction of society into privileged and excluded groups. This intuitive understanding is reflected in the interpretation of public policies for social protection restricting the scope of social security and justifying a restrictive interpretation of the Constitution as well as the perpetuation of outdated understanding of an opposition between security and legitimizing assistance and enabling as acceptable a consistent social protection limited to integrated workers into the formal productive system, partially complemented by social assistance.

Keywords Social security • Social assistance • Post-industrial society • Social exclusion • Inequality • Poverty

2.1 Introduction

As the wording of the Article 194 of the Federal Constitution of Brazil, the social security comprises an integrated set of initiative actions by the Public Authorities and society, aimed at ensuring the rights to health, social security, and social support.

F.L. dos Passos (✉)
Diretor adjunto de assuntos internacionais do Instituto Brasileiro de Direito Previdenciário, Chapecó, Santa Catarina, Brazil
e-mail: fabiodospassos@passosadvocacia.com.br

M.A. Serau Junior, J.R. Caetano Costa (eds.), *Assistance Benefits in Brazil*,
DOI 10.1007/978-3-319-27046-3_2

The idea of integrating the three areas of activity that compose social security is still relatively new in Brazil, since it was inaugurated with the Federal Constitution of 1988 and, although there have been more than 25 years since then, it is not easily assimilated and understood, either from the government or by the judiciary.

Although the idea of social security is founded on the model created in the 1940s by W. Beveridge, it is still interpreted from the Bismarckian segmented protection perspective, class, and exclusive characteristic of the early industrial era.

Thus, perceiving the existence of a social protection gap between the coverage areas of social security and social support is not difficult; a "limbo" in which the citizen is unassisted by the State as the individual is not formally integrated in the social security to social security benefits, the citizens are still conceived and interpreted under a Bismarckian bias, and are not presented in misery condition that results in this same classic interpretation, the need for assistance protection.

Moreover, there can often be seen, especially in the judicial action, an interpretation of the scope of social support which is detached from the economic and social realities experienced by (and in the) Brazilian State in these early days of the century, and yet grounded in strict legal interpretation and in the limited protection capacity of the state, characteristic of the early 1990s, resulting in an application of social law in contradiction with the fundamental constitutional provisions.

With regard to social support, Boschetti (2003) reports that

> (…) this social policy has faced much resistance to be legally recognized as a right and continues to suffer enormous resistance in its implementation as such because it is a *policy in constant conflict with the forms of social organization of labor.*

To this is added the paternalistic view and electoral interests on social support from politicians as well as the difficulty of assimilation by the very needy citizen of social protection as a right of citizenship.

2.2 The Evolution of the Concepts of Poverty and Social Exclusion

In the period preceding the Industrial Age, poverty was recognized as a natural fact, something inherent in life that just occurred, such as droughts and bad harvests (Giddens 1996), there being no possibility of prediction or correction since it came from the divine will or fate.

Thus, harmful occurrences to the individual, in their physical or social condition, represented the negative aspect of fate, bad luck or literally "dis-grace," and the linking of human luck to the divine plan would justify the understanding of poverty "as something necessary, or even a benefit to people in need whereas it would be the effective guarantee of admission into the Kingdom of God, given the extreme grace and detachment to material goods"(Ibrahim 2011), or, as a representation of divine punishment.

From these concepts, the aid to the poor did not consist as a criterion of social justice, but as charity, a conduct dictated by moral, reflecting the generosity of wealthy individuals (Ibrahim 2011).

In the early sixteenth century, there were propositions which tended to minimize poverty in the interests of society, but still on the basis of Judeo-Christian obligation to provide charity, as shown by the detailed plan of minimum income to needy populations established in 1526, by Professor Johannes Ludovicus Vives, in Louvain, France, called *De Subventione Pauperum,* where the legitimacy of providing assistance to the poor by the government is shown, from:

> alms given voluntarily. However, it would be much more effective than private assistance, for being better distributed - only between those in need (Vanderborght and Van Parij 2006).

From the late seventeenth century, since the dawn of the Industrial Age, the vision on poverty has turned towards the development of national wealth. Poverty was no longer recognized as a natural condition nor limited to the lack of resources, as poor were those who could not or would not work. According to Giddens (1996):

> the pauperism linking with the lack of moral education was very clear: 'work for those who struggle, punishment for those who do not, and bread for those who cannot'. In turn, the moral resolution related directly to social welfare; because [...] poverty 'makes men tumultuous restless', and fighting it is 'an act of civil prudence and political wisdom'.

In this context, the concept of poverty was clearly related to the growing industry needs, "the aid to the needy is not seen as mere virtue, becoming basis of society" (Ibrahim 2011).

The idea of poverty started to be linked to the income sufficiency for the provision of basic needs of subsistence, and strictly evaluated in monetary terms, which led to the development of several tools of social protection from the late nineteenth century, in order to prevent men from "continually find themselves grappling with the horrors of misery" (Leão XIII 1891).

However, one of the difficulties found when "poverty is defined briefly as a sharp restriction on welfare, and, as a rule, meaning in monetary terms" is to establish objective criteria to define it and thus enable effective action to combat it. "The traditional solution is creating *poverty lines,* which, once exceeded, qualify as poor those with income and/or expenditure below a certain frontier" (Ibrahim 2011) which are defined arbitrarily and often are related to the idea of the *minimum existential.*[1]

Rosanvallon (1984), showing another current interpretation says that poverty "cannot be defined simply by an income criterion. The insulation, the place to live (city or countryside) may increase the effects of income." Therefore, poverty can also be recognized for "certain sectors, such as poor health, Social Security, etc., but not forgetting that the broader wellness view reflects the possibility of joining the individual life in society" (Ibrahim 2011), suggests the idea of social vulnerability that is characterized by the possibility of the individual with borderline income regress on its financial and/or social condition, exceeding the poverty line at a future time.[2]

---

[1] According to Bauman (2013), usually appointed overall, as below $2 a day, which is equivalent to the average European subsidy per cow.

[2] As records Associação Internacional De Seguridade Social (2008): "*Aunque no todos aquellos que trabajan en la economía informal son trabajadores pobres, el número total de trabajadores*

Rousseau (1753) when drawing up the discourse on the origin of inequality among men has said that "it is clearly against the law of nature in any way to define, [...] that a handful of people swim the superfluous, while the starving multitude lacks the necessary". However, recognizing the origin of these inequalities in society itself states that

> inequality, being almost null in the state of nature, draws its strength and its growth in the development of our faculties and progress of the human spirit, becoming finally stable and legitimate by the establishment of property and laws.

In this sense, Ibrahim (2011) shows that the evolution of social demands can lead the individual poverty, stating that

> the need for better competitiveness in the global market requires not only lean and functional structures, but also increasingly educated labor, which generates an increase in unemployment, which, in turn, demands greater spending on Social Protection System, creating a real trap of poverty.

From this conception, poverty and inequality are consequences of social settings and legitimized by society, as exemplified by Bauman (2013), to inform that

> Tanzania produces an annual income of US $ 2.2 billion, which divides among its 25 million inhabitants. The Goldman Sachs Bank earns $ 2.6 billion a year, divided among 161 shareholders.
>
> Europe and The United States spend U$ 17 billion a year on pet food, while, according to experts, only U$ 19 billion would be needed to save the hunger of the entire world population.

The consequence of the unequal distribution of resources and opportunities among people and social groups, or even among countries, drives harmful effects to individuals unprovided of these possibilities, resulting in an "exclusion chain reaction" reaching the individual capacity of reaction. In this sense, Muller (2000) states that

> the economic depletion is linked especially to devastating disadvantages of personality formation and vocational training, culture, the level of information, the sense of justice and self-esteem. It is worth adding that the weakening of the sense of self-esteem and lack of "recognition" leads to the paralysis of the affected people as political beings: the excessively low standard of living, to the impoverishment of the family, the stigma of the wrong residential neighborhood, the bank account closure noticing by the bank's management, the growing social and cultural and political exclusion, the worsening of the lack of chances in life. The economic decline leads quickly to the socio-cultural depravity and political apathy - which almost always fits well the designs of the dominant spheres of society.

With a view to this new social conformation, which brings distribution risks that do not observe the standards of industrial society, Sen (2010) records that "there are good reasons to see poverty as a deprivation of basic capabilities, not just as low income." According to the Indian professor, Nobel Prize in economics,

> Deprivation of elementary capabilities can be reflected in premature death, significant undernourishment (especially of children), persistent morbidity, widespread illiteracy and other disabilities. [...] The change of perspective is important because it gives us a different view - and more directly relevant - of poverty, not only *in developing* countries but also in the more *affluent* societies.

---

pobres (aquellos que ganan menos de US$2 al día) en el mundo ha aumentado hasta alcanzar los 1370 millones."

This conception of poverty proposed by Amartya Sen is significantly important to address the social problems that are raised in the new social conformation called post-industrial society, in which the distribution of social and individual risk occurs very differently from the one that was experienced in the Industrial Age.

Bauman (2013) also demonstrates the necessity to overcome the poverty identification from the simple assessment of income, stating that

> 'The end of the national class society' [...] does not herald the 'end of social inequality'. We need now to extend the issue of inequality beyond the mistakenly limited area of per capita income; it must extend to the fatal and mutual attraction between poverty and social vulnerability, corruption, accumulation of dangers, as well as humiliation and denial of dignity; that is to say, until the factors that shape attitudes and behavior and that are responsible for the integration [...] of groups, factors that quickly grow in volume and importance in the global information age.

In this understanding line, the International Social Security Association recognizes social exclusion as "the process by which individuals lose their ability to participate fully in all aspects of society in which they live and therefore are exposed to a higher risk of poverty" (ISSA 2010).

In order to minimize these effects of social exclusion by improving the social protection programs and adjust them to the new reality of the market, new public policies are being adopted by many countries, especially those who are not in the group of developed countries, where social protection seems to have reached its peak from the traditional model.

2.3 The Concept of Poverty and the Reach of the Social Support

Boschetti (2003) questions what are the attributes and functions for social support in its conformation as a social right in a society where "the social order is based on the primacy of work," thus underlining the perpetuation of an interpretation of the social relations and the state's role still from the perspective of industrial society or, more specifically, the salaried society. The author clarifies that

> (...) The legal recognition of social care as a right revivals and maintains a distinction between support and work, between being able and unable that structures the social organization secularly. The liberal rule of work or more precisely, the salaried labor, materialized in history the principle that the man should keep himself and his family with his work gains, or by selling his workforce. This principle is so preserved that the prospect and/or initiative of individuals support through welfare policies, whether those of cash transfer (usually called minimum income programs) or actions of other kinds, are deeply permeated by tense theoretical debates, conflicting and, as could not be otherwise, driven by political and ideological antagonistic perspectives. While the Liberals 'accept' minimum welfare policies aimed at those who are "unfit to work' and recognize that cash transfer programs can ensure the free hand labor supply in the market, authors with social perspective advocate the establishment of large income transfer programs in order to protect the excluded workforce from the production process."

Thus, work and support live a historical and contradictory relationship of tension and attraction, even when being recognized as social rights. According to Boschetti (2003) the tense situation occurs:

> (…) Because those who have the duty to work, even when they cannot work, they need assistance but are not entitled to it. In this way, the work impedes social support. And attraction because the absence of one of them propels the individual to the next, even if he/she cannot, should not, or does not have the right.

This situation is dramatically excluding, especially in a reality in which "the right to support is limited and restrictive" (Boschetti 2003) and although the work is recognized as a right, it is not guaranteed for all. This reality is even more devastating when evidences show that the formal economy sometimes benefit from this exclusion.

It is not hard to see that this clear distinction between social support and social security (social protection eminently intended to those who are included in the labor market), typical of a Bismarckian reading of social protection, is no longer sustainable nor efficient in today's society, either because their basic elements and distinctive features are gradually disappearing or confused, or because this absolute duality is not efficient in the postmodern industrial society.

On the first point, Boschetti (2003) states, from the study of Dufourcq, that

> (…) Social security based on the logic of insurance is nothing but a myth, as: the financing of policies that make up the social security is often less based on direct contributions from employees and employers and increasingly incorporating derived sources of the fiscal budget; social rights are increasingly based on the logic of citizenship and less in contributory; the amount of benefits is increasingly defined in terms of family income and social needs, and less on the payment made; management models are increasingly being nationalized and under the control of the legislative and executive powers and less under the autonomous control of workers and employers.

On the second point, it emphasizes the distinction between the Beveridge's concept of social security, which originated the trend adopted by the Brazilian Constitution in 1988, which aims at protecting citizens from poverty, the Bismarckian design, which aims at supporting the unable employee to provide their livelihood from work (wage, industrial, male). In addition to treating of diametrically opposed views, the second (Bismarckian) does not keep the line with the constitutional principles assumed by Brazil in 1988, because it does not have the power to alleviate poverty and reduce the conditions of social inequality. Conversely, if applied strictly, it can aggravate these situations because it does not include other dimensions of the concepts of poverty and social inequality, beyond the scope of monetary limits.

2.4 The Restrictive (and Outdated) Distinction between Support and Welfare

In the same line of understanding adopted by Amartya Sen, as pointed out above, Boschetti (2003) states that "*poverty and inequality, although closely related, do not express similar situations*" translating misinterpretation commonly given by the

Public Administration and the Judiciary Power to the constitutional right to social support, from a restrictive reading, explaining that

> poverty is commonly qualified and reduced to the absence or insufficient income to meet social minimum necessary for survival. This is a simplistic and reductionist definition in two respects: 1) reducing poverty to the absence or insufficient income, not considering other necessary aspects for the reproduction of human life; 2) lists the standard of poverty to the minimum necessary to survival. This minimalist design aims at, for example, the establishment of 'poverty lines', which is absolutely disgraceful, it is also aimed at a practice of poverty classification, as occurs with the per capita income of a quarter of the minimum wage established in LOAS (Organic Law of Social Support). (Boschetti 2003)

Social inequality is a key factor in maintaining the levels of poverty and legitimizes the adoption of socially exclusionary practices, as well as getting significant benefits from the social exclusion reality in a clear vicious circle that tends to increasingly aggravate the reality of the social inequality as to conform the excluded population a mindset that allows the distinction of society into privileged groups and excluded groups.

Again quoting Boschetti (2003) there has been found that

> There are countries considered 'poor' that do not have high levels of inequality among the population. Conversely, there are countries seen as 'rich' that maintain and exacerbate economic and social inequalities between classes and social groups. On the other hand, the improvement of poverty does not mean, necessarily and automatically, in reducing inequalities. (…)
>
> The existence and persistence of poverty is linked (not only, but decisively) to the distribution of socially produced wealth. Thus, there are two groups of countries where the absolute poverty is predominant: first, the population is poor because the national income, divided among its population, is not capable of ensuring the minimum essential to citizens, even if it were distributed in an equitable way. In the second group, national wealth is high enough to ensure basic living conditions for all citizens, but the distribution of this wealth is so unevenly that situations of poverty live and persist as well as economic and social inequalities.
>
> Brazil certainly is included in the second group, as its gross domestic product (…) places it among the 11 richest countries in the world, but has one of the worst income distributions.

Correa (2013) reports that "inequality was naturalized in Brazil, because a third of the population is prevented from accessing basic rights, a situation that relegates this stratum of society the condition of sub-citizens."

While in the historical process of social struggles and right achievements experienced in Europe enabled the moral understanding on the universal principle of equality between individuals, the absence of this record and the personal element in the Brazilian society would justify the presence of linked injustices to the very notion of dignity. Correa (2013) reports that

> (…) In central societies this process would have ensured the formation of a primary *habitus*, which is characterized by the establishment of a minimum respect between all subjects of a given society, allowing them to incorporate the notion of dignity into their claims. In contrast, this process does not occur in the peripheral countries, where the rights and modernization are driven by the state. This situation forms a precarious *habitus*, which is characterized by fragmentation, in other words, the respect between all the population is not established, affecting a significant part of the individuals to the status of useless and unproductive.

The referred author clarifies that in interpersonal relations

> The way we look at ourselves and at the world is how we justify the demand for justice. It is guided here, for beyond the formal equality, the individual consideration among themselves, proposing a deepening of civic horizon underpinned by the need to think the daily relationships - which involves parents and children and even the contact between different professionals. That is, if the relationships are formed, they must be permeated by civic recognition, because otherwise, when the development of visions guided by meritocracy is possible, the hierarchies will be justified. (Correa 2013)

However, it is found that in Brazilian society, a dissonance remains "between the institutionalized form of justice, based on liberal constitutional principles, and hierarchical patterns admitted to the social reality" (Correa 2013), which has on the principle of personhood the filter of justice, in order to enable the intuitive and permanent judgment on the existence, on the interacting partner and on the moral substance of dignity. Citing Cardoso de Oliveira, Correa (2013) concludes that "only those people in whom we can identify the particular moral substance of worthy people deserve full recognition and (almost) automatic citizenship rights."

This intuitive understanding that permeates the unconscious collective is reflected in the public policies interpretation for social protection by the agents of the public administration and in the judiciary decisions, restricting the scope of social security and justifying a restrictive interpretation of the constitutional text.

Assuming that equality, fairness, and dignity are intertwined concepts, the concept of citizenship "entails the respect toward the rights and consideration to the person" (Correa 2013). However, as in Brazil "there has not been established a respect between the individuals, which could ensure the inclusion of all people into the civic universe, in which legal rights would be respected and the possibility of mutual esteem, that is to say, recognition, would be honored" (Correa 2013) the notion of citizenship is in deficit, to admit, as opposed to that equal condition, the existence of worthy individuals and others who are unworthy:

> For the latter, the egalitarian norms would be settled with limitations, so the premise of a previous equality is not established (...).That is, if the individuals consider that some people are worth a kind of recognition and others not, it is natural that some will be disqualified (Correa 2013)

This deficit conception of citizenship justifies the perpetuation of obsolete understanding of an opposition between security and services and, as mentioned above, the conflict between (not) working and support, legitimizing and enabling to admit coherently a limited social protection to workers integrated into the formal production system, partially complemented by social support to the disabled ones to integrate this same formal production system, but seriously excluding for individuals that are not part of it.

What aggravates the situation is the social exclusion of individuals who, although used by the industrial capitalist production system, are not included in its formal boundaries. Several examples show how activities carried out informally by workers usually considered as excluded, leverage the movement of capital accumulation, which reinforces the dichotomy inclusion/exclusion (Ferraz 2013).

Ferraz (2013) exemplifies that in the recyclable material collection activity, "the collectors are integrated into the financial accumulation process and (...) the qualification required for this type of activity is precisely the alleged exclusion condition." The same author justifies this conclusion citing A.P. *Bosi:*

> (...) Recycling in Brazil only became possible when the large-scale collection and waste separation proved to be a viable and cost-effective task, i.e., achievable by workers whose remuneration compensates technology investments for the emergence of the recycled material production sector. Whatever the organization of this type of work would have been, their profits should compete with certain prices, for example, the world market responsible for oil products [...] and the aluminum and cellulose production. In these terms, it explains why this workforce emerged composed of workers without a contract and with a productivity that could be set by pay for production: a population reprimanded from the labor market and with no attributes to return to formal jobs.[...] Thus, unlike what could be thought, a large labor force of refuse collectors has made such technologies possible to be employed, enabling the expansion of the recycling business in Brazil (Ferraz 2013).

Two other examples cited by the author mentioned above deserve to be presented for having significant relevance to the central theme of this work.

The first, related to the beauty industry. According to the author "the popular sectors ensure a relatively stable market because of the proximity between consumer and reseller" (Ferraz 2013) which results in the recognition of logistics effectiveness used in this sector. However, the economic success also stems from "the precariousness work because in addition to the low cost of labor, the contract between employer and reseller does not guarantee workers' rights (...)" (Ferraz 2013).

The study that bolstered the author shows that "the so-called 'beauty consultants' have an average family income of two minimum wages and have generally low education" (Ferraz 2013). While the informality of the activity excludes this group of workers from rights of social security protection, the middle income reference shows that they will not be supported by social support either, thus integrating the group of workers allocated in the "limbo of social protection" and private from the right of dignity:

> The companies seek to 'compensate' this low investment distributing gifts to the workers and offering discount on product purchases. Thus, in addition to investing in brand image by improving the seller's appearance, the company ensures customers' loyalty by offering discount quotas and also ensures a wide coverage of the consumer market at a relatively low cost making use of the 'invisible work' of women who feed and move the cosmetics industry (Ferraz 2013)

The second example concerns the "women who live in urban peripheries [that (...)] perform domestic work in the homes of those who are occupied in specialized and qualified activities" (Ferraz 2013), with low formalization of employment relationship, getting low remuneration, and experiencing situations of social and spatial segregation in the homes where they work (and often live):

> Workers with low visibility (...) who are fundamental in maintaining the lifestyle of those at middle and upper segments of the Brazilian social hierarchy, who do not hesitate at the delegation of daily tasks to people who serve them privately in exchange for little pay and, often without any social protection. (Holzmann 2006).

Social (and social protection) exclusion of formal or informal workers, in favor of the dominant capitalism evolution in the post-industrial era is evident also in "outsourced" labor relations where the

> segregation and disregard of human dignity that the outsourcing produces in the workplace is seen, where the 'outsourced ones' are shifted from the living of other employees at the company; use specific lifts; have lunch at separate dining room or at different time; are not subjected to any kind of subordination, as they say 'so as not to generate bonds'; i.e., they are treated as a thing or are simply not seen. (Souto Maior 2005)

Clearly, one can see from the considerations, the existence of an unsupported social layer for social protection when the social security tools are interpreted from the classic Bismarckian reading.

As Souto Maior (2005) states, "social rights so far have not been fully implemented because they imply significant change in the social context and are always hindered by political and economic arrangements that act to the contrary."

However, we must keep in mind that for years, gradual changes are taking place on the national scene, which enable the construction of a new interpretation on the application of social security.

The Benefit of Continued Provision of social support, known in Brazil as (BPC) was established by the Organic Law of Social Support (LOAS) in 1993, and implemented only in 1996, allowing the payment of income in an amount equal to the minimum wage to those individuals with a monthly per capita family income no superior than 25 % of the minimum wage and for those older than 70 or with permanent disability, which would prevent their independent living.

At that time (early nineties, that is, two decades ago) the Brazilian State started a dignity rescue work which had consonant limitations with more than half a century of a typically Bismarckian social protection model and a clearly populism social service model, characteristic of the 1980s, limited to milk donations and market basket as populist political interests.[3]

The reality experienced by the state in the early existence of the Organic Law of Social Support justified the understanding that even today is constantly identified in court decisions that do not realize the evolution of society and of the Brazilian government, adding that the state should concentrate efforts in rescuing people in more extreme condition of misery, leaving those who were "only" in disrepair relegated to their own devices.

It is important to realize that reality has changed significantly as the Brazilian government has proposed the creation of public policies for social protection at new levels, even though this implementation is hampered by a restrictive and retrograde interpretation.

---

[3] *"The Constituent orders to incorporate in the pension funds the collection of FINSOCIAL, taking resources of school meals, the free school milk, the housing programs for low-income people; and financing for small farmers. These programs will have to be drastically reduced, canceled, and will be a tragedy because reach those most in need ..."* (Quoted from the speech of Mr. President of the Republic José Sarney, delivered on July 27, 1988 on national radio and television, showing the paternalistic/welfare interpretation which until then was rooted in Brazilian culture to criticize the implementation of Social Security and from it, an active program of Social Support in Brazil!) *in* Carvalho Filho (2008).

In this sense, we can highlight some indications of this development for new social protection levels that apparently have gone unnoticed.

In 2003, with the Brazilian Elderly Statute (Law 10.741), the minimum age to access the continued provision of social support benefit was reduced to 65, significantly expanding the list of people who are protected by social protection. The same law showed the overcoming of that initial situation in which the social service was target only at social layers in extreme poverty condition, by raising the criterion of per capita income for access to the benefits of social care for the elderly to half minimum wage, by disregarding the income of equal value paid to the also considered elderly's spouse for the granting of that benefit.

Also in 2003, there was established the psychosocial rehabilitation aid to people who had been hospitalized and were affected for mental disorders through Law 10.708/03 Article 3, II of the referred Act establishes as a requirement for obtaining this income "II - clinical and social situation of the patient does not justify the stay in hospital, technically indicate the possibility of inclusion in social reintegration program **and the need to financial aid**." By not establishing an objective income criterion but a subjective criterion that the patient's social situation justifies the need for financial aid, the State again demonstrates with solar clarity, the adoption of a new level of social protection, showing that the restriction of social welfare protection to the portion of the population in extreme poverty had already been overcome.

The overcoming of that limited scope of social support is also evidenced by the Law 12.435/2011, whereby the benefit of continued provision of social assistance was also extended to people who have no permanent disability, starting to include those with a long-term temporary disability, again in clear extension of social protection.

It is also possible to determine the evolution of social care in Brazil also assisting population that is not in extreme poverty, with the creation of PRONATEC (National Program for Access to Technical Education and Employment) with Law 12.513/2011, which aims resources at the training of the population in social *risk conditions*. In addition to the allocation of funds for the financing of training programs, this law brings a forecast of income transfer to the Student and Worker Training Grant (art. 4, IV). In June 2013, this federal program of social assistance had expanded its list of beneficiaries by Law 12.816/2013.

There is no denying that this government program of care and qualification to the population at risk condition already includes more than just those individuals in extreme poverty condition. It clearly assists the unemployed population who is benefited from the unemployment insurance that, with no doubt, is in a much higher social and economic level than that at which he had focused social support in the early 1990s.

It is no different with the BolsaFamília (Family Grant program), which originally was intended to meet the sections of the population who were in extreme poverty and has already expanded its range of beneficiaries, as shown by the Law 12.817/2013. It is also evident the evolution of the assistance protection towards the financing program institution created by Law 12.868/2013, which allocated 8 billion reais (Brazilian currency) to enable beneficiaries of the Brazilian assistance program "My Home, My Life" buying durable goods to improve their condition of domestic life.

There is no doubt that allocating this amount of resources to enable the low-income population to acquisitions such as blenders, refrigerators, television, telephone, and other appliances, makes it clear that the Social Support reach has far exceeded the focus on the condition of the population of extreme poverty.

It should also be reminded that in 2004, the Law 10.835/04 was published, which established in Brazil, the Citizen Basic Income, which is "the right of all Brazilians residing in the country and foreign residents for at least five (5) years in Brazil, **regardless of their socioeconomic status,** receive an annual **monetary benefit.**"

Although this income has not yet been implemented, it is clear that a country that instituted the right of all citizens, national and foreign residents to a financial income, regardless of their socioeconomic status and which has conditions to "give public supplies of food for international humanitarian assistance" (Law 12.429/2011) and "make donations to international initiatives of development aid"(Law 12.413 / 2011), has already far surpassed that social care setting exclusively for social strata in condition of extreme poverty and who denies the right to social protection and dignity of individuals in the next higher social spectrum, characterized as the "limbo of social protection between security and support."

2.5 Conclusion

Despite the need to respect the intervention limits between the Government Branches in their reciprocal responsibilities, this limitation may not matter in disregard, even by the Judiciary Power, regarding the social and economic evolution of the Brazilian state in the two and a half decades elapsed since the publication of the constitutional text.

Evolution that authorizes this new readings about the fundamental social rights set out in Article 6 of the Constitutional Charter and detailed in Articles 194 to 204 of the same Constitution, in line with the fundamentals of the Brazilian Republic of citizenship (CF/88, art. 1, II) and human dignity (CF/88, art. 1, III), which underpin the construction of the Brazilian state whose ultimate goal is the eradication of poverty and the reduction of social inequalities (CF/88, art. 3, III).

The Brazilian state objectives, established in Article 3 of the Federal Constitution, can only be fully achieved from a new reading of social rights, which overcomes the classical distinction between security and social support, as well as overcoming the traditional restrictive interpretation of the social support scope.

The existence of a significant portion of the population in the limbo of social protection mentioned in this text highlights the inefficiency of the traditional interpretation of social security and has as a consequence the scope of a contrary result to the objectives set out in the Constitution, not leading to reducing social inequalities but to its aggravation.

References

Associação Internacional De Seguridade Social (2008) Perspectivas de política social n° 04. AISS, Genebra. Available in http://www.issa.int/esl/Recursos/Perspectivas-de-Politica-Social. Accessed 4 May 2010

Associação Internacional De Seguridade Social (2010) Perspectivas de política social n° 14. AISS, Genebra. Available in http://www.issa.int/esl/Recursos/Perspectivas-de-Politica-Social. Accessed 24 Aug 2010

Bauman Z (2013) Danos colaterais. Desigualdades sociais numa era global. Zahar, Rio de Janeiro

Boschetti I (2003) Assistência social no Brasil: um direito entre originalidade e conservadorismo, 2ª Ed. Ed. UNB, Brasília

Bosi AP (2008) A organização capitalista do trabalho "informal": o caso dos catadores de recicláveis. Revista Brasileira de ciências sociais 23(67):101–116 [citado por Ferraz DLS (2013) Pelo fim da dicotomia exclusão/inclusão. A questão do exército de reserva no capitalismo contemporâneo. In: Catani AD, Díaz LM, Cohen N (eds) A construção da Justiça Social na América Latina. Tomo Editorial, Porto Alegre]

Carvalho Filho C (2008) A constituição de 88 e a previdência social, 20 anos depois. In: Carvalho Filho C (ed) Sonho ou realidade? 20 anos da seguridade social na constituição. Fundação ANFIP, Brasília

Corrêa AS (2013) Economia solidária. Um meio social disponível para ensejar lutas por reconhecimento e reduzir desigualdades? In: Catani AD, Díaz LM, Cohen N (eds) A construção da Justiça Social na América Latina. Tomo Editorial, Porto Alegre

Ferraz DLS (2013) Pelo fim da dicotomia exclusão/inclusão. A questão do exercito de reserva no capitalismo contemporâneo. In: Catani AD, Díaz LM, Cohen N (eds) A construção da justiça social na América Latina. Tomo Editorial, Porto Alegre

Giddens A (1996) Más allá de la izquierda y la derecha. El futuro de las políticas radicales. Cátedra, Madrid

Holzmann L (2006) A dimensão do trabalho precário no Brasil no início do século XXI. In: Piccinini V, Holzmann L, Kovács I, Guimarães VN (Org) O mosaico do trabalho na sociedade contemporânea: persistências e inovações. Editora da UFRGS, Porto Alegre [citado por Ferraz DLS (2013) Pelo fim da dicotomia exclusão/inclusão. A questão do exército de reserva no capitalismo contemporâneo. In: Catani AD, Díaz LM, Cohen N (eds) A construção da justiça social na América Latina. Tomo Editorial, Porto Alegre]

Ibrahim FZ (2011) A previdência social no estado contemporâneo. Fundamentos, financiamento e regulação. Ímpetus, Niterói

Leão XIII P (1891) Encíclica *RerumNovarum*. Vaticano. Available in http://www.joaosocial.com.br/enciclicas/revum_novarum.html. Accessed 6 Apr 2013

Muller F (2000) Que grau de exclusão ainda pode ser tolerado? Revista da Procuradoria-Geral do Município de Porto Alegre, Porto Alegre

Passos FL (2013) Previdência social e sociedade pós-industrial. Ed. Juruá, Curitiba

Rosanvallon P (1984) A crise do estado providência. Inquérito, Lisboa

Rousseau JJ (1753) Discurso sobre a origem da desigualdade entre os homens e se é autorizada pela lei natural. Amsterdam. Available in http://www.dominiopublico.gov.br/download/texto/cv000053.pdf. Accessed 1 Apr 2013

Sen A (2010) Desenvolvimento como liberdade. Companhia das Letras, São Paulo

Souto Maior JL (2005) A seita Secreta para a efetivação dos direitos sociais. Revista LTR, v. 69, p. 1170–1177

Vanderborght Y, Van Parij P (2006) Renda básica de cidadania: fundamentos éticos e econômicos. Civilização Brasileira, Rio de Janeiro

Chapter 3
A Contribution to the Study of Social Assistance to the Persons with Deficiency: Labor and Efficiency in the Capitalist Mode of Production

Flávio Roberto Batista

Abstract This paper deals with the meaning of a social assistance system to the persons with deficiency in the context of a social security system based in the primacy of labor. Its objective is related to the demonstration that the very concept of deficiency is linked to a nuclear point to the capitalist society, so that law faces difficulties when trying to treat persons with deficiency as a whole, not only focusing on their labor disability. To get this achievement, the paper discusses the meaning of the primacy of labor as the basis of social order, the concepts of efficiency and deficiency in the capitalist mode of production, the possibilities for inclusion of persons with disabilities in labor market and in community life and, finally, the changes in the concept of deficiency in Brazilian law.

Keywords Social assistance • Persons with deficiency • Primacy of labor • Efficiency • Capitalist mode of production

3.1 Introduction

Since 1988, with the enactment of the new Brazilian Constitution, social assistance lies, by virtue of Article 194,[1] organically articulated to health and social insurance forming the social security system. The social security system is the most important dimension of what the constituent called *social order*, not defined in the text, but identified in Article 193 from its foundations: "*The social order is based on the primacy of labor and aimed at well-being and social justice.*"

---

[1] Art. 194. Social security comprises an integrated set of actions initiated by the public authorities and society, to ensure the rights to health, social security, and social assistance.

F.R. Batista (✉)
Department of Labor and Social Security Law, University of São Paulo, São Paulo, Brazil
e-mail: flavio@usp.br

M.A. Serau Junior, J.R. Caetano Costa (eds.), *Assistance Benefits in Brazil*,
DOI 10.1007/978-3-319-27046-3_3

It follows that social assistance must be inescapably based on the primacy of labor. This information is quite counterintuitive, since the most common recipients of social assistance are precisely the ones that are for any reason unable to work, or in any way excluded from the labor market. Nevertheless, it shows in several passages of the constitutional text itself, revealing even the meaning of be based on the primacy of labor. See, about this, the text of Article 203 of the Constitution:

> Art. 203. The social assistance will be provided to those who need it, regardless of contribution to social security, and aims to:
>
> I – the protection of the family, maternity, childhood, adolescence and old age;
>
> II – the protection of children and teenagers;
>
> III – to promote integration into the labor market;
>
> IV – the habilitation and rehabilitation of persons with disabilities and promoting their integration into community life;
>
> V – ensuring a minimum wage of monthly benefit to the handicapped and the elderly who prove not to have means to provide their own support or having it provided by their family, according to the law.

Note that the first two goals confirm the most ordinary intuition before social assistance. They enumerate social groups that are completely apart to the world of labor. On the other hand, the following two goals make clear the willingness to integrate recipients of social assistance to the labor market and, hence, the constraints of the capitalist mode of production. The item IV even suggests a link between the habilitation and rehabilitation for the labor market of disabled persons and their integration into community life, demonstrating that the social assistance system obeys the constitutional command that determines that it must be based on the primacy of labor.[2]

From what was exposed until now, it is evident the need of a deep understanding of the meaning of the submission of the social assistance system to primacy of labor for a good reading of it, particularly the social assistance to the persons with deficiency. To achieve this understanding, it is imperative to secure the understanding of *primacy of labor* and especially the consequences of its adoption in the Constitution; pass through the debate of the meaning of the pair of opposites *efficiency/deficiency*, especially from its use in the capitalist mode of production; examine possibilities of inclusion of persons with disabilities in the labor market and in community life; and in the end, moving towards a more practical point of view, examine the transformation of the concept of deficiency served by Law No. 8.742/93 from a comparison between the original wording and the current text adopted by Law No. 12.435/11 and 12.470/11, that incorporated the provisions of *United Nations Convention on the rights of persons with deficiencies*. These are, briefly, the objectives of this paper and the intended path to meet them. The text was intended as a single reasoning. Its division into sections lends itself only to facilitate reading organization.

---

[2] The determination is reiterated by Law No. 8.742/93, in Article 2.

3.2 The Meaning of the Primacy of Labor as the Basis of Social Order

As mentioned above, the primacy of labor appears as the basis of social order under Article 193 of the Constitution. There are references to the same concept in the Constitution in its Article 1, IV, establishing that "*the social values of labor and freedom of enterprise*" are foundations of the Republic, and even in the heading of Article 170, which provides that the economic order is "*founded on the value of human labor and on freedom of enterprise.*" Therefore, we can say that in Brazil, pursuant to its Constitution, political order—the Republic, economic order, and social order have as their basis the labor, which appears sometimes in the form of *primacy of labor*, and other times in its variant form *social value of labor*. The Constitution, however, at no time clarifies the meaning of all this appreciation for the labor.

It is clear from reading the mentioned constitutional provisions, especially given its location at the most abstract and conceptual parts of the Constitution, that the concept of primacy of labor[3] is not juridical, that it apprehends a reality external and previous to law and that it triggers legal consequences. As the reasoning continues, it will be clear that, in fact, law could not fail to take the primacy of labor as the foundation of political, social, and economic orders. In other words, the non-juridical reality of primacy of labor would trigger consequences on law although the constituent said nothing at this respect. This section will treat about this.

Clearly, stating that the primacy of labor triggers consequences on law does not mean that from this may arise technical and legal solutions to practical problems of law operation. The caveat is important because certain group of authors that focus on the legal phenomenon, particularly in the field of human rights, search, in a naïve way, to derive directly the provision of certain fundamental rights from the primacy of labor, even invoking the historical and dialectical materialism as their method.[4]

It should be noted that the use of historical and dialectical materialism, taken as the key to understanding the law, can only have scientific and critical objectives,[5] never intending any kind of dogmatic construction. In other words, the first paragraphs of this section are intended to convey the idea that the election of the historical and dialectical materialism as a method in this paper means that the primacy of labor will be investigated from a critical understanding of the legal

[3] This paper will continue making use of the expression "primacy of labor" by reason of having been chosen by the constitution to address the issue in the relevant context for the legal treatment of social assistance. Do not forget, however, that this debate is made in sociology, philosophy, and law with the name of "centrality of labor."

[4] A notable example is in Escrivão Filho (2011). In this article, the author endeavors to derive the right to work, stated in Article 6 of the Constitution, from labor ontology identified by György Lukács as constitutive of the human social being.

[5] *Science* and *criticism*, from the perspective of historical and dialectical materialism, are so close that they become almost synonymous. The observation, however, is only indicated, due to the impossibility to examine the subject in the narrow limits of this paper.

system of social assistance, not from a dogmatic point of view. Still, the historical and dialectical materialist science of law cannot neglect the legal dogmatic and, instead, should be a critique of legal dogmatic, like the critique of political economy undertaken by the founder of this method, Karl Marx, as proposed by Eugeny Pasukanis.[6]

For this reason, without fear of any inconsistency, this paper will be ended by the critical treatment of Law No. 8.742/93. Note the difference between formulating, from scientific considerations whose method is the historical and dialectical materialism, a critique of legal dogmatic and, on the other hand, derive technical solutions of the same scientific considerations.

After clarifying methodological issues, it is essential to treat the concept of labor.

It is not difficult to find the treatment of the concept of labor in the legal literature. Virtually any labor law book tries to define it. However, it is rare to find authors that provide *a single* definition of labor. Indeed, two characters are quite common in this treatment: the observation that the concept of labor is different in philosophy, economy, or law (de Barros 2009); and the historical feature of the concept of labor, that is, the recognition that the various historical eras have interpreted differently the same phenomenon (Souto Maior 2011). It is crucial to realize that these are not only several different interpretations throughout history. Rather, it is the labor itself, being historical, that changes with the succession of the various modes of production. In fact, in the light of historical and dialectical materialism, it is the labor, with its historicity, which creates the social human being and its same historicity:

> The first *historical* act of these individuals, by which they differ from animals, is not the fact of thinking, but to start *producing their means of life*. (…). However, they begin to distinguish themselves from animals as soon as they begin to *produce* their means of life, which is conditioned by the organization of their body. By producing their means of life, men produce, indirectly, its own material life (Marx and Engels 2007, 87).

There is the most fundamental statement of historical and dialectical materialism about labor: it is the production by human beings[7] of their own means of life and consequently of their own material life. Hence, the perception that labor is also transformed with successive changes in mode of production and the interpretations that humans formulate on it by producing their own material life in the production process of their means of life. That leads to the statement of Karl Marx and Friedrich Engels in the same study mentioned above: "*It is not consciousness that determines life, but life that determines consciousness*" (Marx and Engels 2007).

---

[6] The theme of these paragraphs has been object of the author's doctoral thesis, later adapted for publication in book (Batista 2013). It is recommended to those interested by methodological issue reading the first chapter, which epistemologically limits the historical and dialectical materialism. For the source of the idea that the science, in the field of law, is the criticism of the legal dogmatic, see Pasukanis (1989).

[7] Although translations of the works of Marx normally use the expression *men*, here it is replaced by *human beings*, when they are not in literal quotes, honoring a less inadequate option from a perspective of gender oppression.

In short, interpretations on labor varied throughout history because they were determined by the changes in labor, which is inherently historical. The meaning of putting the primacy of labor as the foundation of political, social, and economic orders in the Brazilian Constitution must be sought in the historical feature of labor.

Most of authors in Brazilian legal literature support the adoption, by the 1988 Constitution, of capitalism.[8] Eros Grau affirms that supported by ideas of José Afonso da Silva:

> (...) The Constitution is capitalist, but freedom is only permitted as exercised in the interests of social justice, and Constitution gives priority to the values of human labor over all other values of the market economy (Grau 2004).

Given the fact that the Brazilian Constitution is capitalist—which is consequence, in fact, of the social value of labor and freedom of enterprise—there would be no choice but to give priority to the value of human labor. Capitalist society is organized around the value or, more specifically, around the continuous value valorization,[9] its indefinite reproduction. Moreover, the value has, historically, a unique way of determining its substance and dimension:

> Leaving aside then the use value of commodities, it remains to them only one property, which is that of being products of labor. (...). What these things still represent is just that in their production was expended human labor power, they have accumulated human labor. As a crystallization of this common social substance to them all, they are values – exchange values (Marx 1996).

The 1988 Constitution therefore does not carry any innovation or regulatory dirigisme to establish the primacy of labor as the basis of social order. It is limited to make legally positive what the political economy had long identified on the basis of the organization of any society in capitalist mode of production: human labor is the substance of exchange value, which also allows quantifying it from its duration. The core of capitalism lies in continuous value valorization from the repetition of production cycles.

---

[8] In this regard, Eros Grau, dedicated to summarize the most relevant contributions of the legal literature to the treatment of the economic order in the 1988 Constitution, identifies references to capitalism or market regime in the contributions of Geraldo Vidigal, Miguel Reale, Washington Peluso Albino de Souza, Tercio Sampaio Ferraz Junior, and José Afonso da Silva (Grau 2004).

[9] The term *value valorization* is marxian and it integrates the explanation about the transformation of money into capital. Money, by itself, is only a medium of exchange and is not immediately considered capital. To become capital, it must be inserted in a specific social relation of production, characteristic of the capitalist mode of production in which it is used to reproduce itself through the ongoing maintenance of the production process. See: "*The simple circulation of commodities – sale for purchase – serves as a mean to a goal that is out of circulation, appropriation of use values, satisfaction of needs. The circulation of money as capital is, however, an end in itself, for the value valorization exists only within this constantly renewed movement. So the movement of capital is insatiable*" (Marx 1996).

3.3 Efficiency and Deficiency in the Capitalist Mode of Production

It is essential to remember, in this step, that the definition of labor as production of means of life and the material life for human beings, given the historicity of the phenomenon, will trigger the effect that labor will take peculiar features in the various modes of production at each particular time. This perception is important to deny the idealizing interpretation—contrary to the historical and dialectical materialist method—under which labor would have a concept ahistorical and eternal, namely the human exchange with nature, which could lead, in the end, to excessive expansion of the concept extent, with the improper inclusion in it of physiological activities such as eating or breathing.

Labor takes its own configuration in the capitalist mode of production, linked to the determination of the substance and magnitude of value of commodities. For this, the most evident dimension of labor in capitalism is the *abstract labor*. Labor is relevant in the capitalist mode of production as pure and simple expenditure of human energy, allowing its equalization, comparison, and capture by market system. The abstract feature of labor allows labor force to be socially assimilated to the condition of commodity, which is at the basis of political economy of the capitalist mode of production.

> Let us now consider the residue of the products of labor. Nothing left of them unless the same ghostly objectivity, a mere jelly of homogeneous human labor, of labor power expended without regard to the mode of its expenditure. (…). A use value, or useful article, therefore, has value only because human labor in the abstract has been embodied or materialized in it. How, then, is the magnitude of this value to be measured? Plainly, by the quantity of the value-creating substance, the labor, contained in the article. The quantity of labor, however, is measured by its duration, and labor time in its turn finds its standard in weeks, days, and hours. (Marx 1996).

Pasukanis identified brilliantly the interference of determining the labor power as a commodity on law. If capitalist society is based on the exchange of commodities and they obviously cannot lead themselves to the market, human interference for its occurrence is required. Establishing its most basic category, the *subject of rights*, whose physical support is human person, law transports to it two fundamental characteristics that are, in fact, contained in the commodity itself, because of its unrestricted comparability: the freedom and equality. The condition of subject of rights, therefore, is a fetishization of the condition of owner of commodities (Pasukanis 1989).

In capitalist society, however, being subject of rights is not enough. The central role of value valorization in capitalist society has the consequence that a certain exchange of commodities assumes the primordial social role: the exchange of the commodity labor power for wages. Given the fact that the commodity labor power, as well as the legal category subject of rights, has human beings as their substrate, each person undertake to law in the capitalist mode of production the double condition of subject and object of rights, an owner of his own human energy as a commodity that leads to the exchange market. Edelman first noticed this phenomenon, when investigating the double appropriation of the photographed person's image rights (Edelman 1976), which led him to continue his studies in labor law, in which, in an ingenious way, similarly identified the same assignment situation to one person of dual condition of concomitant physical support of a subject and an object of rights (Edelman 1978).

If the exchange of wages for labor power assumes the role of fundamental exchange of capitalist society, the best human being before the law of such a society is the one that will fit perfectly to its dual role of supporting the categories of subject of rights and the labor power commodity, the object of rights par excellence in law of the capitalist mode of production. This perception demands also some additional details about the qualification of the labor power commodity as provision of abstract labor, which will lead directly to the theme of this section, about the idea of efficiency and deficiency. Marx warns:

> Some persons might think that if the value of a commodity is determined by the quantity of labor spent on it, the more idle and unskillful the laborer, the more valuable would his commodity be, because more time would be required in its production. The labor, however, that forms the substance of value, is homogeneous human labor, expenditure of one uniform labor power. The total labor power of society, which is embodied in the sum total of the values of all commodities produced by that society, counts here as one homogeneous mass of human labor power, composed though it be of innumerable individual units. Each of these units is the same as any other, so far as it has the character of the average labor power of society, and takes effect as such; that is, so far as it requires for producing a commodity, no more time than is needed on an average, no more than is socially necessary. The labor time socially necessary is that required to produce an article under the normal conditions of production, and with the average degree of skill and intensity prevalent at the time. (Marx 1996).

In other words, the characterization of abstract labor already carries with it the idea of normality, which is inherent to law, transpiring also in the most sophisticated positivist elaborations (Batista 2013). Labor power as a commodity constitutes as such from a normal—socially necessary—amount of abstract labor provided by the worker. The worker, therefore, will only fit capitalist mode of production to the extent that is able to provide the normal amount of abstract labor in an exchange for wages. Their efficiency is linked to the normalprovision of abstract labor in a social comparative perspective.

Notice, however, that the supply of abstract labor is not an accidental feature of human beings to the law in capitalism. On the contrary, part of its own constitution as a person before law, that is, its constitution as a subject of rights. The subject of rights arises primarily as an owner of itself as labor power.

Add to this the fact that law mediates sociability in the capitalist mode of production. Indeed, the affirmation of bourgeois society as such, their self-understanding, is based on the naturalization of human rights, that is, the attribution to persons of innate rights derived from their condition of human being. Its main core is precisely the characteristics that the subject of right takes from the commodities: freedom and equality.

In a context in which sociability is mediated by the law, in which the placement of the human being as a person depends on their dual constitution as subject and object of rights, being not able to providing abstract labor in exchange of wages or being able to provide fewer abstract labor than the normal amount means having some form of deficiency, understood as opposed to efficiency,[10] by the standards of the capitalist mode of production. Thus, the person with deficiency is, in the essence of capitalist society, less person than the others are. Hence the exclusionary nomenclature used in legal jargon until a few years ago and still common in colloquial language: deficient. Deficiency, to capitalism, affects personhood as such.

Notice that the exclusion of persons with deficiency in capitalist society carries no moral or evaluative aspect. It is not a choice, but an imposition of political economy of social relations of capitalist production. This is why the exclusion of persons with deficiency causes discomfort when confronted with each individual in particular—leading even the struggle for inclusion of these persons—but remains being so difficult to fight at business world.

In other words, any aspect properly human, that is, not belonging to the sphere of reproduction of value, is deemed irrelevant for the qualification of the person as useful and profitable for community life in capitalist society. Hence the constitutional provision, also full of prejudice, that links the integration into the community of persons with disabilities to their integration into the labor market.

3.4 The Possibilities for Inclusion of Persons with Deficiency in Labor Market and in Community Life

Given the reasoning developed so far, it is certain that contemporary capitalist society is only able to integrate the persons with deficiency into community life through its inclusion in the labor market. That is why the Constitution elects the integration into the labor market as an aim of social assistance. Social assistance is provided as an end in itself only in cases of absolute impossibility of providing abstract labor by the person.

The integration of disabled persons in the labor market is often a fiction. It should be noted, first of all, that persons with disabilities do not fit the logic of the average supply of abstract labor, so that they have their acceptance imposed on employers by law, in order to correct—with measures of humanitarian content—the operation of a labor market that discards any individual—not just persons with disabilities—to provide less abstract labor that the average population. In that sense, the provision of Article 93 of Law No. 8.213/91 imposes hiring persons with disabilities by medium and large enterprises and their continuity at employment:

> Art. 93. The company with one hundred (100) or more employees are required to fill 2% (two percent) to 5% (five percent) of its positions with rehabilitated or disabled persons, at the following proportion:
>
> I – up to 200 employees: 2%;
>
> II – 201–500: 3%;

[10] The dialectical thinking works always with pairs of contradictory concepts. These are the determined contradictions, in which the contrary concepts are inextricably linked and are mutually defined. Accordingly, it is impossible to understand the idea of deficiency without investigating what efficiency means in the capitalist mode of production.

III – 501–1000: 4%;
IV – of 1001 onwards: 5%.
§ 1. The disabled worker dismissal, at the end of a definite time contract – up to ninety (90) days – and the unmotivated dismissal in a contract for an indefinite period may take place only after the hiring of a substitute worker in the same condition.

Clearly, the labor market does not accept passively such provisions. It is known the controversy about the failure to fulfill the quota for lack of capable persons with disabilities to places offered. This conduct often gets sympathy of Labor Courts, that should, in theory, ensure the proper application of the law. This decision is surprisingly based on the common sense of businessmen and newspapers, as can be seen from the following excerpt from a trial:

> There are, however, many newspapers and magazines treat about the "hunt for the handicapped", phenomenon produced by fines imposed by the supervision of the regional labor offices, and articles of business administration specialists on the issue of "lack of persons with disabilities to meet the existing vacancies in the labor market", all in the sense that it is not that easy today to find persons with disabilities who are able to fill the vacancies that are available to them.[11]

Not being able to provide the same amount of abstract labor that a person without disabilities, persons with disabilities are often offered jobs that have as their object the provision of so-called complex labor, intellectualized and specialized (Marx 1996), which is not characterized by pure and simple expenditure of human energy, but requires qualification and training. Then, as throughout the rest of the population, it is much harder to find workers able to perform this kind of function. The mode of production finds a way, approved by the state structure, to maintain the exclusion of persons with disabilities within the same system that should protect them.[12]

In the capitalist mode of production, integration to social life outside the labor market can happen in just one way: in the condition of a commodities consumer. The optimal operating of the system puts as commodities consumers the very participants in the production process, that is, workers and owners of means of production. The so-called welfare state is based on the perception, arising from the crisis of overproduction that was behind the breakdown of the New York Stock Exchange in 1929, that it would be necessary to include in the capitalist mode of production, as consumers, persons who were pushed out of the commodities process of production. Hence, the greater participation of the state in the economy, sponsoring the expansion of employment levels and the distribution of social benefits, expanding the consumer market.

---

[11] Case No. 006.2007.023.02.00-1. Interesting to note that the Superior Labor Court, deciding the issue on appeal, maintained the judgment on the grounds that, being a legal standardization of court, could not return to discuss evidentiary question, understand, therefore, that the aforementioned "many materials" constituting question concerning the evidential whole of the file.

[12] Even the militants of the rights of persons with disabilities now bend to such determinations and focus their academic production in the qualification of persons with disabilities for the selective funnel of labor market. In this respect, the interesting research of Cezar (2012).

In other words, given the impossibility of access to the labor market—derived from the severity of the disability or, as seen, of the business logic, inclusion in community life is based on the provision of resources for the disabled persons to participate in the consumer market, helping to realize the value enshrined in commodities.

It has been investigated elsewhere (Batista 2013) that social assistance presents an incomplete assimilation by legal form, submitted to the logic of equivalence underlying the exchange of commodities, triggering the emergence of a welfare system based on moral counterparts, such as acting in work areas, school attendance, submission to health procedures, among others—the so-called *workfare*, *learnfare*, and similar policies. It is a problem that exists in every social care system and it is due to inherent characteristics of the legal phenomenon. However, specifically concerning social assistance to the disabled persons, their integration into community life does not depend only on access to consumption, as envisioned by the law from their inclusion in the capitalist mode of production. It takes a lot more than that to overcome the barriers that prevent a disabled person to have the same social relevance than any other. Moreover, that goes beyond the limited horizon of the labor and consumer market, involving issues related to the human condition. This takes the research to its culmination, in which there will be the consequences of the ideas here exposed to the treatment of the social assistance system to persons with disabilities.

3.5 The Transformation of the Concept of Disability Served by Law No. 8.742/93: A Conclusion

Giving concreteness to the constitutional provisions of items III, IV, and V of Article 203, the original wording of the Organic Law of Social Assistance provided:

> Art. 20. (…).
> § 2. To grant this benefit, the disabled person is one incapacitated for independent life and labor.

It is clear that the legislation incorporated the idea of incapacity for labor on the concept of person with disabilities, in line with what was developed in the previous sections about the efficiency and deficiency in the capitalist mode of production. The device, however, created room for a discussion that has lasted for many years: the content of the expression *incapacitated for independent living*.

It is imperative to note that the term *incapacity* is used in Brazilian law in two very different directions. On the one hand, in civil law, incapacity is linked to civil minority, that is, the impossibility of autonomous practice of legal transactions. Of course, in addition to the general rule of age, are also considered civilly incapable those who, duc to illness or mental disability,[13] do not have the necessary insight to

[13] Thus improperly denominated in civil law. Today, it is preferred to use the term *intellectual disability*.

the practice of acts of civil life and those who, even by a transient cause, cannot express their will; besides that, in relative terms, the usual drunks, toxic addicts, and those who, by mental disability, have reduced discernment; the exceptional without full mental development; and prodigal. On the other hand, in the social security law, incapacity is linked to the impossibility of exercise of normal labor.

Observed that the social security legislation treats incapacity as inability to labor, concept already incorporated into the organic law of social assistance parallel to the incapacity for independent life, it is clear that this is not limited to that. Therefore, it is necessary to consider whether the inability for independent life in social assistance legislation is synonymous with civil incapacity or it configures a third concept. It is easy to see that the inability for independent life—remembering that it is in the context of the definition of disability—cannot be equated with civil disability. Indeed, there are several civilly unable that do not have any kind of disability, such as the prodigal. On the other hand, there are persons who clearly have disabilities, such as moving or sensorial ones, but are fully able to express their will in acts of civil life. Therefore, the inability for independent life in the social assistance law can only be a different idea of the other two, requiring individualized interpretation.

Case law has established itself to broaden the scope of incapacity for independent life, as appears from the following excerpt from the judgment of the Superior Court of Justice:

> The expert report attesting to the inability to labor and the capacity for independent life, simply because the person does not need help from others to feed, do her hygiene or dressing, cannot prevent the perception of the benefit, because if this was the concept of independent life, the social assistance benefit would only be due to the persons with disabilities so severe that suppresses the individual's ability to move – which does not seem to be the legislator's intention.[14]

This understanding has always been object of complaint by the social movements fighting for the rights of persons with disabilities, for it banalizes the concept of disability. That is correct, because if you cannot understand the inability for independent life as the impossibility of movement and personal care, virtually all incapacity would be framed as disability. This complaint, however, although justifiable in appearance, do not match the essential reality that underlies the capitalist mode of production. Indeed, as detailed above, the determined contradiction of deficiency is efficiency, which is consistent in supply the normal amount of abstract labor by a person. Any disruption in this normal supply put the person as disabled to the operation of the production cycle. The legal provision, with all its formulation defects, had reached a hermeneutics that pacified the theme just by matching the legal solution to the structural demands of the social relations of production.

As reported above, however, in 2007 Brazil came to sign the *New York Convention on the rights of persons with disabilities*. Later on, in 2008, the international document has been incorporated into national law by following the procedures of Article 5°, § 3°, of the Constitution, acquiring legal status of constitutional amendment. With this, it became necessary to adapt the legislation to its provisions,

---

[14] STJ. REsp 360202. Rapporteur Minister Gilson Dipp.

and the organic law on social assistance was amended by Law No. 12.435/11 and 12.470/11 and is currently worded as follows:

> Art. 20. (…).
> § 2. To grant this benefit, disabled person is considered one that has long-term physical, mental, intellectual or sensorial disabilities, which in interaction with various barriers may block their full and effective participation in society on an equal condition with others.

The current legal provision confronts the social relations of production that underlies it. It is true that the personal substrate of disability apparently remains the same, because every incapacity is to be derived from a physical, mental, intellectual, or sensorial disability. In addition, not every person who has such impediments will be unable to perform labor activity. The concept of disability was, in this sense, extended. This idea is even more evident taking into account that defining disability as a form of labor incapacity, as did the previous text, the possibility of entering the labor market is the only way of interaction between the peculiar conditions of the person and its surroundings; while in the new text the existence of disability, with respect to the integration of the person to her social environment, depends on the interaction of the person impediments with *various barriers*, which not only block the labor of the disabled person, but somehow also *block her full and effective participation in society on an equal basis with others*.

In other words, the new legal provision focuses on a different problem. Indeed, labor incapacity and inability to maintain oneself are the only spheres of activity that interest to the capitalist mode of production. When the legal measure treat of any barrier that blocks the full and effective social participation, it vocalized a desire to address the issue of disability in addition to the labor and consumer commodities market. It seeks to address the issue from the aspect of human life of the disabled person as a whole. It seeks to revalue the human being beyond its reduction involved in the condition of subject of rights.

The intention is meritorious. One must not forget, however, that the legislative texts are idealizations and, more importantly, the social conflicts are not fought in them. It remains, therefore, wait for the facts reveal what demands will be triggered by the new concept of disability, and especially how state agents will behave in treating such demands. Social assistance can play an important role in internal destabilization of the mode of production order (Batista 2013), causing disruptions that create political action opportunity. The state response to the demands of persons with disabilities that aims something more than the simple insertion in the labor and consumption market is the arena of battle in which will be decided whether the social assistance to the disabled person could represent another loophole for social change or be reabsorbed by the logic of existing social relations of production.

In this process, society will make an important option for the treatment of persons with disabilities: they can be appreciated as whole human beings, regardless of their ability to normal supply of abstract labor, or remain relegated to ostracism of labor market exclusion and insufficient inclusion in the consumer market, attached to the narrow limits of the capitalist mode of production.

References

Batista FR (2013) Crítica da tecnologia dos direitos sociais. Dobra/Outras expressões, São Paulo
Cezar KR (2012) Pessoas com deficiência intelectual: Inclusão trabalhista – Lei de Cotas. LTr, São Paulo
de Barros AM (2009) Curso de direito do trabalho, 5ª ed. LTr, São Paulo
Edelman B (1976) O direito captado pela fotografia: elementos para uma teoria marxista do direito. Centelha, Coimbra
Edelman B (1978) La légalisation de la classe ouvrière. Christian Bourgois, Paris
Escrivão Filho A (2011) Sobre o trabalho e os direitos humanos. O Direito Alternativo, vol 1, no 1. UNESP, Franca, pp 91–111
Grau ER (2004) A ordem econômica na Constituição de 1988, 9ª ed. Malheiros, São Paulo
Marx K (1996) O Capital. Livro I. Tomo I. Nova Cultural, São Paulo
Marx K, Engels F (2007) A ideologia alemã. Boitempo, São Paulo
Pasukanis EB (1989) A teoria geral do direito e o marxismo. Renovar, Rio de Janeiro
Souto Maior JL (2011) Curso de direito do trabalho, vol 1. LTr, São Paulo

Chapter 4
Public Policies, Judicial Activism, and Social Assistance

Miguel Horvath Jr.

Abstract This article aims to analyze public policies adopted in Brazil within the social security system in particular subsystem of social assistance as well as their style of interpretation by the judiciary of the requirement/economic criterion for access to welfare benefits. The Brazilian judiciary to position themselves on the threshold of economic criteria for access turned out to create room for the granting of welfare provision with strong subjectivism, creating a situation of legal uncertainty in that people facing the same situation cannot obtain social protection in the face of hermeneutical component as binding on the judge, in clearly the performance of judicial activism. The latest decision of the Supreme Court helped to extend this form of action.

Keywords Social security • Social rights • Fundamental rights • Public policy • Judicial activism • Legal insecurity

In order for us to reflect on public policies, judicial activism, and social assistance, it is worth analyzing preliminarily the areas of intersection between different areas of knowledge. To talk about social assistance as providing social security benefits, it has become necessary to analyze the concept of public policies. Security as public policy should be seen as a collective economy method. In doing so, the community is called upon to make a technical-economic pact in which social solidarity is the balance point. Social solidarity consists in contribution of majority in benefit of minority (Horvath 2012). To extract the contents and limits of legal provisions of social protection, it is necessary to know and understand the public policies, its purposes, addressees, and limits, as well as the way in which Judiciary has been manipulating the social protection.

Social assistance is an instrument of social transformation, having the mission to promote integration and inclusion of the assisted person into community life.

M. Horvath Jr. (✉)
Município de São Bernardo do Campo, Estado de São Paulo, Brazil
e-mail: miguelhorvathjr@uol.com.br

M.A. Serau Junior, J.R. Caetano Costa (eds.), *Assistance Benefits in Brazil*,
DOI 10.1007/978-3-319-27046-3_4

The art. 1 of Law n. 8,742/93 determines: the social assistance, civil rights and State's duty, is a non-contributory Social Security Policy, providing minimum social standards, carried out through an integrated set of public and society initiative actions to ensure fulfillment of basic needs.

Social assistance is therefore the form of social protection that has the following characteristics: it acts after the state of social need is established and has a non-contributory nature. It is a duty of the State, which will act on a subsidiary basis to the social security protection and in relation to those able to guarantee their vital subsistence minimum.

Social assistance aims to protect the individual who cannot get their livelihood by itself or with the help of their families. The main objectives of social assistance are protecting family, maternity, childhood, adolescence, old age (Senior Citizens), needy children, and teenagers support and to promote integration into the labor market. It is also intended to habilitation and rehabilitation of disabled people promoting their integration into community life; guarantee of a monthly minimum wage benefit to the disabled person and to the senior citizens able to prove having no means to meet their own needs or having it provided by their family.

Social assistance assumes a non-accumulation of means and coverage of needs. The individual must request and prove his/her social need condition. The social protection assistance aims to guarantee and maintain human dignity.

In turn, public policies must be seen as a set of State's options for executing collective interests legally protected by means of public resources.

We emphasize that general tax revenues (indirect financing pursuant to art. 195 of the Constitution of Federative Republic of Brazil) finance social assistance. Budget resources of social security provided for in art. 195 of Constitution, besides other sources (art. 204 of Constitution). Financing of benefits, services, programs, and projects established by Law No. 8,742/93 shall be made through resources of Federal, State, Federal District and Municipalities, and other social contributions provided for in art. 195 of Constitution, apart from those that make up the National Fund for Social Assistance (FNAS). It is the public administration agency's responsibility to coordinate the Social Assistance Policy in the three (3) levels of government, in order to manage the Social Assistance Fund, under the direction and control of social assistance councils. The financing of social assistance in Unified System of Social Welfare (SUAS) should be made by co-financing of three (3) federal entities, being the resources allocated in social assistance funds to be aimed at implementation, provision, improvement and facilitation of services, programs, projects, and benefits of this policy.

The role of interaction between public policy and law becomes important in a state grounded on the Social Welfare way. In a Welfare State, legal standards came to have a great emphasis, since it turns into execution of public goals (public policy). To extract the contents and limits of legal provisions of social protection, it is necessary to know and understand the public policies, its purposes, addressees, and limits.

In Brazil, the understanding and knowledge of public policy, inexorably linked to administrative law, still have the focus on the negative character of activities, directed towards the understanding of discretion limits. That is, in the discussion of what can or cannot be done by Public Administration, while the focus should be in the coordination of State actions, aiming at the realization of public policies in a coordinated, harmonious, and more effectively manner.

Because of this, the phenomenon "judicialization" of public policies can be seen in Brazil, which in a synthetic way, will aim at establishing limits of judiciary intervention in the construction and execution of public policies. Within this phenomenon, it is possible to observe two currents, the first adopts an activist position and vision, in which it is for the judiciary to interfere, remodel, and create public policies. The second current adopts a garantism position in which the judiciary is limited to the formal control (and nonmaterial) of the acts of public managers.

Adhesion to one of the currents is expressed in judicial decisions, particularly in Higher Courts decisions.

Social assistance as a tool of execution of public and economic policy imposes some challenges and obstacles in particular, as regards the coverage level and the acceptable level in order to have assistive protection without undermining or prejudice to the social security policies. Since there will be a difference between the level of assistance and social security coverage, the establishment of such levels and limits is essential to discourage the idea of not working or the idea that it is better to live without working. Always keeping in mind that every generalization is dangerous. In this respect, the social assistance should be a capacity-building instrument in such a way that the addressees of social assistance can resume control of its destiny after being capacitated. Becoming the architects of their own destiny.

The fight against poverty is one of the bulwarks of democracy. Democracy is a sphere in government that helps the country to take decision in the collective sense in fighting poverty to help improving conditions of the people, in favor of the improvement on health, education, and social welfare (Bobbio 1986).

Regarding the income pattern, it is imperative to reflect on the methodology for establishing a minimum income pattern. We emphasize that measures of poverty acquire a capital importance on the definition of social protection level, in addition to which groups are the preferred to be achieved. The current concept of poor has evolved over the years, today the most common concept is that poor is the person who has no way to meet their nutritional needs, which are deprived of access to income, work, housing, and health. Keeping in mind that the poor people can still be classified as structural (the person who is born and will die poor) or circumstantial (people which are in this situation for a misfortune, an adverse circumstance of life).

The big question faced by the public policy manager is to establish the limits of protection in a way that meets the legal requirements and technical limits. The technical limit can be seen as the survival level (subsistence minimum) of an individual or family, and the legal limit is the human dignity. Poverty can be defined as a deprivation of basic capabilities relating to an individual and not just as an income below a preset level. "Capacity" is meant to be the alternative combinations of performance made possible to realize. Therefore, capacity is a kind of freedom: substantial freedom to realize alternative combinations of performance or freedom to have different life styles. For example, a wealthy person who fasts for his free will can have the same completion of functioning that a poor person forced to extreme hunger. However, the first person has a "capacity set" different from the second. The first may choose to eat well and be well nourished, what is impossible for the second (Sen 2000).

Poverty can be measured in several ways, namely: absolute measure, relative measure, and subjective measure. Absolute measure of poverty is used to determine the estimated basic needs and the allocation of resources capable of satisfying them. The big question is to determine the amount of necessary resources to guarantee a decent life (human dignity), as well as the subjective needs variation between people and between countries and regions. The issue in adopting this measure of poverty concerns in establishing the poverty line at 1/3 of the minimum wage. Why not at ½ of the minimum wage?

Relative measure of poverty in turn assumes that the poor person is the one who does not have enough income to achieve the standard of everyday life in a determined society. Accordingly, considering the growing income of countries, no matter how much the income increases for those who are at the base of social substrate, there will always be poor people.

The subjective measure (Sen 2000) states that, to establish poverty line it is necessary to research the basic needs considered directly in its own group.

With the enacted law in Brazil, named LOAS—Lei Orgânica de Assistência Social (Law of Social Assistance), the absolute measure was adopted to set up fixed standards for the minimum level of basic needs for the addressees of the Continuing Benefit Conveyance (CPB). The program was adopted as another reference for assistance activities to meet those who are below the poverty line. Standards of poverty have been adopted by indexing it to the minimum wage (existential minimum), based on the assumption that the minimum wage is the existential minimum.

In the UN study of investments for the end of the poverty, launched during the General Assembly in 2013, Brazil was named as one of the countries that has managed to reduce social inequalities, reaching a substantial reduction of poverty and misery, becoming an important example for the rest of the world. In 2013, Brazil was one of the highlights of international organization in the Development Initiatives report, which recognized the program "Bolsa Família" as an important tool to reduce poverty by 40 %, to enlarge access to food for 52 % of households and reducing child mortality. All this with a low cost, according to the study: "The 24 billion BRL budget [of Bolsa Família] is less than 1 % of the federal budget in 2013, while the investment was 0.46 % of national income in 2012." Brazil and China were recognized in the report for their strategy of social investment to promote sustainable development. According to the document, government resources have grown rapidly in both countries, reaching US$ 4000 (about 9200 BRL) per person in Brazil and US$ 1760 (little over 4000 BRL) per person in China. The Cadastro Único para Programas Sociais do Governo Federal (Single Registry of Social Programs of the Federal Government) was cited as an important initiative for success in the decision of social investments by the large amount of information stored, which allows for a good focus of the programs.[1]

[1] Brazilian government's actions over the past 10 years have reduced social inequalities in the Country. Portal Brasil Published: September 23, 2013 8:19 p.m. Last modified: October 18, 2013 7:11 p.m.

At this point, let us reflect a little on the recent Supreme Court decision in Extraordinary Appeals 567,985/MT and 580,963/PR about economic criterion for access to the Continuing Benefit Conveyance Program with assistance figure, guided by reflection on the role of the Judiciary in the face of public policies and social fundamental rights.

The limitation of the economic criterion for access to social assistance was one of the conditions under the policy viewpoint for the approval of social security in the discussions, which happened prior to the approval of the Constitution of 1988.

Article 203 of the Federal Constitution stipulates:

Art. 203. The social assistance will be provided to those in need of it, regardless of contribution to social security, and aims to:

I – protect families, maternity, childhood, adolescence and old aged people;

II – protect children and teenagers;

III – promote integration into the labor market;

IV – habilitation and rehabilitation of disabled people, promoting their integration into community life;

*V – **guarantee of a monthly minimum wage of benefit to disabled person and the senior citizens who are able to prove to have no means to meet their own needs or having it provided by their family, according to the law.***

The social assistance was only regulated by Law No. 8,742/93, in which the articles 20 and Section 21 state in an infra-constitutional regulation, the assistance benefit provided for in art. 203 of the Federal Constitution. LOAS (Organic Law of Social Assistance) provides for:

Art 20. Continuing Benefit Conveyance Program is a guarantee of a monthly minimum wage to the disabled person and to senior citizens with 65 (sixty-five) or more years, who prove to have no means to meet their own needs or having it provided by their family. (as amended by Law No. 12,435 of 2011).

§ 1 For the purposes of caput, the family consists of the applicant, the spouse or partner, parents and, in the absence of one of them, the stepmother or stepfather, unmarried siblings, unmarried children and stepchildren and minors under tutelage, provided that they live under the same household. (as amended by Law No. 12,435, 2011). Concept of "assistance family".

§ 2 for granting this benefit, it is considered: (as amended by Law No. 12,435, 2011).

I – disabled person: one who has a long-term physical, intellectual and/or sensory impairments, which in interaction with various barriers may hinder their full and effective participation in society with others; (as amended by Law No. 12,435, 2011).

II – long-term impediments: those that disable a person with disabilities to live independently and to work for a minimum of two (2) years. (as amended by Law No. 12,435, 2011).

§2. For the purposes of concession of this benefit, disabled person is considered one that has long-term physical, mental, intellectual and/or sensory impairments, which in interaction with various barriers may hinder their full and effective participation in society on an equal basis with others. (as amended by Law No. 12,470, 2011).

§ 3. **A family with a monthly income per capita less than 1/4 (a quarter) of the minimum wage is considered unable to provide maintenance of disabled or elderly. (as amended by Law No. 12,435, 2011) – measurement criteria of economic need or lack of assets.**

§ 4. The benefit of this article cannot be accumulated by the beneficiary under any other social security sphere or other regimen, except health care and special pension of compensatory nature. (as amended by Law No. 12,435, 2011)

§. The condition in long-term care institutions does not prejudice the right of the elderly or disabled person to Continuing Benefit Conveyance Program provision. (as amended by Law No. 12,435, 2011).

§ 6. The granting of the benefit is subject to the assessment and degree of disability, made up of medical and social assessment carried out by medical experts and social workers of the National Institute of Social Security (INSS). (as amended by Law No. 12,435, 2011).

§ 6. The granting of benefit is subject to the assessment of disability and the degree of impediment mentioned in § 2, consisting of medical and social assessment carried out by medical experts and social workers of the National Institute of Social Security – INSS. (as amended by Law No. 12,470, 2011).

§ 7. In the event that there are no services in the municipality of residence of the addressee, it is assured, as provided by regulation, his submission to the next county that has such a structure shall be done. (Included by Law No. 9,720, of 30.11.1998).

§ 8 the monthly familiar income referred to in § 3 shall be declared by the applicant or his legal representative, subject to the other procedures provided for in the Regulation for grating the application. (Included by Law No. 9,720, of 30.11.1998).

§ 9. The disabled person remuneration as an apprentice will not be considered for purposes of the calculation referred to in § 3 of this article. (included by Law No. 12,470, 2011).

§ 10. It is considered long-term impediment for the purposes of § 2 of this article, the one that takes effect for a minimum period of two (2) years. (included by Law No. 12,470, 2011).

Art. 21. The Continuing Benefit Conveyance Program should be reviewed every two (2) years to evaluate the continuity of the conditions that gave rise to it. (See Law n° 9.720, of 30.11.1998).

§ 1. Payment of benefit ceases at the moment when conditions referred to above overcome, or in case of death of the beneficiary.

§ 2 The benefit will be canceled when it is found irregularities in its granting or usage.

§ 3. The development of cognitive, motor or educational abilities and performing unpaid activities of habilitation and rehabilitation, among others, do not constitute grounds for suspension or termination of benefit of the disabled person. (Included by Law n° 12.435, of 2011).

§ 4 Termination of the Continuing Benefit Conveyance Program provided to the disabled person does not prevent new grant of the benefit, since it met the requirements set by regulation. (as amended by Law No. 12,470, 2011);

Art 21. The licensing body will suspend the Continuing Benefit Conveyance Program when the disabled person is engaged in remunerated activity, including the individual micro entrepreneur condition. (included by Law No. 12,470, 2011).

§ 1. Upon termination of the employment relationship or entrepreneurial activity in the caput of this Article and, where appropriate, ended the period of payment of unemployment insurance and not having acquired the beneficiary entitled to any pension benefit, continuity of payment suspended may be requested. This can occur without conducting medical expertise or reassessment of disability and the degree of incapacity for this purpose, subject to the review period provided for in the caput of art. 21. (included by Law No. 12,470, 2011).

§ 2 The Hiring disabled people as an apprentice does not require the suspension of the Continuous Cash Benefit Program, limited to two (2) years concurrent receipt of remuneration and benefit. (Included by Law No. 12,470, 2011).

The Continuing Benefit Conveyance (BPC) has replaced the provision called Lifelong Monthly Income, pursuant to art. 37 of Law no. 8,742/93 and became effectively required from January 1st, 1996. The criterion of economic need or lack of assets measurement is determined in § 3 where the law expressly establishes the objective criteria for benchmarking, which is the family group not having an income higher than ¼ of the minimum wage per capita. Criterion for economic needs assessment has been questioned since the first moment. Supreme Court, through ADI n. 1232/DF expressed towards to understand this criterion as constitutional, since the Constitution delegated to infra-constitutional legislative the power for establishment of such a criterion.

Until the enactment of Law n. 12,470/2011, the legislation determined the application of the concept of "social security family" (dependents as prescribed in Article 16 of Law no. 8,213/91) as a group in which economic criterion should be observed. After the enactment of Law No. 12,470/2011, the § 1 of Article 20 of LOAS was amended and included the concept of "assistance family." This change, which creates an enlargement in the family composition, is justified as far as it is more compatible with the reality of the composition of the Brazilian family group nowadays. The Law No. 12,435/2011 changed the concept of family for the grant of provision of assistance. For the purpose of granting social assistance benefit, family is composed by the applicant, spouse or partner, parents and, in the absence of one of them, the stepmother or stepfather, unmarried siblings, unmarried children and stepchildren, and minors under tutelage, provided that they live under the same household.

The ADI 1232/DF decided the constitutionality of the objective limitation of the beneficiaries included in § 3 of art. 20 of LOAS according to which, in assessing lack of assets for obtaining the benefit of continued provision, it is considered to be unable to provide for their own subsistence only the member of the family group whose income is less than ¼ of the minimum wage. Such Direct Action of Unconstitutionality (ADI), as an instrument of concentrated control of constitutionality, became *res judicata* in order to assert the constitutionality of the objective criterion. As a result, it As a result, was removed of the application of subjective criterion expenditures such as: medicines, health, housing, education, and other expenses to deduct from the total income of the family group, for measuring the income. This criterion radiates effects in relation to the Judiciary and Brazilian Public Administration bodies.

We feel bound to express our surprise, and why not say astonishment, with the decision handed down by Supreme Court in Extraordinary Appeals 567,985/MT and 580,963/PR. The Plenary of Court decided to dismiss the proceedings that have been lodged by INSS, in which criteria for calculation, used to assess the monthly per capita income for granting assistance to senior citizens and disabled, were discussed. In this decision, the Supreme Court declared unconstitutional, *incidenter tantum*, § 3 of art. 20 of Law No. 8,742/93 and the sole paragraph of art. 34 of Law no. 10.741/2003 (Senior Citizen Statute). It is clear that the Court considered the criterion "circumstantial unconstitutionality."

The "circumstantial unconstitutionality" aims to identify, before a formal constitutional law, that, circumstantially, its application would be unconstitutional, what we might call axiological (Lenza 2013).

Minister Gilmar Mendes declared that it would be possible to change the Supreme Court paradigm, since there was a loss of purpose in the decision-making at ADI 1232/DF. Also according to the Min. Celso de Mello, while exceptional to the measure, would be legitimate the possibility of a jurisdictional intervention by judges and courts in constituting certain public policies, when the State fails to execute its constitutional obligations, without configuring the transgression of the principle of separation of powers.

We understand that in the event of disagreement, there is no failure to comply with constitutional obligations, but the establishment of limits for accessing and verifying the economically needy condition (criterion of lack of assets) that it up to the Legislative to determine. In turn, we highlight the Minister Teori Zavascki's opinion in the sense that the norm in question would have been declared constitutional in concentrated control and a contrary judgment would depend on characterization of supervening unconstitutionality assumption, that not occur in species. Despite of the proposed change in the effects of the decision, in the sense that the contested precepts were valid up to December 31, 2015, quorum of 2/3 was not obtained for its establishment. In such case, this situation created a legal uncertainty with respect to the fulfillment or not of economic criterion for measuring the economic lack of assets to grant the Continuing Benefit Conveyance. As the issue remains to be assessed, we have now a legislative void on this matter. Legal uncertainty that spreads in the scope of Judiciary, as well as the administrative environment.

In this respect, I reflect on the judicial activism issue and distinction between Democratic and Constitutional State, and establishment of public policies. The purpose is a reflection on the role and limits of the Judiciary (judicial function) in the phenomenon called judicial activism over the recent decision in assistance matter.

We must understand by judicial activism, how part of the Judiciary members see the current judicial function. No longer as merely who applies and endorses statutory law, but as part of a core of formation of the legal. We emphasize that there is no consensus in relation to the neologism "judicial activism," neither to its limits.

One of the judicial activism issues concerns to the establishment of Judiciary acting limits, because even among its supporters, there is a consensus that the phenomenon must be accepted with restraints. This is because judicial activity is not an exact and mechanical activity: "to the extent that they are responsible for assigning sense to vague, fluid and indeterminate expressions, such as human dignity, right to privacy or objective good faith, they become, and in many situations, co-participant of the law making process" (Barroso 2012).

By being co-participant in creating law does not necessarily mean establishing and determining the public policy parameters. A declaration of unconstitutionality *incidenter tantum*, in § 3 of art. 20 of Law No. 8,742/93 and in the sole paragraph of art. 34 of Law no. 10.741/2003 (Senior Citizen Statute), creates a legal uncertainty with respect to the fulfillment or not of economic criterion for measuring the economic lack of assets to grant the continued provision of the benefit. As the issue remains to be assessed, we now have a legislative void on this matter. A Legal uncertainty that spreads in the scope of the Judiciary, as well as the administrative environment.

The new functions assumed by the Judiciary arising from judicial activism cause a gap in the power distribution system, provoking or creating a crisis between the powers, although being potential. In addition, it does not allow making a difference in the income levels between assistance and social security protection. "The constitutional jurisdiction operates in interface of the legislation and application of law, legal and politics. Therein lies the danger not despicable of political decisions in an appearance in the form of justice".

I conclude by mentioning the fact that due to the decision of the Supreme Court, the Legislative must act to approve the law, which urgently establishes the new criterion for measuring the lack of assets requirement, being able to authorize the granting of the Continuing Benefit Conveyance, allowing differentiation between assistance and social security coverage levels, especially in a country where much of the economically active population receives between one minimum wage, and in a better projection, up to two minimum wages. The establishment of such levels and limits is essential to discourage the idea of not working or the idea that it is better to live without working, always keeping in mind that every generalization is dangerous. To this extent, social assistance should be a capacity-building instrument in such a way that addressees of social assistance can regain control of its destiny after being capacitated, becoming the architects of their own destiny.

References

Barroso LR (2012) Ano do STF: Judicialização, Ativismo e Legitimidade Democrática. Available at http://www.conjur.com.br. Accessed 03 May 2012

Bobbio N (1986) O Futuro da Democracia: Uma defesa das Regras do Jogo, 2nd edn. Paz e terra, São Paulo, 1986

Horvath Junior, Miguiel. Direito Previdenciário, 10 ed, São Paulo: Quartier Latin, 2014.

Lenza P (2013) Direito Constitucional Esquematizado, 13ª Ed. Saraiva, São Paulo, 2013

Sen AK (2000) Desenvolvimento como Liberdade. Companhia das Letras, São Paulo, 2000

Chapter 5
Social Welfare and *Continuous Benefit Payments*: A Reality To Be Perfected

Theodoro Vicente Agostinho and Sérgio Henrique Salvador

Abstract Guaranteed by the Supreme Constitutional Charter the full social assistance the important planning social welfare, whether Social Security, which since 1988 has brought a new model of social techniques. In addition to the constitutional dimension, the themes discussed here diuturnamente has caused deep discussions and highlighted that well produce the ripening of his fruitful field of study. Generally speaking, it is known that social assistance generally covers various situations and performances, however, the monetary benefit of related legislation is that it has been the main target of today's legal discussions. Issues such as hipossuficiência, gross or net income, as dependents, finally, are some of the issues involving the present and modest article, which aims to demonstrate in essence the urgent need to improve this republican achievement.

Keywords Social assistance • Assistance benefit • Income • Dependent • Improvement • Social welfare

The theme in question is of vital social importance and deals with what is considered to be a solid and necessary boundary for the whole of collective society.

Being so, when speaking of Social Welfare one is by nature setting structure to the entirety of the legal, political, economic, and social structure of a society.

This fact, or better yet, this model was created by those who drafted the Brazilian Constitution in 1988 and who elected to confer upon the Social Welfare Institution an eminently protective function.

By Social Protection it is understood that the highest ideal of a state is to guarantee that social rights, which are non-negotiable, supreme, and fundamental, should be foreseen by law.

T.V. Agostinho (✉)
São Paulo, S. Paulo, Brazil
e-mail: professor.theodoro@terra.com.br

S.H. Salvador
Itajubá, Minas Gerais, Brazil
e-mail: sergiohsalvador@bol.com.br

M.A. Serau Junior, J.R. Caetano Costa (eds.), *Assistance Benefits in Brazil*,
DOI 10.1007/978-3-319-27046-3_5

Therefore, the Brazilian law system created a protective outline seeking to give rise to this end.

In light of this, and to defend and guard these rights as fundamental values and pillars for any organized society, Leite (1973) pointed in this direction, specifically when referring to such a protective plan:

> (…) The basic goal of Social Protection is to secure that human beings have purchasing power, the capacity to satisfy their basic needs, and that this does not result in mere subsistence.

Diniz (1998) also conceptualizes this social right regulated by the Constitution as:

> A set of norms that seeks to attend to the common good, helping those that depend on the fruits of their labor to guarantee their own subsistence, as well as that of their family, to conveniently satisfy their basic needs and to have access to private property.

Thus, it is evident and clear that a politically organized civil society requires prior specific tools necessary to achieve the concept of social well-being that was set forth in the current Brazilian Constitution.

Over time, Social Protection has taken many forms, everything from better working conditions, to a definition of basic living needs.

Nowadays, everything regarding the idea of protection, as it is currently so well constructed, began with assistance protection, as occurred, for example, as public aid in Santa Casa de Misericórdia in the city of Santos.

Strongly influenced by the European system of workers protection, assistance protection then began to be drawn up by specific laws in Brazil, but without also separating itself from the set of Brazilian social ideals.

With the German model, advocated by Otto Von Bismark, the Brazilian social security system gains its direction, but it is with the English model that a specific system of collective protection gains its time and voice, thus going on to condense social security policies as well as social welfare policies.

Here, the beginning of Social Welfare Protection:

This system, inserted within the Brazilian constitutional framework, gaining its own legal structure, specific budget, singular legal topography, and with an accentuated and highly relevant position in society, is composed of a triple structure: Social Security, Public Health, and Social Welfare, regulated by article 194 of the Constitution.

In turn, and as it should, the authoritative doctrine also explains with singular mastery this constitutional organism of protection, as we can see by the writings of Balera (2009) and Berbel (2005), respectively:

> The Social Security System consecrates the individual's protection against all possible risks that may arise, and does this via Public Health, Social Welfare, or Social Security;
>
> In this way, it can be said in principle that the Social Security System is the set of rules and structurally allocated principles, with scope to carry out Social Welfare Protection that, from a purely political view, would be the full protection of the individual from the misfortunes of life, which would otherwise bring about poverty, rather, it is Social Protection from individual misfortune.

It is clear that any constitutional set of ideals dispenses of several mechanisms that enable its concreteness, so that they be not mere abstract achievements without any feasible density.

It is that values, principles, achievements, axioms, or rather, all that is fundamentally elected needs to be protected, built, evolved, and also exercised.

Within this context, we have the evolution of Social Welfare as an active participant in the social welfare protection system as well as the constitutional system, par excellence.

It is true that the former Brazilian Constitutions did not confer the current and structured treatment upon this protective branch, with the current Brazilian Constitution being the apogee of the model of welfare protection.

On the other hand, a specific regulatory system, as well as a political structure, is also required to achieve such a desired constitutional concreteness.

And all this occurred within the context of the homeland.

Indeed, Law 8.472/93 was a great and important landmark for Social Welfare.

Twenty years after the passing of this law, the question that arises is: have we achieved the desired set of constitutional ideals set forth for Social Protection?

We think that we have not yet achieved this, but rather that we have traced a path.

That is because the aforementioned legislation finds itself within a deep and important social evolution, being enhanced, interpreted, complemented, all in order to pursue its ideals.

Within the context of this law it is well known that this piece of legislation brings with it important aspects of welfare policies. However, what interests us is the assessment of the evolution of Assistance Benefits that it has brought in its wake.

First, it is worth mentioning that certainly the law would miss something in essence if it did not carry a prevision for covered benefits for those in need of assistance.

As it is already known, the law concerns itself with a type of benefit that deals with assistance, but without any social security connotation, despite currently being managed by the INSS (National Institute of Social Security), the managing authority of the RGPS (General Social Security Regime).

In truth, this benefit should be maintained and managed by social departments within the cities, but for other reasons this alternative has proven itself still impossible within Brazil.

However, so that the individual in need may be assisted by a state program, it fell upon the Social Security system to exercise this protection directly, although rather irregularly.

The BPC, or the Continuous Cash Benefit Program, is authentic government social aid, but is far from being framed as a benefit payment, being that it is not converted in survivors pensions, neither it is paid out as an allowance in the form of the so-called 13th salary.

Therefore, it is evident that it is not a benefit payment, but rather a government assistance payment.

Specifically, it is paid out to the elderly in need, who are over 60 years of age, and that do not have any income, or it is paid out if the total family income does not exceed ¼ of the minimum wage *per capita*. It is also paid to those who are disabled and unable to perform all the acts required for civil life, be them work related, or be it the ability to conduct an independent life.

These are the objectives of the legislation under discussion with respect to financial and periodic assistance.

It is important to emphasize that these assistance benefits, while very practical in their daily workings, bring within them a medley of eternal legal discussions capable of invoking the intervention of the Supreme Court.

To be sure, a matter worth mentioning is the legal prevision establishing that those in need, without any income due to either age or to other health problems, will be able to exercise their legal right as citizens, and could safeguard their dignity, such as was preserved in beginning of the constitutional provisions.

The question that then arises is: was this particular law satisfactory unto these ends?

Well, Assistance Benefits are merely a minimum wage.

Also, these benefits may be revised periodically, and what is more, they prevent those in need from receiving bank loans. Furthermore, there is no extension to the so-called 13th salary, not to mention the absence of its conversion into pension.

It is clear that we cannot use the social security model in its context, but we should use it in an analogical way, since Social Security and Social Welfare are co-related under Constitutional Social Welfare Protection.

To assist means to attend to, to help those in need, and to confer upon them, at least a certain dignity, not just legal, but also social, and existential.

Moreover, the legislation suffered changes, but still requires many others.

An interesting question is one that concerns income, or rather, the nature of that income, net or gross?

If we think in a real and feasible context, what arrives in the hands of the worker is gross income and not net income.

Moreover, what is meant by a family unit?

If we consider every single person that lives under the same roof, would it be legally more plausible?

For example, an elderly couple that lives with their nephews, all of them of age and with income, but imagine that this elderly couple needs medical treatment and specific drugs.

Would the nephews be the dependents or the ones responsible for that elderly couple?

We think that they would be neither.

So, the current legislation aims indefinitely at a situation which should be limited, but limited subjectively.

A very simple study of Social Welfare in the region, perhaps conducted by the city hall, would bring more certainty and equilibrium to this situation.

On the other hand, the criterion of ¼ of the minimum wage *per capita*, shows itself as an exhaustive or objective parameter?

The Judicial Courts have, for quite some time, understood that it is neither, but let us see:

> JEFs. TNU. Social Security. Assistance Benefits. LOAS. Criteria. State of misery. Monthly income "per capita". Objective criterion. Other means of proof. Possibility. The objective criterion of the assessment of monthly income provided for in § 3 of art. 20 of Law 8.742/1993 (which determines whether or not there exists a state of misery given income "per capita") is not absolute and does not preclude the possibility of the judge, when con-

sidering the case, from resorting to other evidence to confirm whether or not there exists a state of misery in the case of the applicant and his/her family. With this decision, the National Panel of the Standardization of Special Federal Courts (TNU) established a parameter so that the concrete evidence in the case may be re-examined by the Amazon Appeals Panel given this understanding. In the case in question, the insured sought TNU after the Amazon Appeals Panel denied the assistance benefit to the deficient, under the pretense of the absence of the required objective criterion for the benefit being sought (state of misery), whereas income "per capita" determined during the process was more than 1/4 of the minimum wage. However, the TNU, the rapporteur of the case, Federal Judge MARISA CUCIO, gave a different direction to the story. As emphasized by Judge Marisa Cucio, the income "per capita" on the part of the plaintiff, being, or not being, more than 1/4 of the minimum wage is not a determining factor. "It is the understanding espoused by TNU and the Supreme Justice Tribunal that, in all cases, the magistrate may make use of other means to measure the state of misery of the plaintiff, with the income "per capita" not being an absolute criterion". (Case No. 0001332-54.2011.4.01.3200).

And the discussion does not end here.

For example, if a family member already receives welfare benefits, for what reason should these benefits be calculated as income that excludes the participation of the other on the same claim?

Also, if a member of a family already receives benefit payments, but at the minimum legal wage, why does this income become an obstruction for the member who could potentially receive Assistance Benefits, if such value, being equivalent to the minimum legal wage, is not at all near to the amount that would be required for one to maintain a reasonable level of human dignity?

However, we must not forget its importance in structuring a set of constitutional ideals that seeks to protect those who should be covered.

Thus, as happened with the advent of the Statute of the Elderly, other legislation will surely come, and will directly affect these pillars of Social Welfare, causing a necessary and new social interpretation, so that those in need will not be excluded by the restrictions of law.

In this way, with the passing of time, Social Welfare has grown in such a way as to shelter and give home to its recipients instead of limiting access.

However, we are far from this goal, but we must recognize that the path exists and it will always need to be traveled in order to reach the closest version of what is desirable, provided that without the context of Social Protection, no state system can exist nor be justified.

References

Balera W (2009) Sistema de Seguridade Social, 5ªth edn. LTr, São Paulo

Berbel FLV (2005) Teoria Geral da Previdência Social, 1ªth edn. Quartier Latin, São Paulo

Case n° 0001332-54.2011.4.01.3200 (http://www.ibdp.org.br/noticias2.asp?id=1266). Accessed 26 Aug 2015

Diniz MH (1998) Dicionário Jurídico. Saraiva, São Paulo

Leite CB (1973) Previdência Social: Atualidades e Tendências, 1ªth edn. LTr, São Paulo

Chapter 6
Social Assistance: Analysis of the Fundamental Right Based on the 20-Year Experience of Law 8.472/93

Wagner Balera

Abstract There are two essential points that the text deals with: the qualification of social care as a social right and the character of constitutional program granted to social inclusion. Thus, interests on social assistance to identify social needs and, consequently, carrying out the measures—benefits, services, projects, and programs—able to transform the social reality in which the poor live. Everything will be done so that they give full implementation of the task of eradicating poverty and marginalization, qualified by art. 3, III, of the Constitution of Brazil as the magnum social constitutional goal.

Keywords Social security • Social assistance • Fundamental rights • Poverty

6.1 Constitutional Perspective

The historical trajectory of social assistance, in its way, enabled the natural generation of the bases of the Constitutional Social Order regarding the theme being studied.

The call of the National Constitutional Convention was accomplished with the Message forwarded to the National Congress in 1985.

A fundamental political decision had defined that the people's representatives should be elected to draft the Constitution and, after this task was accomplished, they should operate as an ordinary legislative body (Federal Constitution. Constitutional Amendment n. 26, de 27.11.85, published in the Federal Register of November 28th 1985).

It is true that, before that, President JOSÉ SARNEY had created the Provisional Committee of Constitutional Studies, chaired by AFONSO ARINOS, which prepared the *Constitutional Draft*.

W. Balera (✉)
Catholic University, S. Paulo, Brazil
e-mail: wbalera@balera.com.br

M.A. Serau Junior, J.R. Caetano Costa (eds.), *Assistance Benefits in Brazil*,
DOI 10.1007/978-3-319-27046-3_6

The members of the Constitutional Congress did not use this document much, but Title IV of the Draft laid the foundations of the Social Order which, at the proper time, would be thoroughly examined in the works of the thematic committees, especially the one which was focused on the themes of social security and family.

The Draft approaches the theme of social assistance in a manner which is still very modest. However, upon embracing the concept of social security, it created the bases which would allow the future development of the theme at the normative level. The command prescribed as follows:

> Art. 347 – The social security is guaranteed in the form established by the law, by means of social security plans, with the contribution of the Federal Government, and, as applicable, of the companies and of the beneficiaries:
>
> ....
>
> IV – to the social services, according to the needs of the person and of the family:

It also defined, still in a generic way, social service and its main recipients: the person and the family.

Another precept laid the general lines of what would eventually become the social assistance plans:

> Art. 371 prescribed:
>
> SPECIAL REMEDIES
>
> Art. 371 – The assistance to maternity, to childhood, to adolescence, to the elderly, and to the disabled is ensured.
>
> Art. 372 – The Federal Government, the States, and the Municipalities must promote the creation of a national network of maternity-childhood assistance, of a national network of nursery schools, and of an infrastructure of support to the family, regardless of the provision of item XII of Art. 343.
>
> Art. 373 – The minors, especially the orphans and the abandoned ones, regardless of the civil and criminal liability of the parents who abandon them, will be entitled to a special protection provided by the society and by the State, against all forms of discrimination and oppression, with total support, feeding, education, and health care.
>
> Art. 374 – The adolescents enjoy a special protection for the accomplishment of their economic, social, and cultural rights, such as access to education, culture, and work; professional training and promotion, physical education, and sports; good use of free time.
>
> Art. 375 – The elderly are entitled to economic safety and to conditions of housing and family or community contact which avoid and overcome isolation or social exclusion.
>
> Art. 376 – The disabled are entitled to the improvement of their social and economic condition, especially by means of:
>
> I – special and free education;
>
> II – assistance, rehabilitation, and reinsertion into the economic and social life of the country;
>
> III – prohibition of discrimination, also in relation to the admission to work or public service and to salaries;
>
> IV – possibility of access to public buildings and streets.

It thus can be seen that the essential bases of the works to be developed by social assistance, as well as its specific recipients, were already outlined in the first draft of the Constitution that was being prepared in that historic period.

After the National Constitutional Convention was established, in the terms of Constitutional Amendment n. 26, on February 1st 1987, the respective works were organized by themes.

The topic was dealt with by the Committee of Social Order, chaired by the then Senator Almir Gabriel.

The issue of social assistance, sent to the Committee of Classification which, in the capacity of previous collective body, prepared the draft to be analyzed by the Full Constitutional Convention, was already formally classified into the area of Social Security. Here are the terms of the command:

> Art. 333 – Social security in the broad sense includes an integrated set of actions, aimed at ensuring the social rights related to health care, social security, and social assistance.

The Constitutional Convention was technical and precise, as it can be observed. It defined well as constitutional social rights the three components of social security in the broad sense. It systematized well this triple reality.

Therefore, the basis of the constitutional Social Order was already outlined.

The Full Constitutional Convention, on September 22nd 1988, approved the final text of the Constitution, and the Citizen Constitution, as it was called by the Chairman of the Constitutional Convention, Representative Ulisses Guimarães, was enacted on October 5th 1988.

The prescriptions related to the theme being studied readily produce two bulky innovations: it qualifies social assistance as a social right and, in addition to that, it confers upon social inclusion the status of constitutional program.

The normative modeling of social assistance, as it could be realized since the constitutional works, made the basic commitment with social inclusion.

This was about identifying the state of necessity found in the community of the ones in need (or destitute, according to the term used by Art. 6 of the Constitution) and about programming the measures to be used for that state of things to be transformed into definitive.

This is why the Constitution dared include, among the objectives of the Republic, the task of eradicating the poverty and the exclusion (Art. 3, III), which requires more than the creation of social programs.

The *social security* must be in the forefront, of course, but the task must be taken on by all the society.

Social security will certainly lead the initiatives in favor of the poor and the excluded ones, which will be successful if they are supplemented by as many other initiatives led by beneficial entities of social assistance.

The mission of social security, as defined by Almansa Pastor (1991), is sufficiently broad. This mission is:

> El instrumento estatal específico protector de necesidades sociales, individuales y colectivas, a cuya protección preventiva, reparadora y recuperadora, tienen derecho los individuos, en la extensión, límites y condiciones que las normas dispongan, según su organización financiera.

The assistance tasks of social security are not, therefore, exclusively an aid to the poor. The constitutional guideline is more demanding: to eradicate poverty and exclusion.

Therefore, the collectivity must assume the inclusion as its proposal and attitude in face of the giant evil of social exclusion.

This is a true calling of all to the immense social task which Brazil owes to millions and millions of people.

This is the reason why the irradiating effect of social security as an instrument of governmental action can be affirmed, along with Persiani (1981). The master says that such ideal is capable of

> … influenzarre non solo la previdenza sociale, ma in genere ogni attivitá pubblica a scopo sociale.

The protective strategy of the social security is based on the higher principle of the universality of coverage and assistance (Art. 194, sole paragraph, item I, of the Constitution) and; for that reason, all the effort of the social security system must consist in the insertion, into its network of protection, of the most diverse forms of action which the community, throughout history, performs in favor of the ones in need.

Social protection, in its modality of assistance, acquires a more specific meaning, in the interior of this normative universe when, upon identifying the situation of need, the protective device is capable of immediately moving its legal framework to the benefit of the ones in need, especially by means of the provisions.

It has always been difficult to identify the several situations of need which will require the action of social assistance.

The economic perspective, to analyze just one aspect, leads an endless discussion regarding the identification of the so-called extreme poverty line. Several points of view are outlined without reaching a final conclusion.[1]

It must be acknowledged that, under the legal perspective, the concept of extreme poverty may only be reached based on the supreme legal criterion: the legal rule.[2]

The investigation of the causes of poverty and social exclusion must be conducted by several fields of knowledge.

However, the scope of the social security does not consist in the approach of the *causes* of this serious social issue. It must, most importantly, work with the *consequences* deriving from them: the situations of need configured by the destitution and by the exclusion.

The decisive attitude which, in the constitutional reform, the Legislative Power decided to assume, included the requirement for the social assistance programs to have results.

---

[1]Only to cite three recent criteria for definition. The Objectives of the Development of the Millenium qualify as extremely poor those who receive the equivalent to U$ 1,25 *per capita* a Day. The program *Bolsa-Família* (Family Allowance), chief program of the social initiatives of the Brazilian government defines the amount of R$ 70.00 to the *per capita* family monthly income and the program of the LOAS benefit defines the *per capita* family income as up to one fourth of the minimum wage.

[2]*Kelsen* (1974) affirms that "The legal science searches to seize its object "legally", that is, from the point of view of the Law. To legally seize something therefore cannot mean nothing but seize something as Law, which means: as a legal rule, or content of a legal rule, as determined through a legal rule".

Indeed, the creation of the Fund to Fight and Eradicate Poverty by means of Constitutional Amendment n. 31, of 2000, conferred the essential financial basis to support the social assistance programs of social inclusion.[3]

After that, the social security provisions in favor of the poor population could be supported by a certain financial guarantee which would enable, by means of a systematic and rational action of the government, the continuity of the programs.

The social assistance plans and programs, it must be acknowledged, are part of the current reality as emergency measures—and maybe this is what inspired the provisional perspective initially given to the Fund referred to above—capable of remedying the contingencies of poverty.

The structural issue, however, depends on broader measures and perspectives, especially on the economic process of the development.

The constitutional precepts dealing with the issue, upon defining the profile of the social assistance, select the several fronts of work in which the segment will perform.

Art. 203 of the Constitution prescribes:

> Art. 203. The social assistance will be provided to the ones who need it, regardless of contribution to the social security, and it has the following objectives:
>
> I – protection to the family, maternity, childhood, adolescence, and old age;
>
> II – support to destitute children and adolescents;
>
> III – promotion of integration to the labor market;
>
> IV –qualification and rehabilitation of the people with disabilities and the promotion of their integration to community life;
>
> V – guarantee of a minimum wage of monthly benefit to the people with disabilities and to the elderly who demonstrate not to have means to support themselves or to be supported by their families, according to the law.

It can be verified that the list above follows, in general terms, the proposal of social inclusion already dealt with in the draft of the Constitution.

The Constitutional Convention already defines and identifies the protective universe of social assistance.

The phenomenology of poverty and social exclusion, as of that moment, identifies the subjects which are affected by it and, therefore, those who will be the recipients of the social assistance action.

The social issue shows itself, in this aspect, with well-defined boundaries.

The merit of the Constitution, in this aspect, is undisputable.

It not only identified the risks—let's place the sphere of the social assistance as equally apt to face social risks, according to the tradition inaugurated by Beveridge Plan which, among the giant evils to be faced by social security, includes dirtiness, as it manages to engender measures and programs which associate the fight against poverty with the support of development.

It must now be verified, from a historical perspective, whether the 20 years of the Organic Law of Social Assistance have well and adequately accomplished the ideal conceived by the Constitutional Convention.

---

[3] Constitutional Amendments n. 42, of 2003, and 67, of 2010, extended for an indeterminate period the existence of such social fund.

6.2 Legal Perspective

Therefore, representative Raimundo Bezerra introduces Bill n. 3099/89 which later, on September 17th 1990, was fully vetoed by the then President Fernando Collor de Mello, under the argument that the nation had no resources to pay the prescribed benefits, alleging that its principles are not in accordance with a responsible Social Assistance.

After the introduction of Bill n. 3099, of 1989, the configuration of the legal framework of the Brazilian social assistance began.

In a brute violation to the Constitution, the COLLOR Administration fully vetoed that law that had been passed, under the allegation of lack of financial resources for the payment of the social assistance provisions then created.

A new initiative occurred with the introduction of Bill n. 4.100, of 1993, by the Executive Power.

The behind-the-scene political articulation allowed the project to be introduced with the discussions well advanced in the Parliament.

Therefore, the legislative process, under the regime of urgency, was speedily conducted and culminated, after a little over 2 months, with the enactment of the Law.

It was the month of December of 1993.

In this same year, President ITAMAR FRANCO had an important initiative when establishing the National Council of Food Safety.[4]

In the year of 1994, the I National Conference of Food Safety was called and it properly established three objectives:

> A] to increase the conditions of access to food and to reduce its weight in the family budget;
> B] to ensure health, nutrition, and food to certain groups of the population:
> C] to ensure the biological, sanitary, nutritional, and technological quality of food and its utilization, stimulating healthy eating habits and lifestyles.

However, in a severe blow to the still embryonic process of construction of the Brazilian social assistance model—which naturally had to begin with problem number one, the fight against hunger, then pointed as requirement from the impressive movement led by sociologist HERBERT DE SOUZE—President CARDOSO extinguished CONSEA and created a program which was completely apart from LOAS (Organic Law of Social Assistance), the Solidary Community.

In a true revival of *assistencialismo* and *primeiro-damismo*,[5] the Solidary Community received resources without any social control, and was an improper and unruly policy (Raichelis 2000).[6]

---

[4] Decree n. 807, de 1993.

[5] The *primeiro-damismo* began with the creation of LBA—Brazilian Legion of Assistance, one of the pillars of social assistance until the enactment of the Constitution of 1988. LBA would be chaired by the first-lady (*primeira dama*) of the country, DARCY SARMANHO VARGAS and this model set an example… The first-lady is the "mother" of the poor and of the destitute. As well qualified by ALDAISA SPOSATI: "*The "primeiro-damismo" is the institutionalization of* assistencialismo *in the figure of the wife of the ruler (…)* In Núcleo de Seguridade e Assistência Social da PUC/SP. Texto" Assistência x Assistencialismo x Assistência Social. junho/1994.

[6] Raichelis (2000).

During the term of President CARDOSO the I National Conference of Social Assistance was held in 1995.

However, the Executive Power did not listen to this higher democratic instance of the security system management, in its modality of assistance, and did not provided the segment with the essential resources to achieve the objectives of LOAS.

It is true that the creation of the National Council of Social Assistance, the CNAS, result of the restructuring of the National Council of Social Service, represented the first step in the historic march for the accomplishment of LOAS.

Indeed, in the accomplishment of the constitutional objective of the democratic and decentralized nature of social security (Constitution, Art. 194, sole paragraph, item VII), there was the assumption that the bodies of generic resolutions—the Conferences—and of specific resolutions—the Councils would be formed—and they would be capable of establishing policies and controlling the actions of the segment, as also correctly determined by Art. 204 of the Constitution.[7]

6.2.1 The Continuous Provision Benefit

The effective implantation of LOAS will occur, in a concrete manner, with the formal regulation of the first of the respective provisions, the Continuous Provision Benefit, by means of Decree n. 1.744, of December 1995.[8]

It may even be said that this date is the anniversary of LOAS. Before that, the concrete measures were more related to the formal structuring of the structure—in itself subject to disturbances and vacillations—than to the effective compliance with the constitutional duties of the social assistance system.

Indeed, Art. 203, V, of the Constitution of 1988 prescribes that social assistance must provide:

> V – guarantee of a minimum wage of monthly benefit to the people with disabilities and to the elderly who demonstrate not to have means to support themselves or to be supported by their families, according to the law.

This is, therefore, the first of the benefits of the constitutional social assistance, the so-called LOAS Benefit.

---

[7] Art. 204. The governmental actions in the field of social assistance will be performed with resources from the budget of the social security, prescribed in Art. 195, in addition to other sources, and organized by the following guidelines:

I – coordination and for the general rules, and the state and municipal governments are responsible for the coordination and the execution of the respective programs, as well as the beneficial entities and the social assistance entities;

II – participation of the population, by means of representative organizations, in the creation of the policies and in the control of the actions at all levels.

[8] The current Regulation is Decree n. 6.214, of 2007.

The first controversy surrounding the benefit was related to the respective limitation, in the terms of Art. 20, § 3, of LOAS, which only considered eligible to the benefit the ones whose gross family monthly income, divided by the number of the family members, was lower than one fourth of the minimum wage.[9]

Therefore, the first experience of LOAS was successful.

According to data from the Ministry of Social Development and Fight Against Hunger, in March 2012 (last available record), three million and six hundred benefits were given, being 1.0 million for people with disabilities and 1.7 million for elderly included in the provision.

6.2.2 Temporary Benefits

Resolution n. 39, of 2010, of the National Council of Social Assistance demonstrates, by means of documents, that not even the first steps were taken in order to implement this right to the beneficiaries.

LOAS defined, in its Art. 22, that:

> Art. 22. Temporary benefits are those which aim at the payment of a provision in the event of birth or death to the families whose monthly *per capita* income is lower than 1/4 (one fourth) of a minimum wage.
>
> § 1. The concession and the amount of the benefits referred to in this article will be regulated by the Councils of Social Assistance of the States, of the Federal District, and of the Municipalities, by means of criteria and periods defined by the National Council of Social Assistance (CNAS).
>
> § 2. Other temporary benefits may be established to fulfill needs deriving from situations of temporary vulnerability, with priority to children, family, elderly, people with disabilities, pregnant women, breastfeeding mothers, and cases of public calamity.
>
> § 3. The National Council of Social Assistance (CNAS), after hearing the respective representations of States and Municipalities which take part in it, may propose, according to the budget availabilities of the three levels of government, the institution of subsidiary benefits in the amount of up to 25% (twenty-five per cent) of the minimum age to each children of up to 6 (six) years of age, in the terms of the family monthly income established in the head provision.

This was about concretely giving pecuniary provisions in the situations of birth and death to the beneficiaries of social assistance.

In other words, it was about giving that which the social security previously granted under the names of birth-aid and funeral-aid to the beneficiaries of RGPS (General Regime of Social Security).

Although they were the object of regulation, by virtue of the prescription of Decree n. 6.307, of 2007, such provisions were never granted.

---

[9]In COMPLAINT 4.374, whose justice-rapporteur was Justice GILMAR MENDER, the Full Supreme Federal Court, in a decision of April 18th of 2013, changing a previous position, maintained the decision for the special jurisdictional line and considered such restriction unconstitutional (http://redir.stf.jus.br/paginadorpub/paginador.jsp?docTP=TP&docID=4439489).

Law n. 12.435, of 2011, rendering even vaguer the legal configuration of the provisions—what can be said of the expression "organically integrate the guarantees of SUAS (Unified Social Assistance System)"?—prescribes as follows:

> Art. 22. Temporary benefits are the supplementary and provisional provisions which organically integrate the guarantees of SUAS and are given to the citizens and to the families by virtue of birth, death, situations of temporary vulnerability and public calamity.
>
> § 1. The concession and the amount of the benefits referred to in this Article will be defined by the States, Federal District, and Municipalities and prescribed in the respective annual budgets, based on criteria and periods defined by the respective Councils of Social Assistance.
>
> § 3. The CNAS, after hearing the respective representations of States and Municipalities which take part in it, may propose, according to the budget availabilities of the 3 levels of government, the institution of subsidiary benefits in the amount of up to 25% (twenty-five per cent) of the minimum age to each children of up to 6 (six) years of age.

What is the serious danger of the prescriptions of Law n. 12.435?

It is precisely the terms included in the paragraph of the last transcription: "*according to the budget availabilities of the 3 (three) levels of government.*"

It should be remembered that, in the terms of the Organic Law of Social Security, the social assistance would be accomplished only if there were financial resources.

It is evidently a disqualification of social constitutional law.

If there is money, there is the right to the provision. If there is no money, nothing can be done.

The Romans created, in their time, a strange legal category: the quasi-right. This is, in a way, what this is about.

6.2.3 The Social Assistance Programs

LOAS established the respective field of action in three fronts of work: the pecuniary provisions (which include the BPC—the continuous provision benefits—and the temporary benefits), the social assistance programs and, finally, the projects of fight against poverty.

> Art. 24. The social assistance programs include integrated and supplementary actions with objectives, time, and effective areas defined to qualify, encourage, and improve the benefits and the social assistance services.
>
> § 1. The programs referred to in this Article will be defined by the respective Councils of Social Assistance, in conformity with the objectives and principles governing this law, with priority to the professional and social inclusion.

The final part of the prescription allows us to affirm that only one of the programs fully complies with this purpose. It is the **National program of youth inclusion.**

Created by Law n. 11.129, of 2005, amended by Law n. 11.692, of 2008, the *Projovem* is indeed a tool of social inclusion. Its constitutional basis is item III of Art. 203 of the Constitution.

Being this a strategic project of social inclusion, the social assistance must promote the inclusion.

It must be acknowledged, however, that the two most inclusive and known programs—the *Bolsa-Família* (Family Allowance) and the *Brasil sem Miséria* (Brazil Without Poverty) are unmistakably covered with a strong *assistencialista* character, which has always occurred in the actions of social assistance in Brazil.

6.2.4 The Projects of Fight Against Poverty

The last of the fields of action prescribed by LOAS is the one of the projects of fight against poverty.

These are the words of the normative command:

> Art. 25. The projects of fight against poverty include the institution of economic-social investment in the popular groups, searching to financially and technically subsidize initiatives which provide these groups with means, productive capacity, and capacity of management for the improvement of the general conditions of subsistence, increase of the standard of life quality, the preservation of the environment, and their social organization.
>
> Art. 26. The incentive to projects of fight against poverty will be based on mechanisms of articulation and participation of different governmental areas and on a system of cooperation among governmental organisms, non-governmental entities, and the civil society.

The content and the spectrum of such projects are diffuse.

Its diffusion has been derived especially from specific initiatives lacking some sense of organism.

The projects which have a more concrete repercussion on the social means are those which search for the inclusion of well-defined groups: the children, as in the Program of Eradication of Child Labor; the elderly, whose attention is under the care of the National Network of Protection and Defense of the Rights of the Elderly, integrated to the SUS (Unified Health System) and SUAS (Unified Social Assistance System), and the people with disabilities, of the last of the fields of action established by LOAS is the one of the projects of fight against poverty.

It can be verified, also in this aspect, that the list of social actions from an assistance perspective complies, in general terms, with the first design of the theme, such as configured in the constitutional debates and accomplished in the draft of the Constitution.

6.3 Conclusion

It must be acknowledged that, after 20 years of the enactment of LOAS, there have been significant advances in the normative frameworks of social assistance and notable efforts in favor of the consolidation of the programs which this segment of social security is called to accomplish.

With the formal establishment, by means of Resolution n. 145, of 2004, of the National Council of Social Assistance, of a National Policy of Social Assistance, a certain conceptual standard of performance has been imposed to the State and to the administrators, beyond the mere political and *assistencialistas* manipulations which have always disgracefully affected the good performance of the segment.

Moreover, the implementation of the two Basic Operating Rules (the first was approved by Resolution n. 130, of July 2005, and the second by Resolution n. 33, of December 2012, both of the CNAS) reveals that the segment speedily goes in the direction of the implementation of the respective institutional profile.

Let's adopt as a concept the notion of legal experience coined by Reale (1968), to whom:

> The concept of order, of measure, of rule or norm, in the double pointed aspect, of safeguard of the *specific* while concomitantly safeguard of the *whole* is inherent to the notion of legal experience.

In the light of this criterion, it may be said that LOAS as a data of concrete experience of the regulation, in addition to having taken care of the specific—concrete effectiveness of the benefits, services, programs, and projects—also took care of safeguarding the whole, maintaining the segment duly integrated into the system of social security.

It is, therefore, a landmark whose 20 years deserve being mentioned and reflected upon.

References

Almansa Pastor JM (1991) Derecho de La Seguridad Social, 7ª edição. TEcnos, Madrid

Kelsen H (1974) Teoria Pura do Direito, tradução de *João Baptista Machado*, Armênio Amado – Editor, Sucessor, 3ª ed.

Persiani M (1981) Lezioni di Diritto della Previdenza Sociale. CEDAM, Padova

Raichelis R (2000) Esfera Pública e Conselhos de Assistência Social – caminhos da construção democrática, 2ª edição. Cortez, São Paulo

Reale M (1968) O direito como experiência. Saraiva, São Paulo

Part II
Requirements for Granting the Benefit

Chapter 7
Administrative Process for the Purpose of the Concession of Welfare Benefits

Alexandre Schumacher Triches

Abstract This paper consists of, in short, an approach to the administrative process for the purpose of the analysis of the right to receive Continued Contribution Benefits, as stated in Section 20 of Law no 8.742/93. This is the benefit originated from Article 203 of the Federal Constitution that predicts the subsystem of Social Assistance, in relation to the Social Security System. The objective of this paper is to analyze the aforementioned kind of process, from its instauration to its conclusion, searching for definitions for juridical regime, juridical nature, and pragmatic aspects related to the dynamics of the process.

Keywords Social security • Welfare benefits • Administrative process • Purpose • Concession

7.1 Introduction and Justification

This paper consists of, in short, an approach to the administrative process for the purpose of the analysis of the right to receive Continued Contribution Benefits, as stated in Section 20 of Law no 8.742/93—denominated Welfare Benefit. This is the benefit originated from Section 203 of the Federal Constitution that predicts the subsystem of Social Assistance, in relation to the Social Security System. The objective of this paper is to analyze the aforementioned kind of process, defining juridical nature, juridical regime, and process dynamics.

The kind of process that will be discussed is perceived as a group of administrative acts, practiced in the ambit of the National Institute of Social Security—INSS autarchy, that have as objective verifying and operationalizing the act of conceding Welfare Benefits or not.

A.S. Triches (✉)
Pontifical Catholic University of São Paulo – PUC-SP, São Paulo, Brazil

Pontifical Catholic University of Rio Grande do Sul – PUC-RS, Rio Grande do Sul, Brazil
e-mail: astriches@terra.com.br

M.A. Serau Junior, J.R. Caetano Costa (eds.), *Assistance Benefits in Brazil*,
DOI 10.1007/978-3-319-27046-3_7

The choice of the theme is justified as a result of the relevance of the administrative process, in special because of the fact that the public chosen for the concession of the benefit belongs to an important stratum of the population, composed of the elderly and of people in vulnerable conditions.

7.2 Of the Juridical Regime of the Welfare Benefit Predicted in Section 20 of Law no 8.742/93

The Federal Constitution of 1988 grants assistance through benefits and services as stated in Section 203, Subsections I through V, with Subsection V predicting the payment of the welfare benefit. The Organic Law of Social Assistance regulates the concession of eventual benefits in its Section 22: "the provisional and supplemental provisions that organically integrate the guaranties of the SUAS and are given to citizens and families as a result of birth, death, situations of temporary vulnerability and of public calamity."

The eventual benefits are not to be confused with the Continued Contribution Benefits predicted in Section 20 of Law no 8.742/93: "The continued contribution benefit is the guaranty of one minimum wage to people with disabilities and to the elderly with 65 (sixty-five) or more years of age that prove not having a way to provide for themselves nor having their family provide for them."

It's the right of people with long-term life incapacities and of the elderly with 65 or more years of age, that have no means to provide for themselves nor having their family provide for them.

The referred concept of poverty must be determined based on the family of the candidate to the benefit, as stated by §1 of Section 20 of Law no 8.742/93: "the one [family] consisting of the claimant, their spouse or partner, and in their absence, their stepparents, their unmarried siblings, their unmarried children and stepchildren and adopted minors, as long as they live under the same roof. It is verified that the adopted criterion is that of the family composition."

The legal criterion of family composition is very debatable for the fulfillment of the socioeconomic requirement, seeing as relatives that have no relation to the candidate to the benefit are often wrongly considered part of the family group.

The interpretation that must be given to the §1 of Section 20 of Law no 8.742/93 is one that restricts itself to analyzing the concrete case, observing Section 16 of Law no 8.213/91, that is about welfare dependents.

The concept of a person with disabilities is determined by §2 of Section 20 of Law no 8.742/91: "are considered people with disabilities the ones that have long term impediments of physical, mental, intellectual or sensorial nature, which, in interaction with diverse barriers can obstruct their full and effective participation in society with equal conditions to the other people." At this point, the legislator allowed substantial modifications in the methodology to be used in medical and social evaluations.

The welfare benefit cannot be accumulated by the beneficiary with any other benefit in the ambit of social security insurance or another regime, excluding medical assistance and special indemnification benefits, as stated in §4 of Section 20 of Law no 8.742/93, as well as remuneration from learning contracts in the case of people with disabilities.

The prohibition of the accumulation doesn't cater to the constitutional principles linked to the benefit, since the welfare benefit has objective requirements delimitated in the legislation and only through social evaluation the legal context can be verified. In the case that the claimant possesses another benefit and it isn't enough for their subsistence they must be given the opportunity to prove the right to the benefit.

The interruption of the payment may occur in three situations: (1) When the conditions that gave occasion to the concession have been overcome; (2) In the case of the death of the beneficiary; (3) When irregularities in its concession or use are identified. In addition to that, the benefit must be re-examined every 2 years, for the evaluation of the continuity of the conditions that gave occasion to it.

The criteria for the requisite of the incapacity to provide for themselves in the case of the elderly or of people with disabilities are stated in §3 of Section 20 of Law no 8.742/91: "are considered incapable of providing for the elderly or people with disabilities families whose monthly per capita income is lower than 1/4 (one fourth) of the minimum wage."

It is understood that the objective criterion of income defined by the legislator makes difficult the access to the right as it can't be seen in an absolute way. The objective criterion of income was established in order to make the gauging of the right easier, not being able to act as an obstacle to the analysis of this condition through other means.

Depending on the peculiarities of the case, the family's per capita income can be equal or greater than ¼ of the minimum wage and the family of the claimant still isn't capable of providing for them, thus being evidenced the condition of economic hypo-sufficiency.

The limit established by the legislation must be considered as just one of the elements to be observed for the gauging of poverty, as there are other means of proof to be observed. Considering the adopted criterion in an absolute way is an affront to the constitution. Costa (2013a, b) thinks the same way, even in his theoretical aspects, let us then see if this is not the case:

> It is clearly an affront to the principle of legal regression, considering that the benefit of the Lifelong Monthly Income, that preceded it, had more beneficial criteria, when it comes to the monthly income for its concession.

It is not without reason that the courts[1] have been steering away from the objective criterion predicted in §3 of Section 20 of Law no 8.742/93 for a long time now. However, unfortunately, it is known that in the administrative ambit the server must abide by the legislation, which contains an objective criterion.

---

[1] The STF has already declared the legal criterion unconstitutional by defining in Demand (RCL) 4374, with the same meaning of the understanding already established by the Plenary in yesterday's session, when the court judged unconstitutional the two devices by analyzing Extraordinary Appeals (REs) 567985 and 580963, both with widespread repercussion. The minister Gilmar Mendes has proposed the determination of a deadline for the National Congress to create a new set of regulations about the subject, maintaining the validity of the current rules until December 31st of 2015, but this proposal wasn't approved by two thirds of the ministers (quorum for modulation). Only five ministers positioned themselves in favor of the modulation of the effects of the decision (Gilmar Mendes, Rosa Weber, Luiz Fux, Cármen Lúcia and Celso de Mello).

The legislation defines what is a long-term impediment in §10, when it refers to that which has effects for the minimum time of 2 (two) years. It is needed to assert the importance of overcoming the simplistic perspectives that the welfare benefit is restricted to people with physical and mental disabilities, excluding from its coverage people with long-term disabilities that hinder working and independent life activities.

7.3 Of the Juridical Nature of the Administrative Process for the Purpose of the Concession or Not Concession of Welfare Benefits

With the objective of discussing the juridical nature of the administrative process for the purpose of the concession of welfare benefits, it is important to locate it in the legislation. The administrative process defined by Federal Law no 9.784 of 1999/01/29 is called general. It is general because there are other legislations applicable to administrative processes, called special administrative lawsuits, usually established in the ambit of the state.

The rules of the general administrative process are also applicable to the procedures of special processes, in a subsidiary manner. It is what is verified in Section 69 of Law no 9.784/99, when it states:

> Section 69. The specific administrative processes will continue to operate under specific rules, the principles of this law being applied to them only subsidiarily.

The classification of an administrative process is very broad, as it can be classified as taxes, disciplinary, social security, and other kinds of administrative processes. Let's see some elucidative examples: the execution of an entrance exam by a public university, an external selection exam for hiring people to work in Public Administration, the proper procedure to validate taxes, the rules and sequence of acts between the request and the grant of waters or environmental licensing, some cases within government traffic organs, like issuing a driver's permit, a national driver's license or a second copy of one of these documents, among many other examples of administrative processes. We live together with procedural relations and public authority daily.

When the government organ is part of the federal Public Administration, the processes operate under Law no 9.784/99. If they belong to the state or municipal spheres, the procedures are dictated by their own administrative process laws.

In spite of the low practical and scientific profitability of the effort of classifying the types of administrative process, some delimitations are important in order to comprehend the juridical nature of the discussed type of administrative process. Firstly, that the administrative process for the purpose of the concession of welfare benefits possesses the juridical nature of a grant process, and a non-litigious nature, as there is no conflict of interest.

What happens is the performance of the administrative function, which aims to regulate the procedure for the gauging of the right to the Continued Contribution Benefit predicted in Section 20 of Law no 8.742/93.

It has the free of charge and welfare nature of a benefit. This is because it possesses all characteristics related to the social security process, as an object that reclaims interest beyond social security, but inserted in the context of social security Law, which is seen as the science that studies the Law of social security. Thus, the discussed type of process will be called Social Security Administrative Process of Welfare Benefits.

7.4 Dynamics of the Social Security Administrative Process of Welfare Benefits

7.4.1 Of the Instauration

The instauration of the Social Security Administrative Process of Welfare Benefits should happen in conjunction with the National Institute of Social Security—INSS.

The remote support channels are distributed through the Internet (http://www.previdencia.gov.br) and through Central 135. In order to make an electronic appointment, the user must have their social insurance number; their PIS/PASEP number (for workers with a work card); their NIT number (for individual and domestic taxpayers); their employer's CNPJ or CPF number; their CPF number; their benefit number (if they are receiving benefits).

It is worth noting that the majority of the needs in a welfare benefit process must be done personally in the Social Security Agency. It is also worth mentioning that the insured has the right of determining the Request's Entry Date—DER on the date of the appointment's requisition.

The process is accepted or refused in the appointment and the claimant is informed of the decision. In case there is a document in the process that can give occasion to doubt, a demand letter will be printed and a new appointment will be made for the conclusion of the process. If the claimant does not attend the scheduled appointment the process will be closed and the non-fulfillment of the administrative demand will be declared.

By occasion of the administrative request, the following documents will need to be presented: NIT (PIS/PASEP) or registration number; Identity Document; CPF; a Birth or Marriage Certificate; Death certificate of the deceased spouse, if it's the case; Proof of Residence; Proof of income of the family members; Personal Documents of the family members (Identity Document or Birth Certificate for members under 18 years old, CPF, PIS/PASEP/NIT number); Legal Guardianship, in the case of people under 18 years old with deceased or missing parents or parents that have lost guardianship. In the case of legal representation, must be presented the CPF; Identity Document; Guardianship or Curatorship documents if it is the case.

7.4.2 Of the Discovery Process

It is in the discovery process that all kinds of proof are gathered: witnesses, documental, and expert. Section 29 of law 9784/99 thus describes:

> Art. 29. The activities intended to determine and prove the necessary data for the decision making are done *ex officio* or upon impulse from the government organ responsible for the process, without injury of the right of those interested in proposing probationary actions

All means of proof are still valid in the administrative process for the purpose of the concession of welfare benefit when they are intended to clarify the existence of the right to receiving the benefit, except if the law demands a determined form. Obviously, however, this affirmation must be viewed with temperament, seeing that the public administration follows the principle of legality, and the means of proof and probationary procedures must be those predicted in the legislation.

There are three principal probationary procedures in the social security administrative process of welfare benefit: administrative justification, external research, and expert medical examination. In the three cases, the importance of their use in the administrative process means the exercise of the right of proof.

Administrative justification is the procedure intended to supply the lack of documents, or makes proof of a fact or circumstance of the beneficiary's interest before INSS. Section 596 of the INSS Normative Instruction no 45/2010 states that the Administrative Justification is the procedure intended to supply the lack of documents or makes proof of a fact or circumstance of the beneficiary's interest before INSS. Administrative Justification in INSS will be useful for the production of oral proof, aiming to prove the meeting of requirements related to the socioeconomic and medical condition of the candidate to the benefit. Thus, the presenting of witnesses and the hearsay of the claimant for the production of proof is possible.

Nowadays, the procedural practice hasn't been authorizing administrative justification in the discovery of the social security administrative process of welfare benefit. However, it becomes important permitting to the candidate to the benefit the production of oral proof, both in regard to their condition of poverty and their medical condition, which in many cases can't be limited to clinical analysis but also to their social aspects.

Administrative justification won't be accepted when the fact to be comproved requires a public record of marriage, birth or death, or any juridical act for which the law prescribes a special form, according to Section 597 of INSS Normative Instruction no 45/2010.

The proof of exclusion of a family member intends to eliminate from the calculation of the income of the family group those that don't fit in this condition. In this matter, the use of administrative justification gains relevance as a way to eliminate members that aren't part of the family from the calculation of the family's income.

The consideration about the need of the initiation of material proof for the authorization of the processing of the administrative justification is important. In regard to medical proof, medical documents will certainly serve for this desideratum.

In regard to the socioeconomic matter, bank statements and other documents will suffice. According to Section 599 of INSS Normative Instruction no 45/2010 the initiation of material proof will be dismissed in the case of an occurrence of *force majeure* or *cas fortuit,* characterized by the verification of notorious occurrences, like fires, floods, or landslides, that have hit the company in which the insured alleges he has worked in, having to be proved through a police incident report done in the proper time or presenting contemporaneous documents of the facts, and being verified the correlation between the company's activity and the insured's profession.

The procedure will be prosecuted, according to Section 604 of INSS Normative Instruction no 45/2010 by a server specially designated by the manager of the Social Security Agency or its benefit manager, the choice needing to be made by employees that have the ability to give testimony and make declarations and have knowledge of the subject of interest of the administrative justification.

The witnesses indicated by the interested party, in number higher than 3 and lower than 6, must be heard separately, so that one's testimony is never witnessed or heard by the others. And the homologation of the justification in regard to form is the competence of who prosecuted it, this person needing to make a succinct report of the gathered facts, mentioning their impressing in regard to the aptitude of the witnesses and opining conclusively on the produced proof, in order to confirm or not the alleged facts, not being in their competence analyzing the initiation of material proof presented. The procedure of external research comprises the external activities exerted by an INSS employee, previously designated to act in companies, public organs, or in relation to the taxpayers in general and beneficiaries.

The procedure has several objectives, constant in Section 618 of Normative Instruction no 45/2010: "Section 618: Is understood as External Research the external activities exerted by INSS employees, previously designated to act in companies, public organs or in relation to the taxpayers in general and beneficiaries that have as objective: (I) the verification of the veracity of the documents presented by claimants, as well as the search for useful information for the appreciation of the request formulated to the Administration in INSS organs; (II) the conference and increment of constant data of the systems, programs and computerized registers; (III) realizing necessary visits to the performance of the activities of Social Work, expert medical examination, of qualification, of professional rehabilitation and the monitoring of the execution of the contracts with the payer units through the Banking Service Monitoring System – SAAB or for the adoption of measures done by a previously designated employee; (IV) meeting the revision programs of social security and welfare benefits predicted in the legislation; and (V) meeting the requests of PFE along with INSS and other execution organs of the Federal General Procuracy and of the Judiciary for the gathering of information useful for the defense of INSS."

In the present case, it gains relevance as a mean of proof of external research of proof, specially upon external visits to the claimant's place of residence, or in analysis of the socioeconomic conditions, with hearsay of neighbors and relatives. Furthermore, this mean of proof becomes relevant for the realization of medical evaluation in cases of social incapacity.

The expert medical examination is an activity done in INSS for medical verification. It is of exclusive competence of a medic that has passed public a service exam and been trained internally, that must have knowledge of the social security legislation. It is a technical specialization recognized by the Federal Council of Medicine, being a part of the "Medical Expertise and Legal Medicine" specialization that comprises other kinds of expertise besides the social security expertise, like crime expertise in bodily harm.

The relation between the medic and the insured differs of the relation between medic and patient, as their activity is limited to diagnosing the presented symptoms and issue a report on the insured's capability to work, relating it without presenting any treatment for the illness. In the end of the examination, the expert medic writes an expert report, nowadays digitally, and their report becomes part of the administrative process.

The office impulsion must be observed in the ambit of the social security administrative process of welfare benefit. This is because, in spite of the initiative of the instauration of the process, with some exceptions, it is of the beneficiary, through the formalization of the administrative request. We must assume that when fulfilling the request that the claimant is the creditor of a solution, even if the attitudes between the initiative and the conclusion are under the jurisdiction of the Public Administration. We also can't forget to mention that the Administration can officially use their means for the effectuation of the rights of the administered, like the databases that the autarchy has access to.

In regard to the legal requirements for the concession of the benefit, §6 of Section 20 of Law no 8.742/93 predicts:

> § 6: The concession of the benefit will be subject to the evaluation of the degree of impediment and disability that §2 talks about comprised of medical evaluation and social evaluation done my expert medics and social workers of the National Institute of Social Security – INSS

However, two kinds of proof must be produced: expert medical proof, for the purpose of the verification of the fulfillment of the disability criterion, and social proof, through expert social examination, which must be done by a Social Worker.

In regard to this point, we can't forget to mention that the production of proof in the administrative process is in deficit. This is because the social evaluation is done by public employees with no specialization in Social Work.

The proof must be necessarily done by a Social Worker, and the social worker, being a social agent, needs to advise in the elaboration of social politics in all levels.

The form predicted by the legislation for the gauging of the social requirement is supported in §8 of Section 20 of Law no 8.742/93: "§8: The family's monthly income that §3 talks about must be declared by the claimant or their legal representative, being subject to the rest of the procedures predicted in the rulebook for the concession of the request."

It is not possible for all social evaluations to be filed in unilateral and objective forms that don't represent the reality of the candidate to the benefit.

It is possible that the party presents certificates and declarations useful for the validation of the fulfillment of socioeconomic requirements. A certificate is a written affirmation, with the objective of proving an action. Certificates are different from attestations and declarations as it proves permanent facts or actions, while the other two are related to transitory facts or actions.

A declaration is a spoken or written affirmation, declaratory of the existence or not of a right or fact in relation to something or someone, not mattering if it's favorable or not. It is drafted the same way as an attestation.

In regard to the expert medical report, it must be done by the expert medical department, the expert medic having to analyze the fulfillment of the requirements for the election to the benefit.

The expert medical report is a document of extreme importance for the validation of the right to several social security benefits, like benefit for incapacity, death pensions for an invalid child or older sibling, work accident benefit, maternity remuneration, and other situations that can require an expert medical report.

The basic information that the report must contain are: the diagnosis; the consequences that the problem brings on the worker's health; express indication of the existence of incapacity or limitation of going back to work; the estimated time for recovery. If it is not possible to determine how much time will be needed to recover, it must state that it will be not possible to determine the duration of the leave; the record of the data in a readable manner; the identification of the medic, with signature and stamp or the registration number in the Regional Council of Medicine.

The Federal Council of Medicine has already regulated the matter in the national ambit through Resolution no 1851/2008. However, Section 1 of Resolution no 1658/2008 establishes that "the medical attestation is an integrant part of the medical act, its direct supplying an inalienable right of the patient, with no payment involved."

The concept of incapacity and disability suffered a meaningful change from the year of 2001 when the World Health Organization (WHO) issued the International Classification of Functioning, Disability, and Health (ICF).[2]

The medical evaluation of disability and degree of incapacity will consider disabilities in functions and structures of the body, and the social evaluation will consider environmental, social, and personal factors, and both will consider the limitation of the performance of activities and the restriction of social participation, according to their respective specialization.

A fruit of this Convention, which Brazil attested to, is Decree no 6564/08, which meaningfully changed the biomedical criterion used until then for the verification of disability, predicted in the Organic Law of Social Assistance. The evaluation of the disability and of the degree of incapacity becomes comprised of the medical and social evaluations. The National Institute of Social Security—INSS through Joint Order no 1/2010 instituted the instruments for the evaluation of disabilities and the degree of incapacity of the candidates to the Continued Contribution Benefit based on the international convention.

[2] The ICF from 2001 is a revision of the 1980 ICF, published by WHO experimentally. The current CIF is a fruit of five years of work, gathering several countries, including an effective participation of Brazil, being approved by the 54th World Health Assembly, in May 2001. "ICF is useful for many different applications, for example, social security, evaluation of the health aid management and population studies in local, national and international levels. It offers a conceptual structure for the information applicable to individual medical aid, including prevention, promotion of health and improvement of the participation, removing or mitigating the social obstacles and stimulating the provision of social support and facilitators. It is also useful for the study of medical aid systems, both in evaluation terms and formulation of public politics" (ICF-2011).

In the same direction, Normative Instruction no 45 of August 6th 2010 brought in Section VII, Subsection I, which is "Of the Social Work," several devices that converge to an evaluation beyond medical aspect, let us then see if this is not the case:

> Paragraph 4 –The social evaluation in conjunction with the medical evaluation of a person with disabilities consists of an instrument intended to the characterization of the disability and of the degree of incapacity and will consider environmental, social and personal factors, the limitation of the performance of activities and the restriction of social participation of the claimants of the Continued Contribution Benefit of people with disabilities.

In the case of the Continued Contribution Benefit, the elderly are exempt of producing expert medical proof, the validation of their condition of elder, through the chronological criterion.

7.4.3 *Of the Decision*

The administrative acts practiced during the course of the process involve a true dialectic relation between the interested party and the administration, culminating with the conclusion of how much has been produced in the process through their decision.

In the circumstances that the candidate has incomplete documentation, or that they have documents that validates their right to more than one benefit, the employee will need to orientate the insured in a way that better meets the well-being of the beneficiary.

This is the command contained in Enunciation no 5 of JR/CRPS: "Social Security must concede the best benefit that the insured has the right to, the employee needing to orientate them in this matter."

The transcription of the enunciation above is important to clarify that when we talk about the concession of the best benefit, we are referring to the duty of the employee of enlightening the insured in regard to the possibilities that they have, notably which is more beneficial to them. However, the decision regarding the benefit is entirely of the insured's responsibility.

If by occasion of the service, without loss of the formalization of the process, the legal requirements are met, the right will be immediately recognized. And, if by occasion of the dispatch, it is verified that in the date of entry of the request the insured didn't meet the requirements for the concession of the benefit, but that he met them later, a new qualification won't need to be made, with reaffirmation of the request's entry date—DER.

When the discovery process is concluded, the decision must be delivered in 30 days, except if there is a postponement properly specified in Section 49 of Law no 9784/99. The referred deadline can't be mistaken for the 45 days deadline predicted in §5 of Section 41 of Law no 8213/91, which is related to the first benefit payment.

Despite not having the prediction of consequence for the administration in the case of formal inactivity, the Public Administration has the duty of deciding, because besides expressing a regular conducting of administrative activity, it avoids the appearance or aggravation of damage that has occurred with the unjustifiable delay of the administrative process.

In the situations that the public administration passes the predicted deadline without issuing a decision, the acceptance of the thesis of the administrative silence is possible, equating the silence to the denial of the request of the claimant.

The unjustified delay in the analysis of the administrative request of benefit concession affronts several constitutional rights, like those predicted in Letter A, Subsection XXXVII and LXXVII of Section 5 of CF/88.

Thus, the legal deadline that the autarchy has to analyze the process being elapsed, without having issued a decision, the administrative silence is applied, considering the formulated request denied.

In the decisive phase, it is the competent organ's duty to deal with the proposed question, analyzing it before all proof produced in order to conclude in the end through a decision.

In the molds of the prescribed in Section 93, Subsection IX of the Federal Constitution of 1988 the decision must be motivated, which means that the decisive organ must detail the reasons and motives to be decided.

In the same direction, Section 50 of Law no 9784/99 predicts that the administrative acts must be motivated. The grounding must be clear and explicit in order for its content to be intelligible and its conclusion to be easily deduced from the text.

7.4.4 Of the Appeals and Fulfillment Phase

Of the decisions of INSS, in the process of interest of the beneficiaries of Law no 8.742/93 will be appropriate appeals for the Appeals Council of Social Security. It is what the *caput* of Section 126 of Law no 8213/91 states: "of the decisions of the National Institute of Social Security – INSS in the processes of interest of the beneficiaries and taxpayers of Social Security will be appropriate appeals for the Appeals Council of Social Security – CRPS". The rules related to the administrative organization of the Appeals Council of Social Security – CRPS can be found in MPS Order no 548/11.

The competence to judge the administrative appeal is one of the 29 (twenty-nine) Appeal Councils, that have the competence to judge, in first instance, the interposed appeals against the decisions passed by regional organs of the autarchy, in the matter of the interest of its beneficiaries. Furthermore, there are 04 (four) Judgment Chambers, with their headquarters in Brasília, with the competence to judge, in second instance, the interposed appeals against the decisions passed by the Appeal Councils that infringe the laws, rules, enunciations, or ministerial normative acts.

The structures also counts with the Plenary Council, with the competence to standardize the jurisprudence upon enunciations, being able to have other competences defined in the By-laws. Regarding the composition of the organs, it is presided by a Government representative, with notorious knowledge of the legislation, nominated by the State Minister of Social Security and Assistance, being designated to him the duty to direct the administrative services and define the number of monthly sessions, which can't be less than ten, according to the volume of ongoing processes.

In their turn, the Councils and Chambers, presided by a Government representative, are comprised of four members denominated councilors, nominated by the State Minister of Social Security and Assistance, two being Government representatives, one being a representative of the companies and the last being a representative of the workers. The mandate of the members is of 2 years, renewal being allowed.

The appeal deadline is of 30 (thirty) days counted from the date of the acknowledgement of the decision. The appeal protocol must be effectuated directly in Social Security Agencies, preferably in the same organ that issued the decision about the benefit, or through electronic scheduling.

The reasons of the appeal must be presented and accompanied by the documents that prove the formulated allegations. When the 30 days deadline for counter-arguments expires the writs will automatically be forwarded to hypothesis judgment in which will be considered as counter-arguments the motives of the initial dismissal. The organ of origin will state in the writs grounded information regarding the date of the interposition of the appeal, not being able to refuse the reception or oppose the continuance of the appeal to the judging organ based on this circumstance.

After being received by the judging organ, the process is given to a rapporteur who has the responsibility of analyzing and reporting the process. After the inclusion in discussion of the writs will be judged by the collegiate.

In the case of process that involve medical matters, they are also analyzed by the medical advisory council of CRPS. The medical advisory council analyzes the documentation that is known of the process, like: medical attestations, complementary exams, expert medical reports and statements.

Once the decision is passed by the Appeal Council, another appeal will be needed, now denominated "special." About this resource there are 02 (two) considerations to be made: (a) The INSS has legitimacy to interpose special appeals, if it doesn't conform with the passed decision in second degree; and (b) The By-laws of the Appeals Council of Social Security, according to Order no 548/11 of the Social Security Ministry established a set of matters that are of exclusive competence of the Appeal Councils, in a way that, in what is related to these cases, their decisions are unappealable. Regarding the effects in which the appeals will be received, they can be in suspensory or returnable effect.

If during the course of the appeal's judgment the existence of a judicial action with the same subject of the matter discussed in the administrative sphere is verified, will be recognized the resignation to the right of appealing and the waiver of the interposed appeal. It is a measure of extreme importance, as it avoids that conflicting decisions between the administrative and judicial instance are passed.

The judgment is open to the public and the insured can ask beforehand for oral sustention in the appeal form by protocolling it in the Social Security Agency or presenting a request in the judging organ for it to be united with the process. This way, he will receive a communication informing him of the date, time, and place of the judgment, where he will be able to only watch or realize oral sustention or presenting final allegations in the form of memorial briefs.

When the judging organ has too many processes, and its above their capacity of judging, the president of the collegiate, through a provision, redistributes the processes from a judging organ to other that has less processes, in order to guarantee a faster judgment.

Embargos will be appropriate when there are in the judgment obscurities, ambiguity or contradiction between the decision and its foundations, or when a point that the judging organ should have stated something about is omitted. They will be interposed through the parts of the process, upon a grounded petition directed to the President of the judging unit in a time period of 30 days, counted from the acknowledgement of the judgment. The interposition of the embargos will interrupt the time period for the fulfillment of the judgment, the time period of 30 days being fully restituted after its solution, except in the hypothesis of unashamedly postponing embargos.

The standardization, in thesis, of the administrative social security jurisprudence can be evoked in order to end administrative jurisprudencial divergences or to consolidate reiterated jurisprudence in the ambit of the collegiate, upon the editing of enunciations. Such question is of extreme importance, as it generates the binding character of law interpretation. The issuing of enunciations, in any hypothesis, will depend on the approval of the simple majority of the members of the Plenary Council.

In regard to the fulfillment of the decision, it must be done by the Social Security Agency responsible for the process, in a time period of 30 days.

7.5 Conclusion

The objective of the present paper was an approach to the Administrative Process for the purpose of the concession or not concession of welfare benefits. The interest in the choice of the theme resided in the concern of promoting studies about this important theme related to social security in the ambit of the Social Assistance subsystem.

The coverage of social events of the welfare benefit is of extreme importance for the instrumentalization of the guarantee of well-being and social justice, values sought by the legislator inside the constitutional social order.

This paper started with the verification of the juridical regime of the discussed process, its juridical nature, and with the definition of its concept, its classification and principle that are subjacent to it. It was concluded by the definition of the juridical nature of the discussed process as a modality of social security administrative process of benefits.

The vision of the process, set on the logic of the administrative act, in its unilateral form finds itself surpassed by the procedural vision that the Federal Constitution of 1988 brought, through the due legal administrative process.

The dynamics of the administrative process were also discussed, through its five phases: initial, discovery, decisive, appeals, and of fulfillment.

In the discovery process, emphasis was given to the relevant question to the office impulsion of the process, which doesn't relieve the insured of promoting administrative requests. Were also discussed the main means of proof and probationary procedures.

In the decisive phase it was referred about the duty of the administration of delivering the best benefit to the insured, highlighting that this duty is only of orienting the insured about the possibilities they have, the final decision being of the beneficiary. The deadline for the autarchy to decide the process and the effects of passing the deadline were also discussed. In regard to the appeals phase, the main characteristics of the CRPS were described.

References

Costa JRC (2013a) A Quebra de Paradigma na Perícia Médica: da concepção biomédica à concepção biopsicossocial. Revista de Previdência Social 392:591–610

Costa JRC (2013b) Construção e efetivação do benefício de prestação continuada da LOAS: uma análise crítica da assistência social no Brasil e a perspectiva de sua efetivação através da construção jurisprudencial. In: Marco Aurélio Serau Júnior (Org) Comentários à Jurisprudência Previdenciária do STF, 1st edn. Juruá, Curitiba, pp 78–95

Instrução Normativa INSS/PRES No 45, de 06 de agosto de 2010

Lei no 9.784, de 29 de janeiro de 1999

Lei no 8.742, de 7 de dezembro de 1993

Portaria MPS no 548, de 13 de setembro de 2011

Resolução CFM no 1.851, de 18 de agosto de 2008

Chapter 8
The Right to Have Rights: Social Assistance Rights from a Judicial Activism Perspective

Ana Maria Correa Isquierdo and José Ricardo Caetano Costa

Abstract This article raises the origin of social welfare rights, from the "Poor Law" English, investigating how the expression of social assistance joined the social protective system in Brazil. Points the division between welfare, where the rights to social protection for those in need was understood as mere charity or bounty of the rich toward the poor economically, and the understanding of these rights as fundamental social rights, brought by the Federal Constitution of 1988. Investigates also the mangling process for this fundamental social right, which occurred after the promulgation of this Constitution, through various infra-constitutional laws, as happened in 1993 with the establishment of the Organic Law of Social Assistance (Law no 8.742/1993). Be in the design of disability as well as the understanding of what constitutes the family unit, even this right brings anchored in understanding its meaning that only the poor should be entitled to social assistance. So the judiciary is easing the restrictive criteria for access to this benefit, which denotes a strong judicial activism in the protection and realization of these rights.

Keywords Social rights • Social assistance • Judicial activism • Poverty • Social policies

8.1 Introduction

We can initially affirm that Social Assistance in Brazil was closely connected to the notion of charity, benefits, alms, aid, among many other terms.

Maybe this is why we are able to understand the reason for the charitable activities being responsible for providing support for the needy. This role was initially undertaken by the First Ladies who assumed the Presidencies of the LBAs (Brazilian Assistance Legion). Likewise, we are able to understand a certain touchy feeling inherited from the

A.M.C. Isquierdo (✉)
FURG - Universidade Federal do Rio Grande, Pelotas, Rio Grande do Sul, Brazil
e-mail: anamaria.isquierdo@gmail.com

J.R.C. Costa
Isquierdo e Costa Advogados Associados, Pelotas, Rio Grande do Sul, Brazil
e-mail: jrcc.pel@gmail.com

M.A. Serau Junior, J.R. Caetano Costa (eds.), *Assistance Benefits in Brazil*,
DOI 10.1007/978-3-319-27046-3_8

notion of Social Assistance connected to the Catholic Church, whose mission was to distribute benefits, forming an idea of mercy, compassion and sympathy toward the poor.

Unarguably, the 1988 Federal Constitution breaks this paradigm, conceiving Social Assistance as an integral part of Social Security (Art. 194 of CF/88), i.e., in conjunction with Pension Fund and Health Care, it is part of Social Security.

We understand that this is quite important, breaking away from the aforementioned rationale. Now it is a matter of conceiving and introducing social assistance rights in the array of social rights as fundamental rights.

On the other hand, to execute and optimize social assistance rights, making such rights efficient, there is the need to comply with the Constitution, whether through the legislative branch or the executive branch, or whether by proactive action by the Judiciary.

The issue regarding the only continuous cash benefit (BPC) of the Social Assistance Law (Lei 9.874/93) represents well what we intend to develop herein. For example, CF/88 guaranteed in Art. 203, V, the benefit of one minimum wage to disabled people and the elderly (currently people at the age of 65 and above). Note that CF/88 was enacted on 5 October 1988 and the Social Assistance Law only came to light in 1993 (Law No. 8.742/93), and its only pecuniary benefit was implemented as of 1996, with an 8-year delay.

The long road between the validity of CF/88 and the enactment of the LOAS indicates the unwillingness and the lack of interest in complying with the constitutional precept, as we will demonstrate in this paper.

We are interested in reflecting on, at this stage, the criteria used by the social security administration (INSS) with regard to criteria for disability and family income as qualifiers to receive the BPC, respectively, due to incapacity or age.

Finally, we are further interested in investigating the role of the Judiciary in assessing actual cases and the decisions it renders, particularly when the effectiveness and application of constitutional precepts related to Social Assistance are supported by the proactive and developmental position of such Judiciary.

8.1.1 Genesis and the Legacy of Social Assistance Rights

We understand that the "Poor Law," developed in the awakening of the Industrial Revolution, i.e., England, in 1601, is a benchmark of what we interpret today as Assistance Rights.

To make such analysis, we basically focused in the work of Karl Polanyi, entitled "The great transformation," whose title indicates the importance of this period as a turning point for its time.

Within this line of thinking, we will seek to analyze the two events that marked social assistance rights in the western world: the Poor Law of 1601 and the Poor Law Reform of 1834. Also in this context, we seek to analyze Speenhamland (1795–1834), which is, according to Polanyi (2000), the origins of our time.

This first milestone of Assistance Rights, brought by the Poor Law or the Elizabethan Law, as it became known, can only be understood within the context of initial capitalism, represented by the Industrial Revolution (England, late eighteenth century). That is because capitalism led to massive changes in people's life style: the new capitalist order subverted the personal and social relationships of its time. The capitalism which was being formed caused many social problems to the new working class which was being formed: hunger, diseases, instability, etc.

That is the context in which the Poor Law of 1601 was enacted, in an attempt to mitigate the arising social problems. According to this law, revoked as of 1834 by the New Poor Law, Social Assistance was designed as a private policy, connected to the parishes. Therefore, it comprised collecting from the parishes taxes and fees to subsidize the poor and the needy. This system granted pecuniary aid to the invalid (children, the elderly, the disabled) and to the poor considered disabled, in exchange for subsidies, sought work for this large number of people, which increased due to the harmful effects of the Industrial Revolution. Beggary, in turn, "was severely punished; vagrancy, in case of repetition, was a capital offense" (Polanyi 2000).

The 1601 Poor Law also provided for the organization of Workhouses, an embryo of nursing homes. Assistance was located by region, and this created a problem regarding the mobility of the needy that sought the parishes with better economic conditions. This practice was prohibited as of the Act of Settlement of 1662, which "prohibited the parishes from getting rid of the poor, making it mandatory for the poor to stay in their homes" (Rosanvallon 1984). On the other hand, this law clashed with and contradicted the need brought by capitalism in that period, i.e., a large, mobile and flexible workforce, sought for by a demanding and allegedly free and self regulating labor market.

We believe Marshall sums up well this exemplary moment of the Social Assistance Rights by affirming that the Elizabethan Poor Law can be understood as "an item in a broad program of economic planning, whose general goal was not to create a fundamental change." According to this author, it was "a means to alleviate poverty and eliminate vagrancy" (Marshall 1967).

In the Poor Law of 1834, according to Marshall, social rights were eliminated and its former users began to be treated as indigents (Marshall 1967). We note, according to the analyses made by Marshall—an author who, as Polanyi, studied in depth this historical period—that the notion brought by this second Poor Law outlined what modern times conceived as Social Assistance.

In fact, according to this Law, claims could be accepted only if its users were no longer citizens, i.e., the "one had the 'right' to Assistance if one waived in full any other rights" (Schons 1999).

This change brought by the new Poor Law of 1834 can only be understood if we comprehend the dialectic movement of capitalism which arose from the developing Industrial Revolution. It was not possible to reconcile the interests of the free market with an interventionist system as the one from the first Poor Law. This historical moment calls for the free mobility of potential workers, with the formation of a new working class. It is specifically for this reason that Polanyi states that Speenhamland (1795–1834, when the new Poor Law revoked the former Law) represents the end of an era and the beginning of another one.

Schons (1999) makes a noteworthy analysis in relation to these two Poor Laws. She states:

> Finally, this period clarifies us how an Assistance benefit mechanism contributed to delay the process as a whole. This process, obviously, with the uprising of the market economy, was beginning to become established. On the other hand, it also clarifies us how the 1601 Poor assistance law – basically a neighbor and 'parish' assistance service (Work houses) and beggary is subject to punishment – is resumed in the 1834 New Poor Law, although from the perspective of Public Assistance, restricted to those who abstained from other rights. Assistance in this period had the stigma of being designed for those who gave up fighting, i.e., Assistance for the sick, the elderly and/or lazy people.

Since this was the context in which Social Assistance Rights were born, we believe it is of utmost importance to ponder about such matters, which definitely underlie these rights in modern times.

8.1.2 Social Assistance and Assistencialism in Brazil

Social Assistance in Brazil has always been linked to a notion of benefits and assistencialism, rather than of Social Rights, maybe due to the legacy brought by the Poor Laws, as exposed in the previous item. All the more so that the beginning of the granting of aid to the poor in Brazil has been historically connected to religious philanthropy, at first, and to the care provided by public institutions with private management, such as the LBA.

The LBA had a private nature to it because its top position was usually occupied by first ladies, with no technical criteria to define the priorities and management of funds.

While the Brazilian State, up to 1920, did not intervene in work relationships, and, likewise, in Social Rights in general, as of 1930, with Brazilian president Getúlio Vargas, the State clashes with the liberal oligarchy, indicating new outlooks (Mendonça 2009). But in opposition to Marshall's view, social rights in Brazil precede political rights. By this line of thinking, it is possible to understand the commonly called "regulated citizenship" or the citizenship protected by the State. Vargas's legacy, in fact, proves this affirmation.[1]

On the other hand, a large portion of the population, represented by rural workers, self-employed workers, domestic workers, unemployed and underemployed workers, remained deprived from any social protection (Costa 2010).

In this sense, we can affirm that in Brazil Social Rights as a whole are associate with specific income classes: this is how the Retirement Funds (*Caixas de Aposentadoria*—CAPs) were created in the 1920s, by "protecting one of the most

[1] Vargas' legacy is unique as an example of this regulation of social movements: unions protected by and linked to the government; the verticalization of social policies; the standardization and regulation of conflicts through the Judiciary, with the intermediation of the Labor Court; finally, the regulation of social relationships with the alienation of the working class in an yet incipient industrial capitalism, but that needed this structure to develop itself.

active categories, the railway workers" (Cohn 1980), and the Retirement and Pension Institutes (*Institutos de Aposentadorias e Pensões*—IAPs), which followed such CAPs in the next decade, were also organized by professional category (Costa 2011).

Although we have the Social Security Law (LOPS) of 1960, somewhat an advancement in unifying social rights by unifying the six largest Institutes which existed back then, the rural workers, domestic workers, and informal workers remained excluded.[2]

In fact, if the Social Rights related to Social Security were granted by the Brazilian State to workers in officially recognized professions—and it was not by chance that the Workers' Card (*Carteira de Trabalho*) served as a passport to receive said rights—in relation to Social Assistance, the situation is different: "those excluded from the process had reserved for them social assistance philanthropy to help them survive misery" (Mendonça 2009). Social Assistance, from this perspective, "follows a secondary, decentralized path, through the articulation between the State and the private philanthropy responsible for providing to the destitute the elements of citizenship" (Mendonça 2009).

This notion of Social Right, as analyzed, is to take another path after the enactment of the 1988 Federal Constitution, as a result of a long dispute between the social forces which conceived them.

8.1.3 Social Assistance as a Fundamental Right Under CF/88

Elevated as one of the foundations of Social Security, jointly with Health Care and Pension Funds, by the 1988 Federal Constitution, Social Assistance has been from then on understood as a fundamental right. Therefore, it is a significant advance because it conceives social assistance rights as rights to which political actors, deprived from the minimum social standards, are eligible to receive a minimum wage which can afford them minimum dignity amidst the savage capitalism we live in.

We note, on the other hand, that the assurance of such right by CF/88 is not enough. An example of this is the fact that the LOAS was only enacted in 1993, virtually 5 years after the enactment of CF/88, and its only continuous cash benefit came in force as of 1996.

---

[2] Note that in the case of rural workers the extension of social rights to this large number of workers, which represented the largest share of the active labor force in 1960, the rural oligarchies did not allow the participation of such rural workers in said social rights (Couto 2006). Actually, the exclusion of rural workers was only mitigated with the Constitution of 1988. Until April 1991 rural retirees still received half a minimum wage and rural workers' pensioners only received 30 % of the Minimum Wage in their proceeds.

Moreover, the criteria of a monthly wage "per capita" lower than ¼ of the legal minimum wage, as exposed in Article 20, paragraph 3, as well as the criteria of disability, as exposed in Article 20, paragraph 2, both set forth in Law no 8.742/93, further restrict the possibility of granting such rights.

These are the matters we will examine in the subsequent item.

8.1.4 Criteria for Characterizing the Beneficiary of the LOAS' BPC: Misery, Poverty, and Need

The wording of Article 203 of CF/88 states that Social Assistance will be provided when needed. The criteria used by the constitutional law maker is necessity.

The INSS, the agency which administrates social security, by screening, granting, preserving, and paying the Assistance Benefit, began to require social misery to be eligible to receive such benefit.

The Social Security Independent Agency interprets in a literal manner the provisions in paragraph 3, Law no 8.742/93, which states: "to be considered unable to support a disabled or elderly person, the family has to earn wage per capita lower than ¼ of the minimum wage."

The gap between the notions of "necessity" and "misery" is gigantic. If it is correct to state that every extremely poor person is needy, the reverse is not always true. That is because, according to the criteria used by Márcio Pochmann, an extremely poor person is the one who receives less than 25 % of a minimum wage as income *per capita* (Pochmann 2012).

It is not credible that social assistance policy in Brazil might consider a beneficiary of the Assistance Benefit only those who are below the poverty line, i.e., those who are in absolute misery.

Accepting such reference is to severely hurt the social assistance right set forth in Art. 203 of the 1988 Federal Constitution, which states: "Social Assistance will be provided to those who need it, regardless of their contribution to social security… ." That is because "the Constitution mentions necessity, but does not require a situation of misery to grant this benefit" (Savaris 2009).

These harmful criteria which elect misery as a requirement to grant assistance benefit reinforces the historically proven notion that social assistance must be designed as an aid to the extremely poor. Such fact also explains why it is that Social Assistance was the last policy in the scope of social security to be regulated.

This is evidenced by the data showing in 2011 a total of 155,725 requested benefits, by age, of which only 64,136 were granted, less than half of what was requested.

We can affirm, in this sense, that "there is general unawareness about social assistance policy in Brazil. We also note the notion found in common believe that such policy represents the benevolence of a solidary civil society or of the State toward the poor" (Sposati et al. 2006).

To prove how surreal is the criteria of income *per capita* used as a parameter to provide the administrative/bureaucratic grant of the LOAS's BPC, we only need to imagine a very common example: a family with four members, among which one of them is disabled, whose only income comes from the work of another member of the family, who receives one minimum wage for such work. The BPC grant, from the administrative perspective, is denied based on the argument that this family's income surpasses the restrictive criteria provided for in Law No. 8.742/93.

It is therefore unarguable that this family is socially vulnerable, and is below the poverty line, as per the cited criteria.

The struggle to include the Social Assistance BPC among the rights to which citizens are entitled, and even include them in this factual situation, perspasses the analysis of the criteria used by the INSS.

Through the judgment of Adin No. 1232, the Federal Supreme Court (STF) had the historical opportunity to repair the mistake in relation to the criteria of an income *per capita*, through inaction.

Actually, the STF refused to assess the constitutionality or unconstitutionality of the criteria set forth in Law no. 8.742/93, alleging that it is the ordinary legislative that has to set out which criteria is to be used for assistance policy. The arguments of the votes by Justice Gilmar Mendes and Justice Ellen Gracie, in turn, suggest as ground for decision the incapacity of the State to bear the costs of a possible increase in the number of the beneficiaries of the LOAS's BPC.

On the other hand, other STF judgments which followed the one exposed above amended the court's position to broaden the criteria of family income used by state bureaucracy.

Such as:

> APPEAL. Extraordinary. Continuous Cash Benefit. Art. 203, V, of CF/88. Objective criteria to grant benefit. Art. 20, paragraph 3, of Law No. 8742/93 c.c. Art. 34, sole paragraph, Law No. 10741/2003. Infringement of the understanding applied in the ADI No. 1.322/DF judgment. Inexistence. Extraordinary appeal not provided. Not opposed to the understanding applied by the Court in the ADI No. 1.232/DF judgment, deduction of the income from benefit received by another family member (Art. 34, sole paragraph, of the Elderly Statute), to measure the objective criteria provided for in Art. 20, paragraph 3, of Law No. 8742/93 (monthly family income *per capita* lower than ¼ of the minimum wage). (RE 561936/Pr. – Reporting Justice Cezar Peluso – 2nd Panel. DJE – 083 de 09-05-2008).

The Judiciary, in turn, not only excluded the income from another one of the LOAS's BPC, and by analogy another benefit that a family member may receive, but it also began to use as criteria for income "per capita" half a minimum wage.

The explanation to this value lies in the fact that social programs, specifically income transfer programs, such as the "*auxílio-gás*," programs deriving from "*fome zero*," "*bolsa família*," determine as a parameter half the minimum wage in force.

Accordingly, unless the ordinary law assures minimum living standards through the fundamental social right of an assistance benefit, the criteria of half a minimum wage will support court rulings, remarkably advancing the application of such right.

Actually, we can vindicate the following criteria: if the potential beneficiaries of the Social Assistance Law's Assistance Benefit earn a family income below ¼ of the minimum wage, they are automatically entitled to such benefit, without the need of a social-economic report or opinion. It is objective evidence.

Otherwise, if the income is above this level, analyses should be conducted case by case, because only the actual reality will be able to indicate the need to receive the benefit to meet the minimal living standards of citizens.

8.1.5 Disputes on Disability: The Disastrous Social Security Expert System and Its Incompetence to Assess Disability

The definition of "disability," set forth in Art. 20, paragraph 2 of Law No. 8.742/93, links this condition to those unable to perform work and to have an independent life. In Article 1 of the Disabled People Act, to which Brazil is a signatory (Legislative Decree No. 186/08), a disabled person is defined as a person who "has a long-term handicap of physical, mental, intellectual or sensorial nature, which in interaction with many obstacles may curb their full and real participation in society in equal conditions with other people."

In light of such Act, which has the "status" of a Constitutional Amendment, the notion of disableness needs to be completely reconsidered. This notion has been underlined social security policies.

Otherwise, there should also be the analysis of the bureaucratic and inefficient expert system under the responsibility of the INSS, which is responsible for screening applicants to the Social Assistance Law's Assistance Benefit.

As it is widely known, not only it does not have a body of experts skilled in many different specialties of medicine, following the example of psychiatrists that rarely transit though the dark corridors of the National Institute of Social Security (the INSS), the education of the experts it does have is not in line with the spirit raised by the continuous cash benefit of the Social Assistance Law.

When the expert doctor analyzes actual cases, it uses as reference the incapacity for work demonstrated by secured individuals, i.e., this doctor works from the perspective of the "world of labor".[3]

Certainly, this is not what should direct Assistance Benefit. It has another nature, completely different from that of the social security benefits of contributive nature.

This equation results in the disastrous expert evidence conducted by the INSS. This is demonstrated by the objective data we found in a study about the requested and granted benefits for 2011. According to data from the INSS, from a total of 430,959 requests from disabled people, only 286,973 were granted. When analyzing the reasons for these denials, we note that the principal reason is the unfulfillment of the requirement "incapacity to work and to have and independent life," representing a total of 117,041 denied benefits under this item.

Another significant data we extracted from the data obtained from the INSS refers to the amount of benefits under the "family income" item, corresponding to 26,023

[3] For a more detailed analysis of the expert system, see Costa (2013), particularly the exhibit about Biopsychosocial Expert Evidence.

covered people whose family is considered "self-sustainable," plus 36,452 whose income "per capita" was equal to or higher than ¼ of the Minimum Wage. Summing them up, we achieve 62,475. The number of people with temporary disability (maybe permanent?) is also revealing, with a total of 55,590 denied benefits.

We highlight that, despite proving to fall under this strict criteria of deficiency, virtually 36 thousand people did not receive this important benefit, due to their family income.

Another important issue is the disregard toward the criteria for incapacity to work and to have an independent life when it concerns people under age (0–16 years of age). That is because the incapacity of under-age people is an assumption, so there is no need to provide evidence of work incapacity in this case. The INSS itself has already regulated this matter through Internal Guidance INSS/Dirben No. 61/02.

In fact, we note that only an interdisciplinary work involving several types of practitioners (psychologists, doctors, social assistants, among others) can respond to the criteria of necessity under the LOAS's BPC, as set forth in CF/88, whether from the perspective of deficiency or in relation to benefits by age.

8.1.6 The Concept of "Family" from the Perspective of Assistance Benefits

The notion of family, for the purposes of granting the Assistance Benefit, is restrictive. That is because, according to the provisions in Law No. 9720/98, it applies the same list set forth in Article 16 of Law No. 8213/91, namely: spouses, partners, under-age or disabled daughters and sons, dependent parents, and under-age or disabled siblings.

Once again, the criteria of social security direct assistance policies. This results in disaster, with the loss of purpose of this benefit.

Firstly, we must note that all other assistance and income transfer programs outline a different notion of family. Here are some examples:

(a) *BOLSA FAMÍLIA* = an income transfer program destined to deprived families, established by Law 10836/04, whose notion of family can be understood as a core unit of people with family or affinity bonds that live under the same roof, therefore being a domestic unit that survives from the income of its members.
(b) *BOLSA ESCOLA* = established by Law 10219/01, it is also destined to deprived families, seeking to keep children in school. In this case, just as the first cited group, the notion of family is understood as a core unit of individuals, relatives, or nonrelatives, who compose the domestic group and live under the same roof, and whose earnings derive from the work of everyone.
(c) *BOLSA ALIMENTAÇÃO* = a program that aims to complement the family income, strengthening the health conditions of pregnant women. In this case, it is the core unit composed of parents and children, whether with family or affinity bonds, and that live under the same roof, under the same terms of the first two programs.

Consequently, the designated "socio-affective parenting" is harmed since in the less economically privileged social classes it is quite common to have complex and differentiated core family units. In these core family units we find several socio-affective combinations and various family bonds: a disabled nephew, a nonrelative child, a stepson, both grandparents and a son over 18, all living under the same roof in mutual support.

When assessing the criteria for granting the Assistance Benefit, taking as example the aforementioned actual case, where two components of the same group receive one minimum wage each, the disabled nephew will not be eligible to the LOAS's BPC, even though his disability is unarguably confirmed.

As stated by Simone Barbisan Fortes, "it is not possible to disregard other relatives, such as daughters and sons over 18 years of age, or even non-blood or affinity related individuals whose family bonds exist due to affection, since they certainly are part of the family" (Fortes 2009).

8.2 Conclusions

Based on the foregoing exposition, we can conclude that the Assistance Benefit, subject to an assistencial and paternal system that considered social assistance policy as "an act of giving alms" as a result of cynic social solidarity, or monetary populist actions by the State, is, in fact, still not addressed as a Fundamental Social Right.

Social Assistance in Brazil assimilates as its signatories those who abstain from their citizenship and other rights, inversely to what should be their founding role: promoting citizenship through the social inclusion of those eligible to such rights.

There are several examples we can cite to illustrate and confirm this conclusion.

This inversion of principles, as analyzed herein, was already something bad when Social Security was designed to screen, maintain and pay this important social benefit. Firstly, the perspective from which the experts assess the notion of disability, whose parameter is the "work of labor," is a criteria which is completely useless for the purposes underlying Social Assistance as an institutional policy to promote and integrate individuals with some type of deficiency. Secondly, the perspective from which these experts assess the criteria of income and family also provide social security notions which are equally useless in relation to Social Assistance, e.g., the notion of family exposed in Article 16 of the Social Security Benefit Law (Law No. 8213/91). The consequences of this perverse rationale could not be any different and the indicative data shown herein confirm this reality.

Among many other examples that we could cite, we highlight those that impact thousands of disabled people who try to enter or re-enter the labor market. The dilemma is always there when it comes to social rights: in case they manage to get a formal job, occupying, furthermore, the quotas destined to disabled individuals, they no longer fulfill the requirements which authorize them to receive the assistance benefits. If they have already worked with a signed Work Card and lose their jobs, which is quite common, their subsequent requests will be received with distrust by the Social Security for the reason that they no longer fulfill the criteria of disability, since they have already worked. This dynamic, which confirms the theory that the recipients of the assistance benefits should abstain from the other rights, leads to a catastrophic result: individuals, afraid of losing or not receiving their benefits, stop working in formal jobs.

We understand that Assistance Rights, especially as it is the only continuous cash benefit set forth in the Social Assistance Law, should be a transitory benefit. This means that they cannot be an end in themselves. As contradicting as it may seem, Social Assistance should have as an end its own elimination. The recipients of social benefits should not become accommodated due to the aid receive, but instead be encouraged to emerge from their condition of assistance receivers. Their benefits should ultimately be eliminated and not perpetuated.

On the other hand, how is it possible to reconcile these purposes when those eligible to such Rights are discouraged to elevate their citizenship rights, seek a better condition in life, since they must provide evidence of their misery and remain in it to be eligible to said assistance rights.

In fact, there is very little articulation between Social Assistance and other social, political, and cultural rights. An example of this is the fact that receivers of the Social Assistance Organic Law cannot contribute to Social Security, because if they do so their benefits will be automatically suspended.

From our perspective, there should be a certain type of incentive to receivers of Assistance Rights for them to participate in Social Security plans. Stating it differently, if such receivers stop being assisted and start paying Social Security, their condition will change: they will become insured persons under the social security system, in case of death, those depending on them will receive a pension due to death (and the benefit under the Social Assistance Law is fully personal, thus cannot be transferred), and consequently will be eligible to receive several other rights which they did not have as receivers of assistance benefits. It is exactly in this sense that we propose the notion of *temporary benefit (benefício de passagem)*, to make the ultimate objective of the assistance benefit be its own elimination, as we stated above.

References

Cohn A (1980) Previdência Social e Processo Político no Brasil. Ed. Moderna, São Paulo

Costa JRC (2011) A Previdência Social ao Alcance dos Assistentes Sociais. Paco Editorial, São Paulo

Costa JRC (2013) Direito do Trabalho e Direito Previdenciário: subsídios ao trabalho social. Paco Editorial, São Paulo

Costa JRC (2010) Previdência: os direitos sociais previdenciários no cenário neoliberal. Editora Juruá, Curitiba, Pr.

Couto BR (2006) O Direito Social e a Assistência Social na Sociedade Brasileira: uma equação possível? 2nd edn. Cortez, São Paulo

Fortes SB (2009) Conceito Aberto de Família e Seguridade Social. In: VAZ, Paulo Afonso Brum e SAVARIS, José Antonio (Orgs) Direito da Previdência Social: elementos para uma compreensão interdisciplinar. Conceito Editorial, Florianópolis, pp 251–280

Marshall TH (1967) Cidadania, Classe Social e Status. Rio de Janeiro, Zahar
Mendonça AMÁ (2009) Estado e Direitos Sociais no Brasil: entre a modernidade e o retrocesso. Editora da UFAL, Maceió
Pochmann M (2012) A nova economia política brasileira. Jornal Le Monde Diplomatique-Brasil, Ano 3, No 58, maio, pp 22–24
Polanyi K (2000) A Grande Transformação. As origens de nossa época. Campus, Rio de Janeiro
Rosanvallon P (1984) A Crise do Estado-Providência, 2nd edn. Editorial Inquérito, Lisboa
Savaris JA (2009) Direito Processual Previdenciário. Juruá, Curitiba
Schons SM (1999) Assistência Social entre a Ordem e a "des-ordem": mistificação dos direitos sociais e da cidadania. Cortez, São Paulo
Sposati AdO, Falção MdC, Fleury SMT (2006) Os Direitos (Dos Desassistidos) Sociais, 5th edn. Cortez, São Paulo

Chapter 9
Specifics of Claim Preclusion in Lawsuits Involving Welfare Benefits

Bruno Takahashi and Karina Carla Lopes Garcia

Abstract This study considers to which extent the proceedings regarding welfare benefits in Brazil under Law 8742/1993 can be changed due to its own nature, namely the modulation exerted by welfare specifics in general civil procedural law. In particular, it focuses on the procedural institute of *res judicata* (or claim preclusion), opposing its natural idea of decisiveness with two major points: (a) the temporary nature of the welfare benefit; (b) the possibility of putting it in perspective after the evolved constitutional construction of the benefit's legal requirements. It also tries to lay down the limits of the 2-year review set forth by law, and the possibility of reshaping *res judicata* according to new constitutional case law of the Brazilian Supreme Court.

Keywords Social security • Welfare benefit • Civil procedural law • *Res judicata* • Claim preclusion • Limits

9.1 Introduction

Welfare, within the Brazilian constitutional system, was created to help the poorer layers of society that are not usually assisted by social security rendered against social contributions.[1] It acts in order to guarantee minimum levels of subsistence for those who need the most, and one of the goals is to "guarantee a monthly minimum

[1] In this work, when we talk about welfare benefits, we are focusing on the one established by the article 203 of the Brazilian Constitution and regulated by the Law 8742/93.

B. Takahashi (✉)
Federal Judge, Master of Laws (University of São Paulo) University of Sao Paulo, Sao Paulo, Brazil
e-mail: btakahas@trf3.jus.br

K.C.L. Garcia
State Attoney. Advocacia-Geral da União, Brasília, Distrito Federal, Brazil
e-mail: karina.carla@gmail.com

M.A. Serau Junior, J.R. Caetano Costa (eds.), *Assistance Benefits in Brazil*,
DOI 10.1007/978-3-319-27046-3_9

wage to those with disabilities, or to elders that can prove not having means to support themselves or to be supported by their families, as legally set forth".[2]

Granting of such welfare benefit quite often happens by court order, under which the specifics of such case must be taken into consideration in the procedural context. Long gone are the days when procedural law—eager to be acknowledged as an autonomous science—strayed away from substantive law. Nowadays its importance is clear as an instrument that takes into consideration not only the substantive law to be ruled, but also the social reality into which it is inserted.[3]

In this context, what we strive to analyse in this study[4] is the modulation exerted by welfare specifics in general civil procedural law, especially given the temporary nature of its requirements, and also the controversy regarding their legal and case law interpretations. In particular, the analysis shall focus on the procedural institute of *res judicata*, the claim preclusion, opposing its natural idea of decisiveness with two major points: (a) the temporary nature of the welfare benefit; (b) the possibility of putting it in perspective after the evolved constitutional construction of the benefit's legal requirements. Finally, we will try to lay down the limits of the 2-year review set forth by law, and the possibility of reshaping *res judicata* according to new constitutional case law of the Brazilian Supreme Court (STF).

9.2 Welfare Benefit: Types and Requirements

There are two types of welfare benefit according to Article 203(V) of the Brazilian Constitution: one for the physically disabled and one for the elderly. The common requirement to both is extreme poverty, that is, the impossibility of one supporting oneself or being supported by one's family.

The legal definition of "disability", "elderly", "extreme poverty" and even "family", for all purposes of granting or not said benefit, can be found mainly in Article 20 of Law 8742/1993.

Disabled was defined as those bearing "long term constraints of physical, mental, intellectual or sensory nature" capable of "obstructing their full and effective participation in society under the same conditions as the others" (paragraph 2). It was determined that "long term" would be "at least 2 (two) years" long (paragraph 10). Elderly, on its turn, would be 65-year-olds or older (main part of the article).

---

[2] Brazilian Constitution, article 203(V).

[3] Revising a previous point of view, we hereby adopt a more comprehensive take on instrumentality, which dictates that one should not only care to seek answers in procedural law for posed substantive law questions, but also in the social reality where such law is inserted into and that is much more complex than what is regulated by law. Such broader point of view is called by de Salles (2011, pp. 13–27) methodological instrumentality.

[4] Many ideas exposed here, with proper adaptations, have been initially broached in article "Legal Aspects Concerning Disability Security Benefits" ("Aspectos Processuais dos Benefícios Previdenciários por Incapacidade"), by Bruno Takahashi (2012).

Regarding extreme poverty, it would be considered a fact in case of household income below one-fourth of the minimum wage (paragraph 3),[5] and, for the purposes of welfare granting, family comprised "the applicant; the spouse or partner; the parents and, in the absence of one of them, the step mother or step father; the single siblings; single offspring and step sons and daughters; and minors under their guard, as long as they live under the same roof" (paragraph 1). Also with an impact on the concept of extreme poverty is the exclusion, for household income purposes, of income from the disabled who are apprentices (paragraph 9), and welfare amounts earned by an elder in the family, as per Article 34, sole paragraph of the Elderly Act (Law 10741/2003).

9.2.1 *Temporary Nature of the Requirements and Two-Year Review*

From the brief exposure of the legal requirements for the concession of welfare benefits, one can infer that they have a distinctly provisional nature. The disability, depending on its nature, can become better or worse, and the household income can vary, or even the household members.

Because of that, the legal provision in Article 21 of Law 8742/1993 is correct in establishing 2-year reviews "in order to assess that the conditions that caused the welfare benefit to be granted in the first place are still there".

9.2.2 *Court Granting and Specific Attributes of Proof*

Despite those who defend the opposite theory, the adopted understanding is that the interest to request welfare in court, except for those cases where the substantive law is at risk, only emerges when the claim is rejected at administrative level, since a litigation doesn't seem likely if public Social Security Agency (INSS) hasn't even had the opportunity to previously accept or reject the presented request.[6]

[5] Since January 2015, the national minimum wage is R$ 788,00 Brazilian Reais or approximately $262,00 US Dollars.

[6] Such understanding, with a few dissenting voices, has recently been adopted by the Brazilian Supreme Court (STF) in a decision with the following syllabus: "EXTRAORDINARY APPEAL. GENERAL REPERCUSSION. PREVIOUS REQUEST. ADMINISTRATIVE AND INTEREST TO SUE. 1. The definition of conditions for regularly exercising the right to file a lawsuit is compatible with Article 5(XXXV) of the Constitution. The existence of the interest to sue is characterized by the need to bring matters to court. 2. The concession of welfare benefits depends on the request of the interested party, and there is no threat or loss of rights before its analysis and rejection by INSS, or if the legal deadline for analysis has expired. One must observe, however, that the previous claim requirement cannot be understood as the need to go through all administrative instances. 3. The need for previous administrative claim must not prevail when the Government's understanding is clearly and consistently contrary to the applicant's claim. 4. In case

Another relevant aspect of the previous administrative rejection, albeit less remembered, is the role of dispute outline, since the Judiciary has the power to review administrative acts. Therefore, the matter subject to proof is already outlined, which also has an impact on the limits of the *res judicata*.

Except for the age requirement, which is easy to prove, the other requirements involved in granting welfare benefits have relevant probative aspects that cannot be dismissed. Regarding disability, the importance of technical evidence is well known, especially the expert report carried out by a doctor trusted by the court, even though medical exams, statements and reports from private doctors are also taken into consideration. Extreme poverty, on its turn, since case law has broadened the legal concept of income per head up to ¼ of the minimum wage, can now be proved in many different ways. In both cases, producing proves is a little more complex, and requires more of a hands-on approach by the judge, especially regarding the "economic and informational weakness" of the applicant in proceedings of this nature, beside the imbalance of power between the parties, which is clearly explained by Savaris (2010):

> The plaintiff is presumably weak. It's an economic and informational weakness, thus considered the lack of knowledge about their rights and duties. Once the plaintiff is at court seeking support, it is assumed that they don't have enough resources to guarantee their own subsistence. (…) In a lawsuit with the purpose to obtain a continuous welfare benefit, the

---

of requests to review, re-establish or keep a benefit that has been previously granted, considering that INSS is legally bound to grant the most advantageous service, such claim may be brought directly to court – unless it is a substantive matter that has not yet come to the Government's attention – since, in this case, INSS' conduct already anticipates the claim's rejection, at least an implied rejection. 5. Given that case law on the subject has a wide range, even in the Supreme Court, a transition formula must be devised to deal with ongoing lawsuits, and shall be done as follows. 6. As for actions filed until the conclusion of this session (Sept. 3rd, 2014), if they have not come from a previous administrative claim when it was so required, the following shall apply: (i) in case the lawsuit has been filed in a itinerant court (Juizado Itinerante), the lack of previous administrative claim shall not imply dismissal; (ii) in case INSS has already filed an answer, the interest to sue will be characterized by the claim's dispute; (iii) the other lawsuits that do not fit in items (i) and (ii) will be stayed, observed the system below. 7. In stayed actions, the plaintiff shall be notified to file the administrative claim within 30 days, otherwise the action shall be dismissed. Once the proof of filing an administrative claim is produced, INSS shall be notified to answer the claim within 90 days, within which the autonomous agency shall gather all evidence they might need and decide upon the subject. If the claim is accepted at administrative level, or if it's the applicant's fault that the merit cannot be analysed, then the action shall be dismissed. Otherwise, the interest to sue is characterized and the case shall proceed. 8. In all cases above – items (i), (ii), and (iii) – both the administrative and the judicial analyses must take the administrative lawsuit filing date into consideration for all legal purposes. 9. We hereby partially accept the extraordinary appeal to correct the previous decision so as to order the case records to be sent back to the 1st instance court, and the plaintiff – who claims to be a rural worker – to be notified to file the administrative claim within 30 days, otherwise this lawsuit shall be dismissed. Once the proof of filing an administrative claim is produced, INSS shall be notified to answer the claim within 90 days, within which the autonomous agency shall gather all evidence they might need and decide upon the subject, taking the lawsuit filing date into consideration for all legal purposes. The result shall be informed to the court, which will analyse whether or not there is interest to sue. (RE 631240, Reporting Judge: Chief Judge ROBERTO BARROSO, Full Bench, session on 03/09/2014, ELECTRONIC DECISION. GENERAL REPERCUSSION – Merit DJe-220 DISCL 07-11-2014 PUBLISH 10-11-2014)".

> presumed economic frailty, unless the claim is shady, cannot be weakened, since the substantive law itself is meant for those in need (Article 203, Constitution) who cannot provide for themselves or be supported by their family (Article 203(V) of the Constitution).
>
> (…)
>
> If the plaintiff is presumably weak, the defendant, on its turn, is a public entity, the Government in a broader sense. If the former is not fully aware of his rights, the latter has all the information that may lead to granting the needed welfare benefit.

In this context, it is incumbent on the court to see to the proper production of evidence, within the collaborative process laid out by Mitidiero (2007), who states that "the collaboration imposes an open attitude of dialog with the court, committed to the goal of attaining what is fair in a case instead of being caught up in the form just for the sake of it".

It is also worth mentioning that the quality of evidence must be analysed according to the existing social context. In case of welfare benefits, there is an obvious discrepancy between the information levels of plaintiffs and INSS arising from knowledge of the details of the legislation and even the plaintiffs' level of education. Such informational hardship must be weighted in by the judge when analysing evidence, to prevent him from demanding proof that is out of the plaintiff's reality.

As well explained by Marinoni and Arenhart (2009):

> the judicial conviction cannot aspire to uniformity, as if the judge could be certain of the facts without looking at the specific case. The judge must consider the circumstances of each case that may hinder the production of evidence (…) the judge's conviction cannot be thought as something only in the realm of procedural law, as opposed to and isolated from substantive law. In order to adequately rule the proposed claims, the judge cannot disregard the differences between the many statuses of substantive law.

This is the relationship between the produced evidence, the plaintiff's informational hardship and the specifics of the welfare benefit that allows a direct association between the *res judicata* and the proved fact.

9.3 Substantive *Res Judicata*. Types

According to Article 502 of the New Code of Civil Procedure, "substantive *res judicata* is the authority that makes the decision on merit unappealable, undisputable and unchangeable". In a similar way, Article 467 of the former Code of Civil Procedure stated that "substantive *res judicata* is the effectiveness that makes the decision unchangeable and undisputable, and no longer appealable to the Supreme Court or Superior Court of Justice (STJ)".[7]

As a rule, the substantive *res judicata* arises regardless of the outcome (whether in favour or against the plaintiff), but it could also follow the *secundum eventum*

[7] The New Code of Civil Procedure (CPC) was enacted by Law 13105, of March 16th, 2015, published on March 17th, 2015. According to its Article 1045, the new CPC shall come into effect 1 year after the official publication, that is, March 17th, 2016. Since it's a recent law, we chose to maintain references to the former Code of Civil Procedure (Law 5869, of January 11th, 1973).

litis regime, unappealable, undisputable and unchangeable claim depending on favourable or unfavourable outcome; or, yet, *secundum eventum probationes*, taking place according to the means of proof that are depleted. Under the latter, dismissal for lack of evidence does not create substantive *res judicata*, and its application within social security cases is defended by Savaris (2010, pp. 90–92), also extended to welfare benefits.

9.3.1 Res Judicata Secundum Eventum Probationes *in Welfare Litigation*

To start out this topic, it is important to point out that an allegation of claim preclusion can only exist when there is an action that is identical to another that has been previously filed, that is, both have the same parties, the same claim and the same cause of action (Article 301, paragraph 2 of CPC/73 and Article 337, paragraph 2 of CPC/15). Thus, if the alleged disability in an action is different from another, there are two different causes of action and two different actions. This is so because there are two separate legal facts that, though capable of resulting in the same legal consequence, have autonomous attributes; unless, of course, the disability is a combination of deficiencies. On this subject, it is worth quoting Marinoni and Arenhart (2007a) in the sense that:

> (…) many "groups" of *legal facts* could enable the same *legal consequence*; in this case, each *set of legal facts* – which can autonomously result in said effect – *must be considered an autonomous cause of action*, capable of representing an isolated action. Thus, even if there's one claim, the existence of many causes of action will also reveal the possibility of many actions.

The same authors stress that it occurs even when the direct or remote cause of action is changed, saying that:

> What we mean is that creating another cause of action does not require, in the new action, that new legal basis is presented for facts that are absolutely alien to those presented in the first action. There may only be factual changes capable of pointing towards a different legal basis.
>
> (…)
>
> From everything that has been explained herein, it is clear that the objective extension of *res judicata* is limited to the order imposed by the decision, making its declaratory effect unchangeable. However, such unchangeability is outlined by the examination of the three elements that identify the action, that is, the *parties*, the *claim* and the *cause of action*. If one of those elements is changed, we would be clearly looking at a new action, and therefore *res judicata* in a previous action becomes absolutely irrelevant.

It must be stressed that the mere change in *a portion* of the cause of action (that is, one of its elements) implies a new action, *since it most certainly implies change in the cause of action, and, therefore, change in action.*

Thus, even if the disabilities arise in the same period, the individual can file two actions, first alleging a deficiency, and then another, without implying *res judicata*.

However, it is believed that such understanding cannot be radical to the point of one single administrative rejection causing two lawsuits. If the purpose of the lawsuit is to correct the administrative rejection act, it is obvious that the analysis in court must be on all deficiencies that had been presented by the individual to INSS, since, as we've seen above, the rejection is what outlines the matter in controversy. Nonetheless, nothing would prevent alleging a disability under administrative proceedings and, once the benefit has been rejected, making a new administrative claim regarding the other disability, since the factual basis would have been changed and would lead to two separate lawsuits.

On the other hand, if the event evidence has been produced in court regarding the non-alleged disability, *res judicata* would be effective upon it. This is so because *res judicata* under disability benefit claims—which implies at least one of the welfare benefits—is closely associated with the evidence produced in court. From the moment proof is made of a certain disability, the effects of the *res judicata* apply. This means that it's not enough to allege the disability in the complaint. It is necessary that such disability is analysed in court from the set of evidence that has been entered of record. If there's no such analysis, then there's no *res judicata*.

In a reverse reasoning, if expert evidence is produced for a disability that is not the one alleged under administrative proceedings, such disability can be considered in court as a supervening cause that is interfering in the case ruling, so Article 493 of the New CPC (match to Article 462 of CPC/73) would apply under analogy. Obviously, waiving previous administrative claim can only be accepted if the plaintiff is in good-faith and the case development shows that such solution is advisable. It is worth mentioning that, in such event, INSS shall only acknowledge the disability through the report produced by the court-appointed doctor. Thus, it is sensible that the benefit's start date is set as the date when such expert report is entered of record.

Such perspective is based on the idea of claim preclusion following what is proved in the lawsuit, a concept that Savaris (2010, p. 87) identifies as the "social security claim preclusion" concept itself, one that is extended to the welfare benefits.

Thus, the concept of cause of action itself is reviewed. Cause of action is traditionally defined as factual and legal basis that justify the claim, divided into remote cause of action (the fact itself) and direct cause of action (fact's legal repercussion) (Theodoro Jr. 2001). However, in lawsuits involving disability benefits, the cause of action is no longer what is alleged by the plaintiff and is more associated to what is subjected to proof. Therefore, there is a direct association between proof and cause of action, resulting in *res judicata* according to the evidence entered of record (*secundum eventum probationis*).

On this subject, it is certain that Article 474 of the Code of Civil Procedure/73 already established that "Once the decision on merit can no longer be subject to appeals, all allegations and defences that a party could file in favour or against the claim shall be deemed presented and rejected". An identical provision can be found in Article 508 of the new Code of Civil Procedure, according to which "Once the decision on merit is unappealable, all allegations and defences that a party could file in favour or against the claim shall be considered presented and rejected". Both provisions confirm the preclusive effectiveness of the *res judicata* or the so-called implied ruling. However, it is worth stressing that the reach of such provision is not as wide as it seems.

Indeed, Marinoni and Arenhart (2007a, b), while commenting Article 474 of CPC/73, but reasoning in a way that seems to apply also to Article 508 of the new CPC, question what would be the topics not presented that would be covered by the provision, presuming that they have been alleged and rejected. For such, they start with the following example: if an eviction lawsuit claim on grounds of property damage is rejected, could a new claim based on unpaid rent be filed? Since there are two distinctive causes of action (property damage and unpaid rent), the answer is yes. This is why such authors state that "only matters regarding the same cause of action can preclude under Article 474. All the others can be presented in a later claim".

In other terms:

> The idea of "implied ruling", therefore (considering the elements that identify the action, of course), involves only *the matters whose examination is a necessary premise for the conclusion to be reached in the case.*
>
> (…)
>
> In a nutshell, it is necessary to keep the following conclusion: the preclusion that can apply under Article 474 of the Code of Civil Procedure is connected only with matters regarding the same cause of action. Only certain internal matters regarding the proposed action – therefore, referring to the same parties, the same claim and the same cause of action – will be affected by the preclusive effect that will make them no longer presentable in a different claim. Any other matter that does not belong in that specific action, even if it's indirectly connected to it – since it is a different cause of action capable of resulting in the same claim, or because it is about some other party's interest on the same object, etc. – *cannot be subject to this preclusive effectiveness.*

Thus, there's a limitation of *res judicata*'s preclusive effectiveness regarding the cause of action of a given case. If the factual basis is the same, once the relevant expert proof is made, then the *res judicata*'s preclusive effectiveness applies.

As explained before, we don't deny that this theory takes the specifics of welfare benefits into consideration, thus learning the lessons of Savaris (2010, p. 87):

> *Res judicata* must not mean a formidable technique to sweep famine and social insecurity under the rug of procedural form, for the sake of legal security. Everything that happens, then, would "only be procedural, even if the consequences were disastrous to those in real life".

In that way, the notion of cause of action becomes more associated with the notion of fact subject to proof, so as to prevent preclusion that would hinder individuals' substantive rights and prevent justice from being done.

Briefly put, *res judicata* in action involving the welfare benefit under Law 8742/93 is about a certain fact that has been subjected to proof. As a consequence, a new action can only be filed if such factual basis is changed. And, following the same sequence of ideas, such change can happen in two ways: a future change in fact and a change in fact due to a past situation that has not been examined before.

9.3.2 Rebus Sic Stantibus *Clause with* Res Judicata *in Continued Relationships*

As a rule, the claim preclusion concept applies to past situations, solving conflicts that have already taken place. As an exception, however, their effects can project to the future, as in permanent or successive relationships, when such effectiveness implies the *rebus sic stantibus* clause.

Granting the welfare benefit, given its clearly provisional attribute, is within said exception, and the study on *res judicata* cannot leave aside the impact of such fact on the concept's expected decisiveness.

9.3.2.1 Future Factual Changes. Limits of Reviewing Court-Granted Benefits

According to Savaris (2010), the "courts in social security claims grant the benefit under legal terms, that is, give a definitive order to grant a temporary benefit". This is, then, a continued relationship, since a disability that did not incapacitate the plaintiff at a moment in life and would cause the claim to be rejected at one point can become incapacitating, and so can an incapacitating disability be treated and cured, entailing the legitimate extinction of the benefit, even if granted in court. Likewise, an economic situation can get worse, creating an extreme poverty that wasn't the case until then, or it can get better, removing an individual from an extreme poverty condition for welfare purposes. Therefore, provision in Article 505(I) of the new CPC, matching Article 471(I) of CPC/73, shall apply.

So, if there's a change in fact after the decision has become unappealable, it's not hard to address it, in terms of doctrine. If there's a supervening change in fact, there's a new cause of action that was not comprehended in the previous *res judicata.*[8]

If the previous claim was dismissed, nothing prevents the plaintiff from filing a new administrative claim and, in case it is rejected, filing a new lawsuit, and INSS and the Judiciary are the ones to assess whether the facts have changed or not.

Likewise, if the previous claim was accepted, the plaintiff can be summoned for a new administrative analysis, pursuant to Article 21 of Law 8742/93, which states that the welfare benefit "must be reviewed every 2 (two) years, so the conditions that have given cause to it can be verified".

[8] As well put by Marinoni and Arenhart (2007a, b) "the unchangeability of the *res judicata* protects the court declaration only while the cause circumstances (factual and legal) are the same, *inserted as they are in the cause of action*". Then, they explain it further as follows: "The decision mirrors the facts and the law that served as grounds, so, if the facts of the law is changed, the cause of action is also changed and, therefore, the action itself. In other words: changes in facts change the cause of action, creating another (new) action and paving way to another (new) unappealable decision. Thus, when factual circumstances change, another (new) unappealable decision will be created, which must be in line with the previous unappealable decision regarding the previous circumstances". In this sense see also: Marinoni (2008).

We are not talking here about an administrative review on an unappealable court decision. We just want to affirm the idea that, insofar as the welfare benefit is clearly provisional, once the factual basis is changed, the cause of action is also changed and, therefore, the *res judicata* cannot prevail in the court case. Thus, the *res judicata* effects only persist if the facts that gave cause to it are the same. If the facts change, there is a new cause of action in the event of a new administrative rejection. However, the opposite is also true, that is, in case the factual basis is the same, there is no new cause of action to justify a new administrative or judicial claim.

In the latter, both the negative and the positive effects of *res judicata* apply (Marinoni and Arenhart 2007a, b). Thus, it prevents the topic that has been decided upon from becoming again object of a court decision on merit (negative effect), and the judges and administrative agents are bound to the judgement that became unappealable in the previous case (positive effect).

It is important to point out that such effects are also present when the claim is accepted and the benefit is granted to the plaintiff. Especially due to *res judicata*'s positive effects, the INSS medical expert cannot, in a later exam, cancel the benefit that has been granted in court without proving that the facts have changed. The same happens when analysing the extreme poverty requirement: if the social and economic reality is the same as the one analysed in court, there can be no administrative review. In other words, a benefit cannot be cancelled exclusively based on a different technical interpretation of the same disability or social and economic status. If the facts are the same, the previous unappealable decision stands.[9]

In this context, it is worth pointing out how important it is to give proper legal guidance to medical experts, social assistants and INSS administrative agents, so they can distinguish between the limits of the *res judicata* or even a provisional remedy given in a previous lawsuit; therefore, it is important to highlight the role to be played by the relevant Counsel to the INSS.

Indeed, when the Counsel to the INSS has to give an opinion in order to cancel a court-granted benefit, the possibility of ignoring the changed factual basis is minimised, since it has to be analysed by the Counsel to the same government body in charge of the legal defence involved in granting the benefit.

However, a different set of debates arise when we talk about a past situation that has not been examined in a precious lawsuit.

9.3.2.2 Unverified Past Situation

The analysis of an unverified past situation regarding the limits of an unappealable decision follows the reasoning exposed above, the proximity between the cause of action and the object of proof, creating *res judicata* effects according to the proof entered of record. In this context, Article 508 of the new Code of Civil Procedure (Article 474 of CPC/73) must be read in line with Article 503 of the same law

[9] It's in this context that Marinoni (2008) warns that "facing continuous relationships, there are circumstances that change (provisional elements) and circumstances that are the same (perennial or stable elements)".

(Article 468 of CPC/73), limiting the *res judicata* effects to the main issues that have been expressly decided upon.

It is worth adding that such understanding, though with different wording, is embraced by national case law.

Indeed, the STJ has broadened the concept of new documents in order to allow actions for relief from judgement to be filed based on Article 485(VII) of CPC/73 (matching Article 966(VII) of the new CPC) when the document already existed at the time the previous lawsuit was filed, especially given the peculiar status of the rural worker.[10] In this sense, for instance:

> ACTION FOR RELIEF FROM JUDGEMENT. SOCIAL SECURITY. NEW DOCUMENT. RETIREMENT UNDER AGE CRITERIA. RURAL WORKER. SUBSTANTIVE PROOF. EXISTENCE.
>
> I – This Bench, considering the unequal conditions experienced by the rural worker and adopting the pro misero solution, understands that the proof, even if existing at the time the action was filed, must be considered for the purposes of Article 485(VII) of the CPC. Precedents.
>
> II – Plaintiff's son's birth certificate showing that her spouse is identified as a landsman is enough to prove his status as a rural worker for social security purposes.
>
> Action for relief from judgement accepted.
>
> (AR 3.520/SP, Rep. Judge FELIX FISCHER, 3rd BENCH, session date 27/02/2008, DJe 30/06/2008)
>
> ACTION FOR RELIEF FROM JUDGEMENT. NEW DOCUMENT AND FACTUAL MISTAKE. ARTICLES 485(VI) AND 487(I) OF THE CPC. RURAL WORKER. DIFFICULTY OBTAINING IN DUE TIME. PRO MISERO SOLUTION.
>
> 1. According to the understanding by higher courts - REsp 15.007/RJ – the new document referred to in Article 485(VI) of the Code of Civil Procedure is "in theory, one that exists at the time of the challenged decision that is not known by the interested party or was impossible to obtain for proper use in the case, and is enough to change the case's outcome".
>
> **2. In the specific case of a rural worker, under unequal and sometimes inhuman conditions of living and education, one is authorized to infer - given the obstacles to find the document, even though it existed at the time the action was filed - that there was not bad-faith or negligence. One can also conclude, without a doubt, that its existence was not known, due to the adverse education background.**
>
> 3. The marriage certificate stating that the plaintiff's spouse was a landsman not taken into consideration by the relieved judgement characterizes a factual mistake that allows for relief from judgement, since it's a reasonable substantive proof of the rural work. Precedent from this Court.
>
> 4. Social security matters. Broad understanding. Pro misero solution.
>
> 5. Action for relief from judgement accepted. (AR 843/SP, Rep. Judge. Fernando Gonçalves, DJU 04-12-2000) (our highlights)

Likewise, the Regional Court—4th Region has decided in some cases that the substantive proof is a pre-requirement of claim admissibility, so the case is dismissed without judging its contents when the proof is not enough. It is understood that the substantive proof is an essential document that must accompany the complaint, otherwise it must be rejected (Article 283 combined with 295(VI) and 267(I), all from CPC/73, that, in general lines, match Articles 320, 330(IV) and 485(I) of the new CPC), and dismissed without analysing its merits. Thus, as an example:

---

[10] What, within the same sequence of ideas, does not prevent the use of the same interpretation when there are unequal conditions in the actual case between the original claim and INSS, even if it's not a rural worker.

SOCIAL SECURITY AND CIVIL PROCEDURE. PRELIMINARY OF VIOLATION TO THE PRINCIPLE OF JUDGE'S PHYSICAL IDENTITY. DISMISSED. EXCEPTION. S ERVICE TIME REGISTRATION. PROSPECTOR. FRAIL DOCUMENT EVIDENCE. LACK OF INITIAL SUBSTANTIVE PROOF. TESTIMONY. IMPOSSIBIL ITY. DISMISSAL WITHOUT PREJUDICE. 1. The principle of the judge's physical identity is not violated when a judgement is rendered by another judge that is not the one who was at the hearing, since it complies with the exception determined by the competent Court. 2. The registration as a prospector in the competent body is not enough to characterize the actual economic exploration of prospection activity. 3. Since the document proof is frail, it is not possible to acknowledge the service time based only on testimony (Article 55, paragraph 3 of Law 8213/91). 4. **The lack of initial substantive evidence implies dismissal without prejudice (Article 267(I) of the CPC), once the substantive proof principle is a pre-requirement to the action's admissibility (Article 283 combined with Article 295(VI) of the CPC). We must add that social security law does not admit preclusion to the right to a benefit for lack of evidence, and whenever possible, once the evidence is renewed, granting is also renewed, and, as a consequence, so is the service time registration.** 5. Appeal rejected. (TRF4, AC 2000.04.01.121383-8, Fifth Bench, Rep. Judge Luiz Carlos Cervi, DJ 17/12/2003) (our highlights)

However, it is understood, that, from the idea of *res judicata* limited to the proof entered of record, there's no need to relieve from previous judgement, since it has been based on different evidence. Likewise, there's no need to try to change the concept of dismissal without prejudice, since what happened previously was in fact a dismissal with the analysis of the contents of a lawsuit, but limited to the evidence at the time, without comprehending the ones produced later.[11]

This way the *res judicata* can be in line with Brazilian reality, where the degree of knowledge of the general population regarding welfare benefits is very low. To ignore such reality, understanding that the plaintiff should present all possible arguments and documents at the time of the first administrative claim would be creating a formalism that impairs the effectiveness of the jurisdiction.[12]

9.3.3 *Evolution of STF's Case Law regarding Extreme Poverty and* Res Judicata

As mentioned above, Article 203(V) of the Constitution delegated the regulation of welfare benefits to nonconstitutional legislation, and Article 20, paragraph 3 of Law 8742/1993 defined extreme poverty using the following criterion: monthly household income per capita less than ¼ (one fourth) of the minimum wage.

A legal criterion that is so objective ended up resulting in judicial claims questioning its unconstitutionality. However, the Supreme Court, exerting a concentrated-abstract control, understood that said provision is constitutional:

[11] Loosening the possibility of dismissing without prejudice, Savaris (2010, p. 89) ponders: "What if the judge starts evaluating the evidence, wouldn't he be examining the merit to, after concluding upon its lack or insufficiency, dismiss the case without prejudice?".

[12] It is clear, on the other hand, that in the event it is evidenced that there were no unequal conditions in the case, that the plaintiff has willingly omitted evidence in the previous case, the unappealable decision still stands, and even the possibility of applying penalties due to malicious prosecution exists.

CONSTITUTIONAL. CHALLENGES THE FEDERAL PROVISION THAT DEFINES THE CRITERION TO ENABLE BENEFIT IN ARTICLE 203(V) OF THE CONSTITUTION. THE ALLEGED RESTRICTION DOES NOT EXIST DUE TO THE CONSTITUTIONAL PROVISION THAT DELEGATES TO NONCONSTITUTIONAL LEGISLATION THE TASK OF DEFINING CRITERIA TO GRANT MINIMUM WAGES BENEFITS TO THE DISABLED AND THE ELDERLY. SUCH LAW BRINGS AN OBJECTIVE CASE OF WELFARE SERVICES BY THE GOVERNMENT. ACTION REJECTED.

(ADI 1232, Rep. Chief Judge ILMAR GALVÃO, Rep. Judge for the Decision: Chief Judge NELSON JOBIM, Full Bench, session date 27/08/1998, DJ 01-06-2001 PP-00075 EMENT VOL-02033-01 PP-00095)

The decision had the majority of votes, and the prevailing theory was the one under which the legal criterion was established as authorised by the Constitution and has the merit of making it applicable. Losing votes were from Chief Judges Ilmar Galvão and Néri da Silveira, who embraced the General Attorney's opinion to construe the provision according to the Constitution, stating that the legal criterion would only constitute an absolute presumption of extreme poverty, not excluding other means to prove lack of resources.

Even though the General Attorney's theory has not prevailed in such judgement, the fact is that, in practice, judges end up embracing it by loosening the analysis on extreme poverty, since they combine other elements to the legal household income per capita criterion, which lead to several INSS complaints being filed on the grounds that the Supreme Court's decision regarding the constitutionality of said provision was being disrespected.

That, combined with other social and political changes, such as the evolution of social inclusion programs, which sometimes adopted different criteria to define extreme poverty, led the Supreme Court to face the issue of constitutionality of said provision again in 2013 under two Extraordinary Appeals: RE n° 567985 and RE 580963.

As the syllabus from both appeals shows, the Supreme Court has concluded that the criteria in Article 20, paragraph 3 of Statutory Law 8742/1993 have suffered a "process of inconstitutionalization", since they no longer allowed the definition of extreme poverty cases, alluding to the principle of prohibited deficient achievement.[13]

In this context, the following question arises: could the parties that had their welfare benefits denied in the past by decisions based on ADI 1232 currently act to substitute such judgements, even when already facing substantive *res judicata* effects?

There are many discussions about the possibility and capable means to challenge the so-called unconstitutional *res judicata* or, as more technically put by Talamini (2005), the "unconstitutional decision with an unappealable status". Said author sums up the problems presented by this issue in a proper way, stating that "it is necessary to define if it's possible to weight in values involved in the actual case to fend off the decision's unchangeability or if such ponderation belongs exclusively to the legislator when creating instruments to review *res judicata* effects" (Talamini 2005).

[13] RE n° 567.985, vote by Chief Judge Marco Aurélio.

Marinoni and Arenhart (2007a, b) cogitate that the "substantive *res judicata* is an essential attribute to the Rule of Law and to the effectiveness of the fundamental right to seek the Judiciary", defending the theory that "if the decisiveness of the *res judicata* can, in some cases, produce effects that are undesirable to the system, it is not correct to assume that, because of that, it can simply be disregarded".

Despite the adopted theory regarding the "loosening of *res judicata* effects", a topic that on its own could result in dozens of articles, the peculiar fact of the decisions regarding extreme poverty in welfare benefits is that they were based on a Supreme Court decision under abstract-concentrated constitutional control. Therefore, this is a constitutional matter. Article 20, paragraph 3 of Statutory Law 8742/1993 was analysed according to Article 203(V) of the Constitution.

Precedent 343 of STF states that "an action for relief from judgement is not admissible against a law provision when said decision is based on a legal text with disputed interpretation in courts".

Thus, one would think that changing the interpretation of the requirement in Article 20, paragraph 3 would not allow a new analysis on cases with unappealable decisions. However, the Supreme Court has solid case law in the sense that such Precedent does not apply to constitutional matters,[14] such as the case at hand. Indeed, the Supreme Court alluded to an unconstitutional case, pointing out that at the time of ADI 1232, the legal criterion was in fact constitutional, though not anymore.

There's an answer to the problem that requires a bit of caution and we'd like to make some brief considerations for exploration purposes by addressing a few issues.

First of all, if there was a change in the factual basis, such as change in the household income of the plaintiff, for instance, there is a possibility of a new ruling or even administrative review. Thus, if one of the plaintiff's offspring is no longer living with the plaintiff or is no longer contributing to the household income, it is possible that a situation of extreme poverty appears. We use the idea explained throughout this article, especially in Sect. 9.3.2.1, in the sense that a future change in fact allows a new decision, since it is not covered by *res judicata* effects.

Likewise, if certain element has not been covered by a previous court decision, such as if no one noticed the existence of additional income from a different welfare program, it can be analysed again without the need to vacate the previous judgement. It is an unverified past event, and what has been explained in Sect. 9.3.2.2 herein applies.

[14] Among others, the following decision is worth mentioning: "Internal interlocutory appeal in the interlocutory appeal. Precedent 343/STF. Non-applicability. Precedents. 1. Case law in this court is solid in the sense that Precedent 343 does not apply when the matters in the case records are of constitutional nature, even if the decision challenged in an action for relief from judgement has been based on disputed interpretation or on previous understanding to a Precedent set by the Supreme Court. 2. Internal interlocutory appeal rejected." (AI 703485 AgR, Rep. Chief Judge Dias Toffoli, 1st Bench, session date 11/12/2012, ELECTRONIC DECISION DJe-027 DISCLOSED 07-02-2013 PUBLISH 08-02-2013).

However, if the factual basis is the same, that is, if there is no future change in fact and no past event to be considered, we understand, at least in this exploratory analysis, that it's not possible to simply ignore the existence of *res judicata.*

That does not prevent the possibility of vacating the previous judgement regarding the extreme poverty issue. This means that the existence of *res judicata* is embraced, but it is understood that the judgement can be vacated. This is so because, given the new interpretation given by the Supreme Court to Article 20, paragraph 3 of Law 8742/1993, it is clear that the requirement of household income per head being less than ¼ (one fourth) of the minimum wage is not absolute. Since it's a constitutional matter, Precedent 343 from the Supreme Court does not apply. Therefore, at first, vacation of judgement due to literal violation of a provision, pursuant to Article 966(V) of the new Code of Civil Procedure, matching Article 485(V) of the Code of Civil Procedure of 1973, would apply.[15]

9.4 Conclusion

The purpose of this work was to analyse how the proceedings regarding welfare benefits under Law 8742/1993 can be changed due to its own nature. Thus, we have highlighted the provisional nature of the requirements to grant said benefit, as well as the specifics involved in the litigation and their implications in the limits of the *res judicata.*

At this point, we came to the following conclusions:

a) assuming that, at first, the Judiciary must act as a reviewer of administrative acts, the previous administrative rejection is important as an outline of what is going to be subjected to proof;
b) once the dispute has been outlined, *res judicata* effects are limited according to the proof entered of record (*secundum eventum probationis*), so the concepts of alleged facts and proved facts are made more similar, and the concept of cause of action is reviewed;
c) likewise, the study on *res judicata* cannot forget the provisional nature of the welfare benefit, showing that there is a new cause of action whenever there's a future change in events, such as when the plaintiff's disability becomes better or worse, or reduced or increased extreme poverty conditions. In this sense, even the administrative cancellation of benefits granted in court is admitted, provided that the adequate procedure is observed, that is, the plaintiff is involved in the review and there's an opinion by the Counsel to the INSS.
d) due to its provisional nature, if, regarding extreme poverty, there has been a future change in events or a past situation that has not been verified, a new claim is pos-

[15] Article 966(V) of the new CPC refers to a manifest violation of a "legal norm" as a case of vacation of judgement, and no longer a "literal law provision". Even so, considering the precedents that gave rise to Precedent 343, we understand that the constitutional matter will keep prevailing, without the need to change the interpretation given by the Supreme Court.

sible, since there was no previous unappealable decision. However, if the factual basis is the same, it is not possible to just ignore the existence of the *res judicata*.

e) the previous conclusion does not prevent the possibility of vacating the judgement regarding the extreme poverty requirement due to a literal legal violation (Article 485(V) of CPC/73 and Article 966(V) of CPC/15) in light of a new constitutional interpretation by the Supreme Court of Article 20, paragraph 3 of Law 8742/93, since Precedent 343 of STF would not apply to this case.

References

de Salles CA (2011) Arbitragem em contratos administrativos. Forense, Rio de Janeiro

Marinoni LG (2008) Coisa Julgada Inconstitucional: a retroatividade da decisão de (in) constitucionalidade do STF sobre a coisa julgada: a questão da relativização da coisa julgada. Editora Revista dos Tribunais, São Paulo

Marinoni LG, Arenhart SC (2007a) Manual do processo de conhecimento. 6ª ed. Editora Revista dos Tribunais, São Paulo

Marinoni LG, Arenhart SC (2007b) Curso de processo civil – processo de Conhecimento, vol 2. Editora Revista dos Tribunais, São Paulo

Marinoni LG, Arenhart SC (2009) Prova. Editora Revista dos Tribunais, São Paulo

Mitidiero D (2007) Bases para construção de um processo civil cooperativo – o direito processual civil no marco teórico do formalismo-valorativo. Disponível em. http://www.academia.edu. Acesso em 10 fev. 2014.

Savaris JA (2010) Direito processual previdenciário. Juruá, Curitiba

Takahashi B (2012) Aspectos processuais dos benefícios previdenciários por incapacidade, de Bruno Takahashi. In: Revista CEJ (ed) Ano XVI, n. 56. Brasília, pp 28–43

Talamini E (2005) Coisa julgada e sua revisão. Editora Revista do Tribunais, São Paulo

Theodoro Jr. H (2001) Curso de direito processual civil, vol I, 37ª ed. Forense, Rio de Janeiro

Chapter 10
Effectiveness of the Social Protection Benefit to Fight Extreme Poverty Under Brazilian Rule of Law

José Carlos Francisco

Abstract The scope of this study is to show the progressive legal and social effectiveness of the monthly pecuniary benefit set forth in article 203, V, of the Constitution of 1988 and in Law 8,742/1993, as one of the public policies to fight social-economic extreme poverty in Brazil. We shall depart from the analysis of data concerning Brazilian reality, in order to prove the statement that this is a country with significant economic potential, but rather unequal regarding the distribution of wealth, with relevant numbers of poverty and extreme poverty. Brazilian historic legal framework brings several obligations to the public administration concerning social rights, guarantees, and duties, but the constitutional system of 1988 was the one that provided for a monthly pecuniary stipend as a systematic social protection benefit to fight extreme poverty and socio-economic inequalities. Under this scenario, Law 8,742/1993 has significant legal effectiveness, shown by relevant figures. There is still a long way to go, with several problems to be solved, but the legal effectiveness of this social protection benefit has been an important measure to efficiently fight extreme poverty in Brazil.

Keywords Brazil • Social security • Social assistance • Unequality • Poverty • Extreme • Fight

10.1 Scope

The scope of this study is to show the progressive legal and social effectiveness of the monthly pecuniary benefit set forth in article 203, V, of the Constitution of 1988 and in Law 8,742/1993, as one of the public policies to fight social-economic extreme poverty in Brazil.

J.C. Francisco (✉)
School of Law, University of Mackenzie, Sao Paulo, Brazil
e-mail: jcarlosfrancisco@hotmail.com

M.A. Serau Junior, J.R. Caetano Costa (eds.), *Assistance Benefits in Brazil*,
DOI 10.1007/978-3-319-27046-3_10

For this purpose, we shall depart from the analysis of data concerning Brazilian reality, in order to prove the statement that this is a country with significant economic potential, but rather unequal regarding the distribution of wealth, with relevant numbers of poverty and extreme poverty. We show that Brazilian historic legal framework brings several obligations to the public administration concerning social rights, guarantees, and duties, but the constitutional system of 1988 was the one that provided for a monthly pecuniary stipend (corresponding to one minimum wage) as a systematic social protection benefit (not a substitute to work) to fight extreme poverty and socio-economic inequalities. Under this scenario, Law 8,742/1993 has significant legal effectiveness, shown by relevant figures. In 2014, it reached approximately 4 million people with this active social protection benefit (around 2 % of Brazilian population).

After that, we conclude there is still a long way to go (with several problems to be solved), but the legal effectiveness of this social protection benefit has been an important measure to efficiently fight extreme poverty in Brazil.

10.2 Data on Brazil

Brazil is not a poor country, but instead a rich one with enormous socio-economic differences and, for that reason, most of its population is poor.[1] Known for its cordiality, Brazilian people is distributed in a territory with the size of a continent (livable and capable of creating a relevant amount of jobs) reflecting a significant socio-economic potential. However, the distribution of wealth and opportunities is mean, triggering several problems with repercussions in several areas (especially child mortality, life expectancy, access to education, and urban violence).

10.2.1 A Rich and Unequal Country

According to governmental data projected for mid-2015, Brazil has 204,548,826 inhabitants from several ethnic and cultural origins, which reflects its pluralism (IBGE 2015a). This population is divided unequally in its territory of 8,515,767 km^2 (with large urban concentrations and low-density areas), divided in a federation with 26 states, 5570 municipalities, and a Federal District (where the capital of Brazil, Brasília, is located), besides several sub-national areas—such as development regions, metropolitan areas, micro-regions, and urban conglomerates (Sogeografia 2015).

Defined as a "tropical country," Brazil has a great diversity of weather, topography, altitude, dynamics of air masses and fronts, and approximately 90 % of its land

[1] We used the terms "rich" and "poor" at their broadest definition, considering specially economic, social, and cultural aspects.

is between the tropics of Cancer and Capricorn; it is crossed by the Equator in the North and by the Tropic of Capricorn in the South. Most of Brazil is located in low-latitude areas, with hot and humid weather and average temperature around 20 °C, adequate to be explored from a socio-economic perspective (Brasil 2015).

Its water and environmental wealth is also exuberant, especially in the Amazon area, whereas other regions (especially in the southeast) are highly industrialized (e.g., the State of São Paulo), with knowledge and cultural centers highly developed. Even considering the relevant environmental protection goals, there is significant capacity of social and economic activities.

All these elements give a great potential to Brazil and, despite the scenario of economic crisis since 2014, this country is in a relevant position in the global context. According to data of the International Monetary Fund, Brazil may fall to 8th place in the ranking of largest economies in 2015 (after the United Kingdom in 2011, it may be surpassed by India in 2015), but Brazil was already 6th on this list in 2011, when it was behind the USA, China, Japan, Germany, and France only (Globo 2015a).

However, social and economic inequalities are clear when we analyze data on life quality and wealth distribution. In 2014, Brazilian *per capita* income was BRL1052.00 per year (equivalent to USD420.80, calculated at the average exchange rate of USD1.00 to BRL2.50). The highest *per capita* income was verified in the Federal District (BRL2055 per year) and the lowest was from the State of Maranhão—only BRL461.00 (IBGE 2015b).

The 2014 Human Development Report—"*Sustaining Human Progress: Reducing Vulnerabilities and Building Resilience*" by the United Nations shows the vulnerability of life conditions in Brazil, from the Human Development Index (HDI).[2] Brazil has indeed advanced one position on HDI ranking, going from 80th in 2012 to 79th in 2013 on that ranking—which comprises 187 nations—because in 2013, its index was 0.744 (in 2012 it was 0.742), being included among the countries with "high" development. During the last three decades, its HDI increased 36.4 % (from 0.545—"low" development in 1980 to 0.744 in 2013—"high" development).[3] Compared to 2012, most countries were stable in 2013, because out of the 187 nations of which the UN collects data, only 38 improved their position, whereas 114 kept stable and 35 countries fell (Globo 2015b).

The HDI figures allow an optimistic analysis, especially of data indicating an improvement of life conditions. However, a comparison with other countries comprises aspects that put at risk this favorable interpretation of data, such as the fact

[2] HDI is an index measured annually by the United Nations in accordance with indicators of wealth, health, and education, ranging from 0 to 1 (1 being the maximum quality indicator). From that study, countries are divided into four categories: "very high," "high," "medium," and "low" human development. 2014 Human Development Report: "Sustaining Human Progress: Reducing Vulnerabilities and Building Resilience" was published by the United Nations' Development Programme (UNDP 2015).

[3] Position 79 is on the general conclusions and on page 167 of the 2014 Human Development Report: "Sustaining Human Progress: Reducing Vulnerabilities and Building Resilience," published by the United Nations' Development Programme (UNDP 2015).

that the global economic crisis (since 2008) did not reach Brazil severely. Several countries were in significant recession until 2012, but are already presenting signals of stabilization and recuperation even, whereas Brazil has presented a lack of control in its economic and political framework since 2013, which resulted in the crisis experienced since 2014 (with perspective of aggravation in 2015). That is, several countries are becoming stable or leaving the crisis, while Brazil has just entered in its crisis.

According to data of 2013 of the National Survey of Households on a Sample Basis (Pesquisa Nacional por Amostra de Domicílios—Pnad), carried out by Brazilian Institute of Geography and Statistics (Instituto Brasileiro de Geografia e Estatística—IBGE), from 2012 to 2013, illiteracy rates fell 0.4 %, although Brazil still has 13 million people who cannot read or write (note that the number of Brazilians with graduate degree increased in the period, especially due to public programmes for stimulating and financing graduation). Concerning sanitation, Pnad showed that 85 % of the households have water network (decrease of 0.1 %) and 64 % have sewerage system (access increased 1 %). The Gini Index (which measures income inequality from zero—absolute equality—to one—absolute inequality) increased again, according to Pnad of 2013, so Brazil did not continue to reduce inequalities although the average income of Brazilians increased in 2013, because the richest Brazilians had an increase of almost double the poorest Brazilians; that is, income inequality stopped decreasing (Globo 2015c).

10.2.2 Poverty and Extreme Poverty

Poverty and extreme poverty are connected socio-economic concepts that cannot be mistaken. Both comprise quantitative and qualitative aspects. Poverty means the lack of monetary resources to purchase goods and services essential for life within regular time/space standards, whereas extreme poverty is a more severe case of poverty, since its victims do not have money even to purchase a minimum amount of food and other items necessary for survival (Singer 2015). Quantity aspects interfere more or less in the qualitative aspect, although poor and extremely poor people are deprived of goods and services indispensable or useful to life, health, etc.

A large portion of Brazilian population is poor and there are also significant people in extreme poverty, despite Brazilian's relevant potential Brazil for production, income, and employment.

According to data of 2013 (before the current economic crisis), the poverty chart was the following (analyzed per family) (Fig. 10.1).

This income pyramid does not show the figures for extreme poverty, which certainly exists and is included in the figures indicated for of poverty. Indeed, the quantification of extreme poverty in Brazil faces some divergences concerning its criteria, and this difficulty is also increased by political speeches (of the government and opposition party).

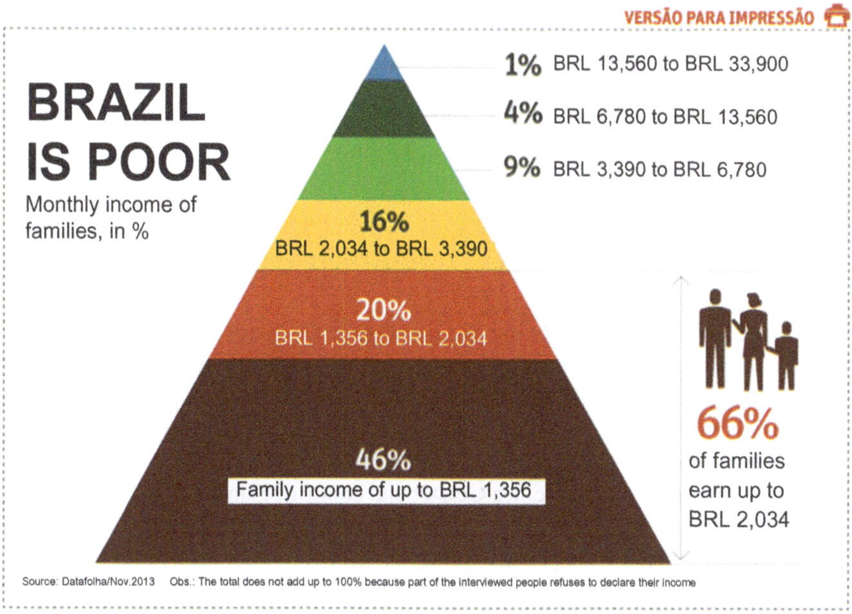

Fig. 10.1 Family income piramyd in Brazil. *Source*: Data Folha/Nov. 2013 Obs.: The total does not add up to 100 % because part of the interviewed people refuses to declare their income

Claiming to follow standards set by the World Bank (according to which, in July, 2009, USD1.00 a day was seen as limit for extreme poverty), the number of extremely poor people acknowledged by the Federal Government considered, in 2013, BRL70.00 of monthly *per capita* income as limit for poverty (under that income we have extreme poverty). Because of several public income transfer programmes (especially "Bolsa Família"), extreme poverty in Brazil has significantly decreased (according to the federal government, it has been eradicated). However, if we adjust these numbers by inflation, the limit would be R$77.56 in 2013 and the number of people in extreme poverty would go from zero to at least 22.3 million (according to data produced by the Ministry of Social Development based on the Single Registry, which assembles data of more than 71 million Brazilians who benefit from social protection programmes), even if adding personal income and transferences by the State (such as Bolsa Família). Moreover, the Federal Government itself estimated that in 2013 there were approximately 700,000 families living below the line of extreme poverty that were not included in official records (Folha De São Paulo 2015). If we consider the estimate population of 201 million Brazilians in 2013, 22.3 million people in extreme poverty correspond to 11.10 % of the Brazilian population (IBGE 2015c).

Therefore, with at least 11.10 % of the population suffering from essential privations, in this country of contradictions and inequalities, fighting against extreme poverty has been the true purpose of Brazilian public policies (by all federation units), besides other measures to raise people out of poverty.

Within the subject matter of this study, the purpose of this analysis is the legal and social effectiveness of the social protection benefit set forth in Law 8,742/1993, which fights economic extreme poverty by offering monthly stipends under standards established by that same law and with its outline also built by precedents (especially by federal courts).

10.3 Legal System to Fight Socio-Economic Extreme Poverty

It is commonplace to state that the historical path of society and State activities in the socio-economical order has progresses and regressions, especially concerning the affirmation and concretization of fundamental rights, regarding which Norberto Bobbio identified evolution in centuries of fighting and suffering, in the eternal controversy between new freedoms and old powers (Bobbio 1992). From the values shed by the Enlightenment, Fleiner-Gerster and colab. of Hänni (2006) remind there was enthusiasm with the role of the State after the French Revolution of 1789 and the nationalist conquests of the nineteenth century, although this confident position weakened throughout the subsequent decades, due to tragic experiences with state practices of Nazism and Red Khmer in Cambodia, among other totalitarian states.

On the other hand, it is also true that accuracies and mistakes are part of the maturation and development process, reason why we agree with Pablo Lucas Verdú (2007) that the idea of Rule of Law is a conquest derived from the struggle of new ideas with contrary power structures, of the Liberal State (against the Old Regime), of the Welfare State (against individualism and Absent State), and of the Democratic Rule of Law—fighting socio-political structures with vestige of individualism and a system of privileges (Ferreira Filho 1999).

The meaning of Rule of Law is not unambiguous. Ferrajoli (2006) indicates two meanings for Rule of Law: 1st) broad, weak, or formal sense, according to which public powers are granted and implemented under the arrangements and procedures set forth by law, the Legislative Rule of Law; 2nd) strict, strong, or substantial sense, under which public powers are equally subject to law concerning the arrangement and content of its implementation, but they are also subject to substantial principles established by the Constitution, the Constitutional Rule of Law.

If there is not one meaning of Rule of Law, the risky reduction of meanings at least leads to the idea that it concerns a quality of the State guided by normative standards (elaborated, understood, and applied according to a democratic system) which apply to all (including to the ones that elaborated them), with the purpose of identifying and implementing fundamental rights, guarantees, and duties.

The meaning of Rule of Law becomes even more complex because it is dynamic, due to the fact that it is under the context of the evolution of experiences of a society and of the State. In any case, in the most familiar types of Rule of Law (classified in accordance with the conception of individual and with the role of the State concerning the promotion of fundamental rights, duties, and guarantees), at least since the beginning of the twentieth century, there has been an increase of public concerns with fighting economic extreme poverty and poverty.

10.3.1 Brazilian Rule of Law and the Fight against Extreme Poverty

In Brazil, the historic fight for social rights, guarantees, and duties reveals that several public activities increased after the 1930s, especially concerning health, education, and social assistance services. Monthly stipends granted by the public administration were mostly related to social security as measures to substitute labor, although there have been periodic social protection stipends and pecuniary benefits in urgent cases. It was only after the constitutional system of 1988 that emerged a structured benefit granting monthly stipends related to social protection (that is, regardless of work) as a measure to fight extreme poverty.

Section 179, XXXI of the Imperial Code of 1824 dealt with public assistance guarantees, followed by section 75 of the Constitution of 1891, which provided for pensions (limited to public employees in case of disability at the nation's service). Legislative Decree 3,724/1919 brought measures to protect the worker if there was a labor accident (attributing to the employer the burden to pay for medical assistance and indemnity insurance).

One of the most important marks on the evolution of welfare state policies is Decree 4,682/1923, known as "Eloy Chaves" (a Federal Deputy at the time), which dealt with workers associated to retirement and pension funds. These policies were then remodeled by Getúlio Vargas with the creation of Retirement and Pension Institutes (Institutos de Aposentadorias e Pensões—IAPs) under section 121 of the Constitution of 1934 (which also dealt with medical and sanitary assistance to workers and to pregnant women and social security funding), and also under section 137 of the Constitution of 1937 (with several types of benefits).

With a social protection nature, in 1942, the government created the Brazilian Assistance Legion ("Legião Brasileira de Assistência"—LBV). Its initial purpose of assisting families of 2nd World War Soldiers was replaced by social protection policies to families in need, until 1990, when it was extinguished by President Fernando Henrique Cardoso after crises related to the alleged corruption of the ex-President Fernando Collor.

In 1946, the Constitution brought several social protection measures (e.g., section 157) and, during the time it was effective, the Legislative Power enacted the Organic Law for the Social Security of Urban Workers (Law 3,807/1960) and created the Assistance Fund to Rural Workers (Fundo de Assistência ao Trabalhador Rural—FUNRURAL) in 1963, followed by the unification of IAPs with the creation of National Welfare Institute (INPS) and of the National Institute for Medical Assistance of Social Security (INAMPS) in 1966, kept in the Constitution of 1967. During the time when this last Constitution was effective, Complementary Law 11/1971 brought benefits to rural workers. Currently, these social security benefits are set forth in the General Social Security Rulings, kept by the National Social Security Institution (INSS), in accordance with Law 8,212/1991 and Law 8,213/1991, while health assistance is managed by the Joint Health System (Sistema Único de Saúde—SUS), which unites the Federal Government, States, the Federal District, and Municipalities.

Despite having implemented services policies (such as sheltering homeless people, health services, etc.), the Brazilian public body had no systematic policy of monthly stipends to people in extreme poverty (although some extraordinary policies were implemented in urgent cases). However, it is also true that the legal system has been stimulating for decades the performance of services by non-profit private institutions (e.g., granting tax relief to social assistance entities, i.e., renouncing State revenues, as set forth in several Constitutions).

10.3.2 Legal Effectiveness: Current Legal Framework

The constitutional system of 1988 was the one to strengthen the legal effectiveness of the normative structure to fight extreme poverty, bringing an original measure of monthly stipends with assistance nature. Along with the longest lists of fundamental rights, duties, and guarantees in comparison with previous constitutions, from the Preamble to the rules indicated in Headings II and VIII, passing through fundamental principles and goals of Heading I, there are several provisions related to the concrete implementation of aspects essential to human nature and life in society with elements of social rights (highlighting social security and social protection systems, especially concerning the fight against extreme poverty). Section 3, III of the Constitution expressly lists among the fundamental goals of Brazilian Rule of Law the eradication of poverty and marginalization, as well as the reduction of social and regional inequalities.

With the nature of systematic stipends, there is a significant list of social security pensions, set forth in the Constitution of 1988 and implemented by Law 8,213/1992, that are clearly benefits that replace work in several situations (especially the payment of contributions to fund the social security system, which comprises the public welfare system).

In the context of fighting extreme poverty, the constitutional framework of 1988 innovated when bringing a pecuniary benefit with social protection nature (regardless of contributions by the interested person and not created as substitute to work) when establishing in section 203, V, the payment of a monthly benefit corresponding to one minimum wage to the person considered to be in a situation of extreme poverty. The constitutional provision of one minimum wage has the purpose of fulfilling basic life needs of the worker and his/her family (with housing, food, education, health, entertainment, clothes, hygiene, transportation, and social security, in accordance with section 7, IV of the Constitution of 1988).

10.3.3 Social Protection Benefit of Law 8,742/1993

Section 203, V, of the Constitution of 1988 was only ruled by Law 8,742/1993, although section 139 of Law 8,213/1991 had created a similar benefit when guaranteeing a monthly stipend of one minimum wage for life to people in situation of extreme poverty. Notwithstanding that, section 139 of Law 8,213/1991 concerned a social security benefit (paid until the date of implementation of the social protection benefit established by section 203, V, of the Constitution), because it demanded a job or remunerated activity and contributions for its funding (even if for modest twelve months), besides other requirements.

Section 203, V, of the Constitution of 1988 gained its current format with Law 8,742/1992, which created the benefit for continue stipends with a clear scope of social protection. Being funded jointly by all society and by the State, this individual monthly benefit (that is, granted to the individual, not to his/her family) does not demand a job or contributions by the interested party. Its grant depends only on the fulfillment of the following cumulative requirements by the applicant: (a) being aged 65 years or more (section 34 of Law 10,741/2003) or having (permanent or temporary) invalidity to perform a remunerated activity (proven by an expert's report); (b) not having other means to provide for him/herself; (c) having family members (or person of which he/she depends, if living in the same house) who are unable to provide for the plaintiff, being characterized as extremely poor in the actual case (generally proven by a socio-economical report). The capacity to perform everyday acts without assistance is not equivalent to the capacity to provide for one's subsistence and does not jeopardize the concession of this benefit. The lack of proof of any of the requirements implies denial of the request by federal administrative agents.

Law 8,742/1993 brought a controversial requirement of per capita family income, which could not surpass ¼ of the minimum wage (an amount that was frequently above the limit of extreme poverty established by the World Bank—of USD1.00 per capita). However, Brazilian judiciary understood that this objective criterion was unconstitutional to the extent that extreme poverty should be analyzed on a case-by-case basis, without this standard factor.[4]

After being granted, this social protection benefit may end due to the possibility of modification of concrete circumstances (e.g., the beneficiary may recover its capacity to work, his/her family may obtain new income sources, etc.).

Despite being individual, the benefit of Law 8,742/1993 fulfills the need of the beneficiary who cannot work (due to his/her age or incapacity), but it is clear that it also favors indirectly all household members, whom the beneficiary would generally help if he/she could work.

Certainly, legal provisions such as Law 8,742/1993 must be interpreted aiming at their maximum social effectiveness, because they concern primary needs essential to human being and to life in society.

---

[4]On April 17th and 18th, 2014, within the scope of Complaint (Reclamação—RCL) 4374 and Extraordinary Appeals (Recursos Extraordinários—REs) 567985 and 580963 (both judged under the general repercussion system), the Supreme Court overcame the decision of ADI 1,232-DF, ruling that the criterion of per capita income of ¼ of the minimum wage no longer applies. For this reason, the characterization as extremely poor must be assessed by an analysis of the concrete circumstances of the case on point, either by the Social Security National Institute (INSS), which regularly grants the benefit, or by the Judiciary, in case of judicial lawsuits.

10.3.4 Social Effectiveness: Quantitative Evolution of the Social Protection Benefit of Law 8,742/1993

After being successful in the stages of ruling and beginning of legal effectiveness, the social protection benefit of Law 8,742/1993 presented important figures already in 1996, when it benefited 346,000 people. Showing the social effectiveness of the constitutional and infra-constitutional legal systems to fight extreme poverty, in April, 2014 (less than 20 years later), this social protection benefit was paid to more than 4 million people, of which 1.84 million were elders (65-years-old or more) and 2.18 millions were handicapped (of all ages). Considering the total estimated population of Brazil in 2014 as 202 million people, the 4 million social protection benefits reached directly 2 % of Brazilian population (without taking into account the indirect benefits to the beneficiary's family members).

According to governmental data, only in 2013 the total resources directly involved in the payment of this social protection benefit surpassed BRL31.4 billions (equivalent to USD 14.3 billion, considering the average exchange rate in 2013 of USD1 to BRL2.20), besides indirect costs with management and judicial control.

The chart below reveals the amount of active benefits (i.e., benefits that are still paid) in April, 2014 (MDS 2015) (Table 10.1).

The concession and maintenance of this social protection benefit by the Federal Executive Power also reveal regional inequalities within the Brazilian Federation, since there is a larger concentration of active benefits in States with lower socio-economical development if compared to more developed States, considering the ratio active benefit/population of the Member State. For instance, the population estimated for the State of Maranhão was 6,850,884 in 2014, when there were 188,998 active benefits (directly reaching 2.76 % of its population, above the Brazilian average of 2 %), whereas the population estimated for the State of São Paulo was 44,035,304 in 2014, when there were 654,956 active benefits—directly reaching 1.49 % of its population, lower than the Brazilian average of 2 % (IBGE 2015d).

10.4 Reflections and Criticism

If we combine the data on Brazilian population considered extremely poor in 2013 (11.10 % of the population, not considering data on non-registered Brazilians), the concession of social protection benefit to only 2 % of the population in 2014 reveals a serious flaw, showing the enormous path still to be covered. However, we must remember that there are several public policies (not analyzed in this study) that range from the improvement of education to economic growth and development, which seem included in the focal point of fighting extreme poverty (improving education and creating job opportunities), to the extent that the social protection benefit is an extreme, complementary, or residual measure, preferentially temporary.

Table 10.1 Social protection benefits implemented in Brazil, by State

Ministry of Social Development and Hunger Combat			
National Secretariat of Social Assistance			
Department of Social Protection Benefits			
General Coordination of Benefit Revision and Control			
Continued Benefit—Benefits active in April, 2014			
Federation unit	Amount of benefits		Total benefits
	Handicapped	Elder	
Brazil	2,178,925	1,842,902	4,021,827
Rondônia	24,642	15,123	39,765
Acre	15,255	6313	21,568
Amazonas	48,048	39,811	87,859
Roraima	7191	3446	10,637
Pará	100,383	84,693	185,076
Amapá	10,511	10,753	21,264
Tocantins	20,629	15,918	36,547
Maranhão	99,614	89,384	188,998
Piauí	41,801	20,208	62,009
Ceará	136,523	84,269	220,792
Rio Grande do Norte	46,628	21,620	68,248
Paraíba	62,658	32,975	95,633
Pernambuco	163,387	111,741	275,128
Alagoas	72,638	34,678	107,316
Sergipe	34,952	15,362	50,314
Bahia	207,265	180,265	387,530
Minas Gerais	222,424	171,779	394,203
Espírito Santo	31,417	27,336	58,753
Rio de Janeiro	110,298	169,868	280,166
São Paulo	299,718	355,238	654,956
Paraná	103,086	86,059	189,145
Santa Catarina	41,270	22,218	63,488
Rio Grande do Sul	107,312	72,697	180,009
Mato Grosso do Sul	34,260	41,536	75,796
Mato Grosso	40,740	39,230	79,970
Goiás	71,544	67,205	138,749
Distrito Federal	24,731	23,177	47,908

Source: DATAPREV/Sintese

Note: The municipality indicated is the payment source

For instance, also with the purpose of retrieving families from extreme poverty, in 2013 programme "Bolsa Família" transferred BRL24.5 billion to low-income families (equivalent to USD11.1 billion, considering the average exchange rate in 2013 of USD1.00 to BRL2.20), benefiting 14.1 million families (in the beginning of

2003, around 3.6 million families were benefited).[5] As presented above, in 2013 the total resources applied to the social protection benefit added up to BRL31.4 billion (equivalent to USD14.3 billion, considering the same exchange rate), reaching more than 4 million families in the beginning of 2014.

It is true that several criticisms may be raised against the Brazilian social protection benefit. One of them is based on the theoretical conceptions of William Henry Beveridge (the Beveridge Plan), which inspired Brazilian social security framework, separating social security (dependent of work and contributions) from social protection policies destined to the population in need (regardless of work and contributions). This theory states that the amount of the social protection benefit could not correspond to the minimum social security benefit, because that would discourage the regular hiring of employees and the contribution system that funds social security. We acknowledge that the amount of a relevant portion of pensions is 13 minimum wages per year (considering 12 months and one Christmas gratification) whereas the social protection benefit corresponds to 12 minimum wages per year (there is no Christmas gratification). Nevertheless, at this moment, we must all acknowledge that not even the minimum wage fulfills the purposes set forth in section 7, IV of the Constitution of 1988, and also that there is a well-known part of recent Brazilian history that disregards the adequate registration of employees and the regular payment of regular contributions (although registration and contributions have been mandatory for decades). This turned the social protection benefit into "the easiest way" to obtain monthly stipends (people seek the social protection benefit instead of pensions, because it does not depend on registration and contribution). Therefore, criticisms according to Beveridge Plan standards seem well grounded, but should be considered with moderation within Brazilian historic framework.

Another relevant matter to be considered is the intense judicial intervention in the concession of the social protection benefit. Despite the fact that the analysis of requirements, concession, and maintenance is attributed to the Social Security National Institute (related to the Federal Executive Power), several problems are taken to judicial courts, among them the analysis of necessary conditions of extreme poverty for the benefit to be paid. Besides increasing public costs with this benefit (with costs derived from judicial lawsuits), this brings problems that characterize Brazilian judicial activism, because the personal opinion of individuals involved in the lawsuit (especially judges) makes the requirements to grant this social protection benefit inaccurate and even unequal.[6]

[5] Programme Bolsa Família benefits families in extreme poverty (per capita income lower than R$70.00 under the standards of the World Bank—without inflation adjustment, as mentioned above, and the amount paid by the Federal Government depends on the size of the family and on the income of family members.

[6] About this subject, Ramos (2010), with an unfavorable perspective, shows judicial activism as a malfunction, a violation of limits imposed to the judge by the legal system. In this situation, the Judiciary Power exceeds its power, characterizing an institutional deviation of conduct and breaching the separation of powers of the Constitutional Rule of Law. Under a perspective favorable to activism but with reservations, see Rothenburg (2007) and Tavares (2007).

We also believe to be mistaken the immediate suspension of payment of this social protection benefit if the beneficiary passes away. In fact, section 34, single paragraph, of Law 10,741/2003 (Elders Act) allows each spouse to receive a social protection benefit established by the Social Protection Law, but if only the deceased one receives the benefit, the immediate suspension will trigger harmful effects during the period (months or years) in which the new benefit will be requested. Considering the presumption of continuity of extreme poverty of the family, we believe the benefit should be paid to the spouse when the beneficiary dies until governmental organs make a new assessment of the situation of extreme poverty (Francisco 2015).

10.5 Conclusion

There are several consistent criticisms that can be raised concerning the social protection benefit of Law 8,742/1993 as an instrument to fight extreme poverty in Brazil. On the other hand, it is also true that decades or centuries of inequalities are not easily corrected in years, even when the measures taken are clearly a priority. And in that context we can see advances in the combat against extreme poverty and inequalities in Brazilian State, with natural advances and regressions.

The legal effectiveness of the constitutional and infra-constitutional legal framework has brought relevant social effectiveness. Based on Law 8,742/1993, from 1996 until the beginning of 2014, there has been a significant increase of the concession and maintenance of this monthly social protection benefit: from 346,000 people to more than 4 million people (around 2 % of Brazilian population in 2014, without taking into account the indirect effects to the beneficiary's families). The total resources applied on this programme in 2013 were BRL31.4 billion (equivalent to USD14.3 billion, considering the average exchange rate in 2013 of USD1 to BRL2.20). Adding these figures to other benefits destined to people in extreme poverty, the data are very meaningful.

These steps are not sufficient in the path to fight extreme poverty in Brazil, but they are firm steps, even if corrections should be made.

References

Bobbio N (1992) A era dos direitos. Campus, Rio de janeiro

Brasil (2015) Governo Federal do: http://www.brasil.gov.br/economia-e-emprego/2013/06/cresce-numero-de-municipios-no-brasil-em-2013. Accessed in 19 Jul 2015

Ferrajoli L (2006) Estado de direito entre o passado e o futuro. In: Costa P, Zolo D (organizers) Estado de Direito: história, teoria, crítica. Martins Fontes, São Paulo

Ferreira Filho MG (1999) Estado de direito e constituição, 2nd issue. Saraiva, São Paulo

Folha De São Paulo (2015) http://www1.folha.uol.com.br/poder/2013/05/1281132-indicador-defasado-esconde-22-milhoes-de-miseraveis-do-pais.shtml. Accessed in 21 Jul 2015

Fleiner-Gerster T, colab. of Hänni P (2006) Teoria geral do estado. Martins Fontes, São Paulo
Francisco JC (2015) Justiça social e manutenção do benefício assistencial da lei n. 8.742/1993 no Óbito do Titular. in Benefício assistencial : Lei n. 8.742/93: temas polêmicos. In: Serau Junior MA, Costa JRC (cordinatores). LTr, São Paulo
Globo R (2015a) Data obtained at: http://g1.globo.com/economia/noticia/2015/05/brasil-deve-cair-para-8-posicao-em-ranking-de-maiores-pibs-mostra-fmi.html. Accessed 19 Jul 2015
Globo R (2015b) A according to the analysis available at http://g1.globo.com/mundo/noticia/2014/07/brasil-avanca-uma-posicao-e-e-79-no-ranking-do-desenvolvimento-humano.html. Accessed 19 Jul 2015
Globo R (2015c) According to the analysis available at http://g1.globo.com/jornal-da-globo/noticia/2014/09/desigualdade-de-renda-parou-de-diminuir-no-brasil-segundo-pnad.html. Accessed 20 Jul 2015
IBGE (2015a) Instituto Brasileiro de Geografia e Estatística (Brazilian Institute of Geography and Statistics). Data projected on 07.19.2015, at 06h40m08s pm, according to http://www.ibge.gov.br/apps/populacao/projecao. Accessed on the same date and time. 2015
IBGE (2015b) Instituto Brasileiro de Geografia e Estatística. This study was carried out by, data obtained at http://www.brasil.gov.br/economia-e-emprego/2015/02/renda-per-capita-dos-brasileiros-aumenta-em-janeiro-em-salvador-recife-e-bh. Accessed 19 Jul 2015
IBGE (2015c) Instituto Brasileiro de Geografia e Estatística: ftp://ftp.ibge.gov.br/Estimativas_de_Populacao/Estimativas_2013/populacoes_estimativas_BR_UF_TCU_31_10_2013.pdf. Accessed 21 Jul 2015
IBGE (2015d) Instituto Brasileiro de Geografia e Estatística. The data on estimated population of the States were obtained on http://www.ibge.gov.br/estadosat/perfil.php?sigla=ma. Accessed 19 Jul 2015
MDS (2015) Ministério do Desenvolvimento Social: http://blog.mds.gov.br/redesuas/?page_id=770. Accessed in 19 Jul 2015
Ramos ES (2010) Ativismo judicial. Parâmetros dogmáticos. Saraiva, São Paulo
Rothenburg WC (2007) A dialética da democracia: entre legisladores e jurisdição constitucional. In Clève CM et al. (org.). Direitos humanos e democracia. Forense, Rio de Janeiro
Singer P (2015) A Erradicação da miséria: uma abordagem inicial, available at: http://portal.mte.gov.br/data/files/8A7C812D3ADC4216013AFAE0D85014C0/A%20ERRADICA%C3%87%C3%83O%20DA%20MIS%C3%89RIA%20UMA%20ABORDAGEM%20INICIAL.pdf. Accessed on 20 Jul 2015
Sogeografia (2015) http://www.sogeografia.com.br/Conteudos/GeografiaFisica/Clima. Accessed in 20 Jul 2015
Tavares AR (2007) O discurso dos direitos fundamentais na legitimidade e deslegitimação de uma Justiça Constitucional substantiva. Revista Brasileira de Estudos Constitucionais, n. 2. Forense, Rio de Janeiro
UNDP (2015) United Nations' Development Programme. http://hdr.undp.org/sites/default/files/hdr2014_pt_web.pdf. Accessed in 19 Jul 2015
Verdú PL (2007) A luta pelo estado de direito. Forense, Rio de Janeiro

Chapter 11
Biopsicossocial Expert Evidence: A Good Example from the Social Assistance Law

José Ricardo Caetano Costa and Marco Aurelio Serau Junior

Abstract This article investigates the meaning of medical expertise, traditionally held to verify the Social Security disability benefits, contrasting what we now call the biopsychosocial expertise. The latter concept, in fact, is based on the International Classification of Functioning, Disability and Health (ICF-2001), promulgated by the World Health Organization in May 2001. In addition to this important reference point also use the International Convention on the Rights of Persons with Disabilities, the UN enacted in 2007 and rectified by Brazil through the Presidential Decree n. 6949 of 25/08/09. These two documents allow us to conclude that the classical system of medical expertise, still in force in Brazil, is all ineffective and inappropriate in view of the purpose brought in the conception of what disability/incapacity for work. We pointed out that the Organic Law of Social Assistance (LOAS) has advanced in the adoption of biopsychosocial expertise, making through various devices analyzed in this article, which should be followed by other public policies.

Keywords Medical expertise • Skill biopsychosocial • Welfare law • Disabilities • Disability

11.1 Introduction

Twenty years after the Social Assistance Law came into force, we are able to provide some analyses and make some conclusions. We have many criticisms about it, but we must highlight a point that is extremely significant in favor of Social

J.R.C. Costa (✉)
Isquierdo e Costa Advogados Associados, Pelotas, Rio Grande do Sul, Brazil
e-mail: jrcc.pel@gmail.com

M.A. Serau Junior
Tribunal Regional Federal, 3a. região, São Paulo, São Paulo, Brazil
e-mail: maseraujunior@hotmail.com

M.A. Serau Junior, J.R. Caetano Costa (eds.), *Assistance Benefits in Brazil*,
DOI 10.1007/978-3-319-27046-3_11

Assistance: the joint expertise assessment, involving doctors and Social Assistants in the dynamics of granting/preserving the only continuous cash benefit set forth in Law No. 8472/93.

This consists in biopsicossocial expert evidence, a procedure in which doctors issue their expert reports within the scope of their skills, and Social Assistants assess the other elements which indicate the long-lasting disability (above 2 years) of those applying to receive the LOAS' BPC. The latter criteria can be roughly translated as social, economic, psychological, attitudinal, and environmental criteria. Only the Social Assistants, as we will further see, can issue these social opinions and reports.

Therefore, the introduction to this new expert evidence model occurred based on two fundamental documents: the International Classification of Functioning, Disability and Health of May 2001 and the United Nations' International Convention on the Rights of Persons with Disability, ratified by Brazil through Legislative Decree No. 189, dated 9 July 2008 and enacted by Decree No. 6949, dated 25 August 2009.

We believe that this new expert evidence model should be highlighted as positive, in view of the need to apply this system to grant other benefits set forth in the RGPS, especially in relation to sick pays and retirements due to disability.

Our approach of this matter in the following five topics considers the implied assumption that the right to social assistance, particularly the right to the BPC, is a substantive fundamental right, since it is necessarily connected to the dignity of the human being (Serau Jr 2009).

11.2 The Meaning of Medical Evidence

Based on the assumption that the Court system is not familiar with the matter in a whole or the full reality, in relation to the actual case developed before such system, Article 145 of the CPC was coined, enabling the Court to elect an expert to help him understand such case.

Although it is evident that the Court does not restrict itself to the report presented by the experts (Article 436 of the CPC), evidence is of utmost importance for it to form its conviction and subsequently make a decision.

We can therefore affirm that "Expert Evidence consists in research, examination, verification to show the fact when there are no means of showing documental evidence in this sense. Since they have skills and knowledge, the expert is able to clarify the facts or the matter, to provide a fair and true solution to the conflict" (da Silva 2007).

In a collective work organized by Savaris (2009), a mandatory read to the entire community dealing with expert evidence matters, this eminent jurist affirms that the expert, in addition to having the technical and specific medical knowledge, must "be aware that his opinion will be pointless if he ignores the social universe and the life history of the examined individual." Only by considering them, he proceeds "the expert can identify the real conditions of an individual to perform a dignifying job that will not worsen their health conditions."

Expertise evidence, in turn, "is the means (of evidence) employed in cases in which the clarification of the *examined fact* is subject to technical or scientific knowledge or furthermore to a differentiated skill or experience" (Ferreira 2012).

With regard to actions that seek to grant benefits in which the incapacity/disability/handicap of the plaintiffs/insured individuals, through (common or accident) sick pay, retirements due to disability (idem), and accident pay, or assistance benefits, Legal Medical Evidence has become a determining factor in the decision-making process of the Court.

This procedure, related to Medical Evidence, took new forms through the actions to which the medical experts have been appointed as assistants to the Court. We can affirm that they have been empowered and their conclusions have become a determining factor to the validity/invalidity equation.

To understand this empowerment, we seek support from Annie Thébaud-Mony, a French researcher, in relation to the perception she had of France and other European countries, alleging that

> ...the history of occupational health is fairly unknown. Until the late 19th century, it was principally a matter of individual and collective battles by the workers to 'not die at work'. On the one hand, the development of clinical and epidemiological medical knowledge about the pathogenic effects of the technical solutions for prevention will transfer occupational health from the hands of workers to the hands of experts who call for a certain technical know-how which the workers themselves will help develop. (Thébaud-Mony 2005).

According to this author, subjectivity and the experience of workers, in this context, are completely disregarded, with the imposition of what was defined as "the tyranny of statistics: if something is not measurable, it does not exist" (Thébaud-Mony 2005).

Among us, Medical Evidence has been developed based on figures, quantitative and etiological analyses, as if the only interest were the bodies and muscle joints of workers/insured individuals. If the body has a problem, this means it is incapable to work.

We will further see which are the consequences of this perception, valid until then, within the scope of both administrative and judicial expert evidence, offering an alternative that surpasses this notion which is no longer able to sustain the actual reality.[1]

---

[1] We cite, for instance, new syndromes caused by the restructuring of production, such as the Panic Disorder, Burnout, as well as repetitive strain injuries, all of which derive from the new organization of labor. The traditionally conducted medical evidence, both within the administrative and judicial scopes, is no longer able to sustain this new historical moment, especially when interdisciplinary works have been indicating the precision of a more holistic analysis.

11.3 Contribution by the WHO's I.C.F/2001 and the United Nations Convention on the Rights of Persons with Disability/2007[2]

By the direction we are taking, it is safe to affirm that expert evidence does not consist only in the assessment of body functions and structures. Actually, they are easily assessable though medical evidence.

But the notion of incapacity and disability changed significantly over the past decade, notably as of 2001, when the World Health Organization (WHO) issued the INTERNATIONAL CLASSIFICATION OF FUNCTIONING, DISABILITY AND HEALTH (ICF).[3]

The foundation of this classification, which should be analyzed jointly with the ICD-10, since the latter offers an etiological model of health conditions, lies in setting out the criteria of assessment based in two domains: body functions and structures and activities and participation (ICF-CY 2011, p. 35).[4]

Perhaps the greatest virtue of the ICF-2001 is to have aggregated other elements, related to health condition, offering another perspective to what is designated as incapacity and disability. As stated in the ICF-2001, "two persons with the same disease may have different levels of functioning, and two persons with the same level of functioning do not necessarily have the same health condition" (ICF-2011).

We will now see the health domains and those related to health, from the perspective of the body, the individual, and society:

> (1) Body functions and structures and (2) Activities and participation. As a classification, the ICF systematically groups different domains of a person in a certain health condition (e.g., what a person with a disease or disorder does or may do). *Functionality* is a term that covers all body functions, activities and participation; likewise, *disability* is a term that covers impairments, handicaps to activities or restriction to participation. The ICF also lists the environmental factors which interact with all these constructs. (ICF-2011).

---

[2] We will use, in order to designate these two documents and making this paper more reader-friendly, the following acronyms: for the International Classification of Functioning, Disability and Health, we will use the term I.C.F-2001, keeping the year of 2011 for citations, since it has been extracted from the Brazilian publication. For the International Convention on the Rights of Persons with Disability we will simply use Convention…2007, the date on which it was approved, in New York, USA.

[3] The 2001 ICF reviews the International Classification of Impairments, Disabilities and Handicaps (ICIDH), published by the WHO in 1980, in an experimental manner. The current ICF is the result of a 5-year work, which gathered several countries, with an effective participation of Brazil, subsequently approved by the 54th World Health Assembly, in May 2001.

[4] We clarify that we will use the ICF version published by the University of São Paulo, whose title is International Classification of Functioning, Disability and Health—Children and Youth Version, jointly with the Pan American Health Organization and the World Health Organization, published by EDUSP. For citation purposes we will only use (ICF-2001). A complete version of the ICF in Portuguese can be accessed on *www.scielo.br/pdf/rbepid/v8n2/11.pdf*.

Consequently, it is advisable to jointly use the ICD-10 with the model built from individuals' environmental conditions and participation.[5] The focus is shifted from the disease to the analysis of health. This means that in order to know if an individual is disabled we must have an etiological view associated with their health state: "The ICF has shifted from a classification of the 'consequence of the disease' (the 1980 version) to a classification of the 'components of health'" (ICF-2011).

In relation to its application in Pension Fund, Health Care, and the formulation of policies, it states that:

> The ICF is useful to a large range of different applications, for example, social security, assessment of the management of health care assistance and population surveys at local, national and international level. It provides a conceptual structure to the information applicable to individual medical assistance, including preservation, health promotion and improvement of participation, eliminating or mitigating social obstacles and encouraging the provision of social tools and facilitators. It is also useful to study medical assistance systems, both in terms of assessment and formulation of public policies. (CIF-2011).

The ICF suggests and analyzes disability and functioning through the dynamic interaction of several factors, as previously noted herein. In Contextual Factors we find environmental and personal factors, and the two latter interact with all the components of functioning and disability. It is noteworthy to recall, due to the importance they take under this notion, the concepts of disability and functioning: the term **disability** includes handicaps, activity limitations, or participation restrictions, while the term **functioning** includes all body functions, activities, and participations.

We can extract from the ICF-2001 the following components and definitions:

(1) **BODY FUNCTIONS** = physiological functions of body systems.
They are classified into:

(1.1) Mental Functions = such as consciousness, orientation, intellectual, psychosocial, and interpersonal functions, functions related to personality, energy and drive, sleep, as well as memory, attention, perception, and thought, cognitive functions in general, psychomotor functions, etc.

(1.2) Sensory Functions and Pain = seeing, functions related to the eyes and adjoining structures, hearing, vestibular, taste, smell, proprioceptive, touch, and sensory functions related to temperature and other stimuli.

---

[5] "The ICF belongs to the family of international classifications by the WHO, whose most widely known member is the ICD-10 (International Classification of Diseases—Tenth Revision). The ICD-10 provides an etiological structure to classify, through the diagnoses of diseases, disorders, and other health conditions. On the other hand, the ICF classifies functioning and disability associated with health conditions. The ICD-10 and the ICF therefore complement one another, and their users are encouraged to use them in a combined manner to gain a broader and more significant view of the health state of individuals and populations. Information on mortality (provided by the ICD-10) and information on health and consequences in health (provided by the ICF) may be coupled in synthetic measures of a population's health" (ICF-2001).

They also include functions related to pain and other unspecified sensory functions.

(1.3) Voice and Speech Functions = voice, articulation, speech fluency and rhythm, vocalization functions, and other unspecified functions.

(1.4) Cardiovascular, Hematological, Immunological, and Respiratory Functions: (A) Cardiovascular: heart, blood vessel, blood pressure functions, and other unspecified functions. (B) Hematological and Immunological = functions of the hematological and immunological systems. (C) Respiratory = respiratory functions and functions of the respiratory system, as well as respiratory muscles.

(1.5) Functions of the Digestive, Metabolic, and Endocrine Systems = ingestion, digestion, assimilation, and defecation functions, weight maintenance functions, water, mineral, and electrolyte functions, endocrine gland, growth maintenance functions, thermoregulatory functions, etc.

(1.6) Genitourinary and Reproductive Functions = urinary, sexual, menstruation, procreation functions, associated with reproductive and genital functions, etc.

(1.7) Neuromusculoskeletal and Movement-Related Functions = in relation to mobility and stability of the joints, those related to mobility of the bones, muscle power, and tone, as well as muscle endurance, as well as motor reflex functions, voluntary and involuntary movements, spontaneous movement functions, gait pattern functions, muscle functions, and neuromusculoskeletal functions.

(1.8) Skin Functions and Related Structures = functions related to skin protection, skin repair, sensation, and other skin functions, as well as hair and skin functions, and other specified and unspecified functions.

(2) **BODY STRUCTURES** = they refer to the anatomical parts of the body, and are composed of:

(2.1) Nervous System Structures: structures related to the brain, the spinal cord, the meninges, the sympathetic and the parasympathetic nervous systems.

(2.2) The Eye, the Ear, and Related Structures: structure of the eye socket, the eyeball, the external ear, the middle ear, and the inner ear.

(2.3) Structures Related to the Voice and Speech: structure of the nose, the mouth, the pharynx, the larynx, and those related to the voice and speech.

(2.4) Structures of the Cardiovascular, Immunological, and Respiratory Systems: structures related to the cardiovascular, immunological, and respiratory systems.

(2.5) Structures of the Digestive, Metabolic, and Endocrine Systems: structures of the salivary glands, the esophagus, the stomach, the intestine, the pancreas, the liver, the gall bladder, and the biliary ducts, and the structures related to the endocrine glands.

(2.6) Structures of the Genitourinary and Reproductive Systems: structures related to the urinary, reproductive, and pelvic systems.

(2.7) Structures Related to Movement: structures related to the head and the neck, the shoulder region, the upper and lower extremities, the pelvic region, the trunk, and additional musculoskeletal structures related to movement.

(2.8) Structures Related to the Skin: structures of the skin, the skin glands, nails, and hair.

(3) **ACTIVITIES AND PARTICIPATION** = the former refers to the undertaking of a task or action by an individual, while the latter refers to the involvement in situations of the daily life. They are divided into:

(3.1) Learning and Applying Knowledge: watching, listening, perceptions, and purposeful experiences, copying, acquiring information, language, rehearsing, acquiring concepts, learning to read, write, and calculate, as well as acquiring skills and basic knowledge. They also include concentration and attention, thought, reading, writing, decision-making, and solving of equations and problems, as well as applying acquired knowledge.

(3.2) General Tasks and Demands: undertaking a single task or several tasks, carrying out a daily routine, own management behavior such as handling stress and undertaking general tasks and demands.

(3.3) Communication: spoken, nonspoken, conventional sign language, and written messages, speaking, pre-speaking, singing, producing formal sign language messages, writing messages, as well as communication and production. This equally applies to conversation, discussion, and the use of devices and communication techniques.

(3.4) Mobility: changing and maintaining basic body positions, lifting and carrying objects, moving objects with lower extremities, fine hand use, hand and arm use, fine foot use, carrying, moving, and handling objects. It also includes walking, moving around (by oneself or using equipment), walking and moving around, in addition to using transportation, driving, riding animals for transportation, and moving around using transportation.

(3.5) Self-Care: washing oneself, caring for body parts, toileting, dressing, eating, drinking, looking after one's health, self-care, safety, and personal care.

(3.6) Domestic Life: acquiring a place to live, undertaking domestic tasks, caring for household objects, and assisting others.

(3.7) Interpersonal Relationships and Interactions: basic and complex interpersonal interactions, relationships with strangers, formal, family, intimate, and particular interpersonal relationships.

(3.8) Major Life Areas: they can be divided into three areas, for a better didactic study. (A) Education: informal, preschool, school education, vocational training, higher education, school life, and related activities. (B) Work and Employment: apprenticeship, acquiring, keeping, and terminating a job, remunerative and non-remunerative employment. (C) Economic Life: basic and complex economic transactions, economic self-sufficiency, economic life, engaging in games and playful activities, and other major life areas.

(3.9) Community, Social, and Civic Life: community life, recreation and leisure, religion and spirituality, human rights, political life, and citizenship.

(4) **ENVIRONMENTAL FACTORS** = physical, social, and attitudinal, through which people live and conduct their lives. They comprise:

(4.1) Products and Technology: products and substances for personal consumption, products and technology for personal use in daily living, mobility, and personal transportation in indoor and outdoor environments, communication, education, work, cultural, recreational, and sports activities, religious practice and spiritual life, products and technology used in the design, architecture, and construction of buildings for public and private use, as well as those related to the use and exploitation of land and assets.

(4.2) Natural Environment and Human-Made Changes to the Environment: physical geography, population, flora and fauna, climate, natural events, human-caused events, light, time-related changes, sound, vibration, and air quality.

(4.3) Support and Relationships: immediate family, extended family, friends, acquaintances, peers, colleagues, neighbors, and other community members, people in positions of authority, people in subordinate positions, personal care providers, personal assistants, strangers, domesticated animals, health professionals, and health-related professionals.

(4.4) Attitudes: individual attitudes of immediate family members and extended family members, friends, acquaintances, peers, colleagues, neighbors, and other community members. Individual attitudes of people in positions of authority, people in subordinate positions, personal care providers, personal assistants, strangers, domesticated animals, health professionals, societal attitudes, and attitudes related to norms, practices, and ideologies.

(4.5) Services, Systems, and Policies: for the production of consumer goods, the architecture, construction, and planning of open spaces, housing, utilities, communication, transportation, civil protection, legal policies, association and organizational policies, the media, economic policies, social security, general social support, health, education, training, work, and employment, the political system, among other policies and services.

Based on this conceptual understanding, we will see that the ICF was divided into two parts, with components, as follows:

PART 1—Functionality and Disability, which are divided into Body Functions and Structures and Activities and Participation.

PART 2—Contextual Factors, which are divided into Environmental and Social Factors.

The question that is being placed, and the ICF-2011 itself sheds light on it (p. 48), is the clash between the "medical model" and the "social model." According to the first system, in force until this day among us, "disability is a personal problem, directly caused by a disease, trauma, or another health state, which requires medical assistance through individual treatment provided by practitioners, as well as care in relation to the cure or adaptation of the individual, as well as a change in behavior."

From the other perspective, represented by the second notion, which has been designated as "biopsicossocial," particularly because it aggregates the biological, individual, and social perspectives, we find disability focused on other foundations. It is a socially created problem, therefore it is not "an attribute of the individual, but instead a complex set of conditions, many of which created by the social environment. Consequently, tackling this problem requires social action and is a collective responsibility of society to make the necessary environmental changes…(…) disability is a political question" (ICF-2011, pp. 48–49).

The ICF itself, in Exhibit 4, cites several variations of an individual's impairments and handicaps. The purpose of these examples is to demonstrate that if a person has an impairment or pathology this does not make him or her automatically disabled for work or for social life. They seek to demonstrate how the environment is crucial to define a certain disability.

The examples of persons that have an impairment should be pondered upon, since they are connected to this paper's purposes. According to the ICF-2001, an individual who is quadriplegic may not be hired by a company which does not have the appropriate equipment for disabled persons, i.e., the workplace does not offer the conditions needed for the development of the work. Another individual, with the same impairment (quadriplegia) is able to perform his work in the company, but he or she uses a wheel chair and the company does not provide accessibility to use this equipment. And another individual, with the same pathology, may use the wheel chair, the company may offer the required conditions (accessibility, software with voice command, etc.), but this individual may face difficulties when interacting interpersonally with his colleagues, in such a way that the difficulty in socializing at work may curb the access to opportunities in the company.

To summarize, all individuals have problems in the work domain due to the interaction of distinct environmental factors with their health condition or impairment (ICF-2011).

Exhibit 5 of the ICF provides a short but fruitful analysis of persons with disabilities. To summarize, in face of this paper's purposes, the ICF does not propose to be a classification of persons. It is, instead, a classification of health characteristics of persons, in a context which considers individual questions and environmental impacts. This rationale, therefore, completely changes our understanding of disability, considering the current traditional meaning. Example: according to the ICF, there are no mentally disabled persons, there are persons with learning problems.

The ICF was careful not to systematically label individuals, hence the categories are neutral, particularly to avoid depreciation, stigma, and inadequate connotations (ICF-2011, p. 252).

To reinforce the thesis about the change of paradigm, in force until now, we understand it is important to analyze another international document, namely the Convention on the Rights of Persons with Disability.

According to this Convention, disability/impairment "is an evolving concept and results from the interaction between persons with impairments and the attitudinal and environmental barriers which curb a full and effective participation of these persons in society under equal conditions of opportunity with the other persons" (as exposed by the United Nations Convention on the Rights of Persons with Disability, ratified by Brazil through Legislative Decree No. 186, of 9 July 2008, and enacted by Decree No. 6949, of 25 August 2009).

Also according to this Convention, persons with disabilities "are those with long-term handicaps, of physical, mental, intellectual, or sensorial nature, which in interaction with several barriers may obstruct their full and effective participation in society under equal conditions of opportunity with the other persons."

The effects of this Convention…2007, as of Brazil's ratification through Legislative Decree No. 186, of 9 July 2008, and enacted by Decree No. 6949, of 25 August 2009 were reflected in the new wordings of Article 20, Law 8742/93, of Law No. 12435/11, which altered the notion of disability, as set forth in paragraphs 2 and 10 of this same provision, as follows:

> Paragraph 2. For the purpose of granting this benefit, persons with impairments are those with long-term handicaps, of physical, mental, intellectual or sensorial nature, which in interaction with several barriers may obstruct their full and effective participation in society under equal conditions of opportunity with the other persons.
>
> Paragraph 10. A long-term handicap, for the purposes of paragraph 2, is a handicap which produces effects for at least 2 (two) years.

While on the one hand, it is a shame that Brazil set a 2-year period to define temporary disability, since we believe in the reduction of some rights over this term, on the other hand it makes significant progress in not considering only full and permanent disability (only disability or impairment) as defining factors to have the right to the assistance benefit set forth in the 1993 LOAS.

The 1st Appeal Panel of the Paraná State Small-Claims Court (JEF), through a precedent whose reporting judge was Dr. José Antônio Savaris, and the National Panel of Standardization (TNU), both precedents dated from 2010, anticipating the position taken by the Brazilian Republic, had already anticipated the position pursuant to the Convention of 2007. We will cite these precedents due to their importance:

> ASSISTANCE BENEFIT TO PERSON WITH IMPAIRMENT. TOTAL AND TEMPORARY DISABILITY. POSSIBILITY OF GRANT. Total and temporary disability calls for the granting of assistance benefit to the person with impairment, and it is the duty of the INSS to review it periodically. (Civil Judgment Appeal No. 2009.70.53.003387-7/PR, 1st Appeal Panel of Paraná State Small-Claims Court, 4th Region, Reporting Justice José Antônio Savaris. j. 02.06.2010, unanimous).
>
> MOTION OF NATIONAL STANDARDIZATION. ASSISTANCE BENEFIT. TEMPORARY DISABILITY. POSSIBILITY. INCIDENT HEARD AND PARTIALLY GRANTED. 1. It refers to an action whose purpose is to grant assistance benefit. 2. The first instance judgment accepted the motion, to determine the granting of assistance benefit

for the plaintiff. 3. The decision of the 2nd Appeal Panel of Rio Grande do Sul State granted the appeal to the INSS, to deny the motion, due to the fact that the expert evidence report decided on the temporary disability of the plaintiff, and the benefit is granted only if the disability is permanent. 4. The plaintiff filed a timely Motion of Standardization on the grounds that temporary disability enables the acceptance of the benefit, as decided by this National Panel of Standardization, in PEDILEF 200770500108659, referred to as a paradigm. 5. The timely Motion of Standardization was not granted by the Chief Federal Judge of the 2nd Appeal Panel. The record was sent to this National Panel, and was assigned to me, the reporting justice, for better analysis. 6. This Motion of Standardization is to be analyzed, since the appealed decision eliminates the possibility of granting the assistance benefit in case of temporary disability, while the paradigm affirms there is no requirement of permanent disability to grant the benefit. 7. On the merits, the Motion of Standardization should be partially granted. In fact, the case law prevailing in this panel understands that the transitoriness of disability does not impede the granting of the assistance benefit. Precedents: PEDILEF 200770530028472, Reporting Judge FEDERAL JUDGE MANOEL ROLIM CAMPBELL PENNA, DOU 08.02.2011 and PEDILEF 200770500108659, Reporting Judge FEDERAL JUDGE OTÁVIO HENRIQUE MARTINS PORT, DJ 11.03.2010. 8. Therefore, I PARTLY GRANT this Motion of Standardization to establish the premise that the transitoriness of disability does not impede the granting of the assistance benefit, and to decide that this process be sent back to its court of origin for a new judgment, under its Point of Order No. 20 (PEDILEF No. 200871520013314, TNU, Reporting Judge Paulo Ricardo Arena Filho. j. 29.03.2012, DOU 20.04.2012).

11.4 The Participation of Social Assistants in Social Security Policies

Social Service has always been connected to social policies, as a whole, and to social security rights in particular, especially as of the creation of the Retirement and Pension Funds (*Caixas de Aposentadorias e Pensões*—1930) and the Retirement and Pension Institutes (*Institutos de Aposentadorias e Pensões*—as of 1933).

This overlapping, as well as all other issues involving social policies, is not untroubled or linear, since the "first Social Assistants—especially those in São Paulo—constantly express great distrust in relation to state insurances and pension funds" (Iamamoto and de Carvalho 2006). There was always distrust regarding the use of the Social Assistance from the perspective of state maneuver, whether to calm down the workers, or to legitimate State policies—especially policies from the New State (*Estado Novo*).

On the other hand, even though some of the IAPs had already included social assistance in their list of benefits, absorbing Social Assistants (Cohn 1980) in their technical-administrative staff, the first experience of implementation of Social Assistance services in the structure of Social Security was in 1942. Ordinance 25, of 1943, drawn by the National Labor Council (*Conselho Nacional do Trabalho*), creates the Social Studies and Social Assistance Department (*Seção de Estudos e Assistência Social*), whose direction was reserved to Luis Carlos Mancini, composed of the first group of São Paulo's Social Security School (*Escola de Serviço Social de São Paulo*).

The duty of the Social Studies and Social Assistance Department was to research how the insured persons lived their lives and their means to do that, and based on such research it should establish the methods and techniques used in Social Security (Iamamoto and de Carvalho 2006).

The research conducted in this period shed light on and provided an outlook of the questions not yet resolved, embedded in Social Security. We cite some examples which, in our opinion, should be further investigated: (a) the application of imported models without any critical reflection; (b) the detachment of the social security policies from their signatories; (c) the lack of knowledge by the insured persons and their dependent of their social security rights, and (d) the humanization of Social Security, due to the stale and rigid bureaucratic structure.

We note that Social Assistants in the second quarter of the twentieth century had a special participation in the design of Social Security. This was when the 1st Social Security and Social Assistance Week was held by the Social Right Institute (*Instituto de Direito Social*), in 1944, and a year later, through Vargas's attempt to standardize the benefits and unify the services through the Brazilian Social Services Institute (*Instituto de Serviços Sociais do Brasil*—ISSB[6]).

The intensification of Social Assistance in the political-administrative structure of Social Security takes place as of 1945, when the Ministry of Labor, through a Ministerial Ordinance, creates intensive Social Service programs for CAPs and IAPs employees (Iamamoto and de Carvalho 2006). Until this date, the participation of Social Assistances was limited to some Institutions, usually to serve residential condominiums (especially from the IAPIs) that arose in Brazil.

On the other hand, it is important to indicate the changes in the plans of Social Security as of 1950. See below the thesis adopted by Cohn (1980):

> In our opinion, the question of economic bonds of social security, in case of Brazil, lies in the fact that until then it was more directed toward investments in strategic areas for the industrializing process, while, especially as of the second half of the 1950s, due to the stage of the industrial development in the country, it sees itself obliged to preserve the production capacity of the employed workforce as well as its reproduction.

The rise in the demand for social services (whether strictly related to social security, or the services and assistance) called for greater investment in the technical-bureaucratic-administrative apparatus. That is why the participation of Social Assistants in the management and organization of social security public policies is important, because since their very beginning Social Assistants showed distrust in that the "staleness" of bureaucracy might dominate the system.[7]

---

[6]This was established through Decree No. 7526 of 7 may 1945. With the deposition of Getúlio Vargas on October 29 of the same year, this important attempt was not developed. The ISBB, due to its importance, was the embryo of the 1960 LOPS, imprinting a significant elgacy in our system (Boschetti 2006).

[7]This distrust, as it seems, had a reason to be, since in any committed research conducted with users (insured persons and dependents) and the INSS carried out today, the weakness is custom care: precarious, inadequate, disregarding the specificities of each region, etc.

While on the one hand authorities and directors had the intention, even if covertly, to use Social Service and Social Assistants to calm down the conflict between the capital and work in this industrialization period in our country, on the other hand there was an awakening of critical awareness of a large number of these agents, to help the user population seek its rights.

The Framework of 1994 (*Matriz-94*) provides three steps in the increasing participation of Social Services in Social Security, obviously before the constitutional phase brought by CF/88. These steps are:

(a) Firstly, Social Service actions were imprinted by the defense of the humanization of large bureaucratic machines, and in this period the profession was legitimized as of the unification of the IAPs in 1966;
(b) Secondly, there was the Basic Action Plan (*Plano Básico de Ação*—PBA), of 1972, whose Social Service purpose was to provide answers to the socio-economic situation influenced by the developmental nature of the military dictatorship period;
(c) Thirdly, there was the creation of the National Social Security System (*Sistema Nacional de Previdência Social*—SINPAS), since the Social Service Centers (*Centros de Serviço Social*) were eliminated. Curiously, by outlining the institutional policy of that time, the services that previously fell in the scope of Social Service were transferred to the LBA, with a prominently assistance nature.

The *Matriz-94*, in turn, was not simply a formal document or a manual of good intentions. This document points out a revolutionary praxis, since it breaks the paradigm in force as of the *Plano Básico de Ação* (1978). Below are excerpts of the *Matriz-94*:

> After 15 (fifteen) years of exercising a model within a theoretical-methodological functionalist framework – *Plano Básico de Ação*-PBA-1978, without any changes over these years, the current paradigm reflects the political drive to revert the reconstruction of the professional performance of Social Service (…).
>
> That is how the social assistants of the National Institute for Social Security (*Instituto Nacional do Seguro Social* – INSS), as historical subjects, rethink their practice and reconstruct it, helping assure a new citizenship statute for the user population, by positioning themselves not only as mere parts of the bureaucratic Institution, but also as the constructors of a historical proposition. (MATRIZ, 1994)
>
> Therefore, the principal action of Social Service is directed to assure the pertinent right, whether through the access to social security benefits and services, or through the contribution to build awareness of work protection with the responsibility of the Government. (MATRIZ, 1994)
>
> With this regard, we understand that the New Paradigm of Social Assistance lies in the commitment to break away from the traditional model, to permanently construct and reconstruct the practice within a theoretical-methodological scope, aiming to put it in force among the social existing powers. (MATRIZ, 1994)

This new paradigm, in turn, exposed in MATRIZ-94, becomes crucial to the pertinent professional category as a whole, since it provides another benchmark about the definitions of social right and social security, understanding the latter as a right of workers:

> Thus, the arising paradigm under discussion since 1991 is an opposition to the functionalist/adjuster framework which for years directed the practice of social assistants in Social Security services, and in this sense it will confront the conservative institutional forces and advance into the direction of renewed practice, constructed from the critical understanding of reality. To this end, the new paradigm will use the support of the critical-dialectical method, providing as foundation new theoretical, strategic, ethical and legal bases to the practitioner's actions, directed by a notion of Social Security as a right of workers. (Yasbek 2007)

Therefore, the importance of Social Assistants in the organization and management of social security public policies is unarguable. Maybe we are currently in debt with the initial criticism made by Social Assistants regarding their distrust of the social security system. Their participation goes beyond the formality in the institutional space.

The 1988 Federal Constitution, resulting from the ideological–political clash and the correlation of social powers in force at that time, after 20 long years of military dictatorship, guaranteed these social rights.

We believe it is interesting to literally cite Article 88 of Law 8213/91, since it provides inputs to the practices and interventions of Social Assistants with social security policies.

> Art. 88 – It is the duty of Social Service to clarify the beneficiaries about their social rights and the means to exercise them and jointly establish with them solutions to problems that arise from their relationship with Social Security, both inside the institution and in the dynamics of society.
>
> Paragraph 1. – Priority will be given to the insured public with temporary disability and special attention will be given to retirees and pensioners.
>
> Paragraph 2. – To assure effective care for users, technical intervention, legal assistance, material aid and social resources will be used, as well as exchange with companies and social survey, including agreements, accords and contracts.
>
> Paragraph 3. – Social Service will use as guideline the participation of the beneficiary user to implement and strengthen the social security policy, in articulation with class associations and entities.
>
> Paragraph 4. – Social Service, considering the universalization of Social Security, will technically assist States and Municipalities to prepare and implement their work propositions.

The excellence of Article 88 cannot be left unnoticed by the pertinent professional category, especially because Social Security has been the favorite target of neoliberal reforms.[8]

Firstly, it was established that Social Assistants will be responsible for clarifying and intervening in favor of the insured persons before Social Security as an Institution (sometimes a "stale" institution, as noted by the first Social Assistants who were present in its inception). This work does not allow for impartiality,

[8] We must not forget that there was an actual attempt by the neoliberal to eliminate Article 88 from the LBPS, in which they failed only because "the resistance by social assistants working in social security engaged several entities of their category, impeding the elimination of this socio-occupational space, and as a result of Article 88 of Law 8213/91, which regulates Social Service in Social Security" (Abramides 2007).

therefore it is their constitutional duty (in addition to ethical obligation under the Professional Code) to correctly instruct the insured persons and their dependents in relation to their rights.

Priority, considering the broad client base, should be given to the temporarily disabled, i.e., to those who intend to apply to social security sick pay. By irony or disgrace, it is the very own Expert Evidence Department which makes the screening of this benefit more problematic: whether due to the lack of experts in the INSS, or the precarious work conditions (due to complementary tests which are troubled by the tardiness of the Unified Health System—SUS), or the lack of specialist doctors, especially, psychiatrists, opticians, and other specialists, i.e., due to the lack of an appropriate policy for this department.

On the other hand, we are not aware of the participation of Social Assistants in the expert evidence department. Social Assistants usually join in to calm down the negative result by incessantly giving explanations to the insured persons, rather than effectively participating in the assessment of their capacity to work.[9]

Social Service is also called to participate in the design of social security guidelines, whether through technical advisory, whether though the preparation of opinions and research. In addition to its essential participation in the management of social security policies, Social Assistants have potential—yet little explored—to contribute as assistant experts to the Court, as we will further see in detail.

11.5 The Need to Train Social Assistants to Act As Social Experts

The history of Social Assistants within the scope of the Judiciary, especially in the designated Child and Youth Court (*Justiça da Infância e da Juventude*), preludes our current objective. Following the steps of Fávero (2010), we will see that in late 1927 Social Assistants were already acting as "watchers," and among their attributions was to investigate minors, their parents, guardians, or those responsible for their custody, assuring the compliance with the resolutions taken by the Judiciary (Art. 152 of the Brazilian Code of Minors—*Código Brasileiro de Menores* of 1927).

As of Decree-Law No. 6026 of 1943, Social Assistants began having a more incisive participation in this process, acting as interns or members of the Watch Committee, and consequently in late 1940 they were already occupying a "formal position in the once designated São Paulo Juvenile Court (*Juizado de Menores de São Paulo*)" (Fávero 2010, p. 20).

As of 1979, with the enactment of the Code of Minors (*Código de Menores*—Law No. 6697/79), the condition of social expert regarding the Social Assistants working in this Court was recognized. Article 4 of the Code of Minors forced this

[9] Except for assistance benefits in relation to the grant of the LOAS's BPC, as we will further see.

participation to the extent that it provided for the study of the socioeconomic and cultural context of the minor and their family, and anticipated that the case study should be conducted "by a team with technical members, whenever possible."

According to Fávero (2010, p. 21), as of the milestone introduced by the Code of Minors, in 1979, the participation of Social Assistants in the Judiciary was intensified in 1990, with the creation of the Child and Youth Statute (*Estatuto da Criança e do Adolescente*—ECA).[10]

We believe a similar path is being taken in relation to the performance of Social Assistants regarding the organization of Biopsicossocial Expert Evidence.[11]

This systematic, engaging medical experts and social assistant experts, is already in operation within the scope of the LOAS's BPC, as we detailed in this paper. It must also operate in relation to social security benefits of contributive nature. There is absolutely no logic or rational explanation to justify the presence of Biopsicossocial Expert Evidence in relation to an assistance benefit and its unnecessity in relation to the continuous cash benefit within the General Social Security System (RGPS).

Purposefully, verifying disability for a definite period—and the diagnosis of the recovery of said disability is not given before a 2-year period—for the purposes of the LOAS's BPC, does not differ from the partial disability for work, for a definite period, of the insured persons seeking the benefits of the social security sick pay.

Therefore, the work of the Social Assistant is necessary to verify all the elements that comprise the ICF-2001, due to the assumption that the expert doctor is unable to assess the social, economic, environmental, personal, and attitudinal requirements.

This new perspective, deriving from Biopsicossocial Expert Evidence, consequently brings to Social Assistants a new challenge: responding to a series of requirements which, until then, was basically the verification of the economic context. Social Assistants, until then, were designated as Social Experts to assess the criteria of poverty, misery, or economic deprivation of the insured public or of those seeking the benefits of the continuous Social Assistance services.

This undoubtedly means going much beyond a simple economic-social assessment. Social assessments should contemplate the several areas and elements introduced by the ICF-2001.

To this end, better training should be provided, which without a question begins in university, i.e., in Social Service Programs. These programs, in turn, should introduce the Social Expertise discipline in their curriculum.[12]

---

[10] Therefore, as of the ECA, it became impossible to think about full protection to the child and adolescent without integrating Social Assistants in the multiprofessional team that is required by its guidelines. From this perspective, it is the duty of the Social Assistant not only to conduct social surveys, but also to issue opinions and reports, as well as to guide, advise, and refer minors accordingly (Art. 150 and 151 of the ECA).

[11] For a more detailed analysis about the participation of Social Assistants as Social Experts, see Costa (2013).

[12] By briefly looking over several researched curriculums, we verified the absence of said discipline, or of a correlated one, even though Social Assistants have been working as Court Experts for quite a while, especially in cases involving minors and offenders.

It is of utmost importance that Social Assistants have a basic understanding of the "world of Law," as well as the intricacies of medical evidence, *stricto sensu*, to satisfactorily respond to this new perspective. By having so, they will make great improvement in assisting the Court, not least because this is the principal reason for their appointment as experts: assist the judge in making a decision, to resolve the conflict in the most just manner.

It is also of utmost importance that they study and understand the social security system, especially in relation to the continuous cash benefits, which to be granted depend on Biopsicossocial Expert Evidence: (common and accident) sick pay, retirement due to disability, and accident pay, among many other benefits.

11.6 Directions Indicated by Biopsicossocial Expert Evidence to Grant the LOAS's BPC

We note, by interpreting what was exposed at the Convention…2007, and the influence of the ICF-2001, that the social barriers may obstruct the effective participation of individuals in society, necessarily leading to a change in the current notion of disease and disability.

As a result of this Convention…2007, which Brazil ratified, gaining the status of Constitutional Amendment, Decree 6564/08 significantly changed the biomedical criteria used until then to verify impairments, set forth in the 1993 LOAS. According to the latter, the assessment of the impairment and the level of disability are to be composed of medical and social assessments, and these specific areas are responsible for:

> The medical assessment of the impairment and the level of disability will consider impairments in body functions and structures, the social assessment will consider environmental, social and personal factors, and both will consider the handicaps to the performance of activities and the restriction to social life, according their specialties.

Likewise, assurance was made, in the assessment of the applications for the LOAS's pecuniary benefits, about assessments through these two specific areas—the medical and the social areas—as the best way to assess long-lasting impairments and disabilities (See Wording of Decree 6564/08).

The INSS, in turn, on May 29, 2009, through Joint Ordinance No. 1, established the instruments to assess the impairment and the level of disability of the applicant to the LOAS's BPC, seeking to comply with the precepts set forth in ICF-2001 and in the Convention mentioned.

In this sense, Normative Instruction No. 45, of 6 August, 2010, establishes in Section VII, Subsection I, which addresses "Social Service," several provisions that converge into the argument herein. For example, Article 385 states that the Social Assistant should prepare their opinion and social survey, and assess the person with impairment. Paragraphs 4 and 6, item V of such Article, all of which in Normative Instruction 45/10, should be literally cited:

Paragraph 4 – Social assessment, in conjunction with medical assessment, is an instrument destined to define impairment and the level of disability, and will consider environmental, social and personal factors, the handicap to the performance of activities and the restriction to the social participation of the applicants of the Continuous Cash Benefit in relation to the disabled person.

However, it is not a matter, as some may think, of having the need for two experts to perform their work detached from one another: the Medical Expert assesses the long-lasting impairment or deficiency of the insured persons, and the Social Expert verifies their income. That is not the case. It is an interdisciplinary work, jointly performed in view of the complexity of the cases about these issues.

We therefore believe in the importance of advancing the operational dynamics of the LOAS's BPC, because in relation to the continuous cash social security benefits in the RGPS this question is definitely not yet solved.

The question to be made is why this very same procedure has not yet been implemented for social security benefits, when there is the need to assess disability to work or disability of the insured persons? Answering that these two milestones (the ICF-2001 and the Convention…2007) only apply to assistance benefits is not valid. As we have seen, they may—and should—be applied in all social security fields.

In fact, it is appropriate to remember that not always this understanding, i.e., Complex and Systematic Expert Evidence (Medical Expert and Social Expert), in relation to the assessment of the applications for the LOAS's BPC, is applied in judicial proceedings which vindicate this benefit. It is fairly common the understanding by the courts which appoint Medical Experts to conduct the analysis of pathologies and Social Assistants, as Social Experts, to verify the monthly income of the applicant's family.

This conclusion is true, as demonstrated in the fact that in face of the negative result of a medical evidence, these courts do not even designate a Social or Socioeconomic Expert, since they understand the first requirement (temporary impairment or disability) was harmed.

Keeping things in perspective, we will see that Social Expert Evidence is not restricted only to assessing the income "per capita" of the family of the applicant to the LOAS's BPC, but also calculating all other components exposed in ICF-2001. Adopting another system would cause great losses to the applicants, especially in relation to assistance benefit.

Nevertheless, the approach started by the assessment system of the LOAS's Continuous Cash Benefit points out the application of this mechanism in other cases concerning social security benefits.

It is a new notion about expert evidence, pointing out a systematic, holistic, complex notion of assessment, designated as BIOPSICOSSOCIAL EXPERT EVIDENCE.

11.7 Conclusions

Social Assistance was the last element of SOCIAL SECURITY to be regulated. The only continuous cash benefit, of pecuniary nature, was regulated 5 years after the validity of Law 8472/93. As indicated by Costa (2011), this reflects the resistance to understand social assistance as a fundamental social right, as provided for in the 1988 Federal Constitution.

On the other hand, even though it was lately regulated, and its management and payment were transferred to the INSS, the understanding of what disability means, whether temporary or not, is noteworthy. The LOAS's BPC was the first social security benefit as a whole to include Biopsicossocial Expert Evidence in the assessment of the insured persons seeking the benefit as a means of subsistence.

By accepting, as we have seen, the new prerequisites introduced by Convention 2007, Social Opinions issued by Social Assistances became mandatory to expert assessments. Medical Evidence, despite certainly being of great importance, is not enough to come to a conclusion about the pathology assessed, since it does not sustain a number of factors surrounding each insured person and each actual case.

In this sense, it is crucial to train Social Assistants. This will most certainly imply the inclusion of a discipline related to complex expert evidence in the curriculum of Social Service Programs, as well as in other similar Courses, to update the knowledge of the practitioners already working in the scope of social policies.

We thus believe that the currently valid system used to grant the LOAS's BPC is a good example, since we point out the use of this grant in other social security benefits, especially those that concern the grant or preservation of benefits due to incapacity to work.

References

Abramides MBC (2007) Prefácio. In: O Serviço Social na Previdência Social.: trajetória, projetos profissionais e saberes. Cortez, São Paulo

Boschetti I (2006) Seguridade Social e Trabalho: paradoxos na construção das políticas de Previdência e Assistência Social no Brasil. Letras Livres, Editora UnB, Brasília

CLASSIFICAÇÃO INTERNACIOINAL DE FUNCIONALIDADE, INCAPACIDADE E SAÚDE – versão para crianças e jovens (2011) Organização Pan-americana da Saúde/ Organização Mundial da Saúde/Centro Colaborador da OMS para a Família de Classificações Internacionais em Português. Editora da Universidade de São Paulo, São Paulo

Cohn A (1980) Previdência Social e Processo Político no Brasil. Ed. Moderna, São Paulo

Costa JRC (2011) A Previdência Social o Alcance dos Assistentes Sociais. Paco Editorial, Jundiaí, São Paulo

Costa JRC (2013) Direito do Trabalho e Direito Previdenciário – subsídios ao trabalho social. Paco Editorial, Jundiaí, São Paulo

da Silva AA (2007) O Serviço social na Previdência Social: entre a necessidade social e o benefício. In: Braga L, Cabral MdSR (eds) O Serviço Social na Previdência Social.: trajetória, projetos profissionais e saberes. Cortez, São Paulo, pp 15–36

Fávero EA (2010) Avanços que ainda se fazem necessários em relação ao benefício assistencial de prestação continuada. In: O Estudo Social em Perícias, Laudos e Pareceres Técnicos. Conselho Federal de Serviço Social – Cefess (Org.). 10. ed. Editora Cortez, São Paulo, pp 9–51

Ferreira WS (2012) Juizados Especiais Federais: reflexões nos dez anos de sua instalação. In: Serau MA Jr (Org.) Juizados Especiais Federais. Juruá, Curitiba, pp 227–242

Iamamoto M, de Carvalho R (2006) Relações Sociais e Serviço Social no Brasil – Esboço de uma interpretação histórico-metodológica. Editora Cortez, São Paulo

Savaris JA (2009) Direito Processual Previdenciário. Juruá, Curitiba

Serau MA Jr (2009) Seguridade Social como direito fundamental material. Juruá, Curitiba

Thébaud-Mony A (2005) Organização do Trabalho e a Saúde: uma questão política. In: Boletim da Saúde Pública, vol 19, no 1. Porto Alegre, pp 91–99

Yasbek MC (2007) Análise da Matriz Teórico-Metodológica do Serviço Social no INSS (1950), considerando a política previdenciária, suas determinações sócio-históricas e o projeto hegemônico do Serviço Social. In: Braga L, Cabral MdSR (eds) O Serviço Social na Previdência Social.: trajetória, projetos profissionais e saberes. Cortez, São Paulo, pp 115–136

Chapter 12
The Continued Payment Benefit in Comparison with Social Security Benefits

Silvio Marques Garcia

Abstract In Brazil, Social Security is conceived as a broad system that comprises three large fields: Social Security in the strict sense (old-age retirement, survivors, disability insurance, etc.), Social Assistance (for needy people), and Healthcare. Amongst the many welfare programs and benefits, the Continued Payment Benefit (CPB) stands out, as it was inserted in the Brazilian Constitution as a right strictly related to the core principle of human dignity. This article seeks to outline the CPB characteristics provided for in Brazilian Constitution and regulated by Law 8742/1993 (LOAS). The contours of the legislative evolution of the benefit in these 20 years of validity of the LOAS are analyzed, as well as the aspects that, in practice of granting benefits, approximate CPB to Social Security benefits, like old-age retirement, disability retirement, and differentiated pensions for handicapped persons. The possibility of differentiated contributions for some categories and the existence of a great number of benefits in the minimum wage demonstrate the close relationship between Social Assistance and Social Security.

Keywords Welfare State • Continued Payment Benefit—Social Assistance • Social Security • Comparison

12.1 Introduction

In Brazilian Constitutional Law, Social Security is conceived as a broad system that comprises three large fields of public policy: Social Security in the strict sense (old-age retirement, survivors, disability insurance, etc.), Social Assistance (for needy people not covered by Social Security), and Healthcare. Amongst the many welfare programs and benefits presently in vigor in Brazil, the Continued Payment Benefit (CPB) stands out, as it was inserted in the Brazilian Constitution as a right strictly related to the core principle of human dignity.

S.M. Garcia (✉)
University of State of Sao Paulo, Franca, Sao Paulo, Brazil
e-mail: escrevaparasilviogarcia@gmail.com

M.A. Serau Junior, J.R. Caetano Costa (eds.), *Assistance Benefits in Brazil*,
DOI 10.1007/978-3-319-27046-3_12

In 20 years of legal regulation of the CPB, there have been many controversies, both in legal doctrine and in Courts, concerning this welfare provision referred in Article 203, Item V, of the Federal Constitution. The forward analysis is intended to outline the main characteristics of said benefit as well as to scrutinize its relations with other existing subsidies of Social Security in Brazilian Law, like old-age retirement and disability insurance.

The Brazilian Republic, founded on the grounds of human dignity and in the social value of work (Constitution, Article 1.), has among its primary objectives (Constitution, Article 3.) the development of a free, just and solidary society, plus the promotion of national development, the eradication of poverty and marginalization, the reduction of social and regional inequalities, and the promotion of the common good. These goals are a decisive point for the understanding of social rights in Brazilian social democracy, aimed at ensuring the dignity of all persons by the means of improving their quality of life without discrimination or marginalization and to reduce social inequalities.

The gains from the Liberal and the Welfare State were kept as fundamental rights and the citizens were included in the process of implementation of public policies, among which stands out those referred to under the macro concept of Social Security defined in Article 194, "caput" of the Brazilian Constitution as an integrated set of actions initiated by the public authorities and society, to ensure the rights to Healthcare, Social Security, and Social Assistance. With the overcoming of the liberal normative paradigm, Social Security became a substantial fundamental right. The implementation of legal provisions governing Social Security shall ensure the dignity of beneficiaries as part of the task of execution of social-civil rights.

Social Security is part of the substantive Constitution, for it is a "structural element of the state" which translates into the implementation of the principle of solidarity in the particular aspect of income redistribution, as well as other public policies related to it (Serau Junior 2009). Recognition of Social Security as a fundamental substantive right entails consequences for the implementation of welfare standards, including the preponderance of constitutional principles (Martinez 2001) that reflect the ethical values shared by the community and therefore must be continuously sought after by the State.

In the coming decades the aging population will exert pressure on the Social Security system (de Oliveira and Givisiez 2011) despite the normative achievements in the social context. In this scenario, the high levels of tax evasion and the government policies to increase the real value of benefits, whose floor is pegged to that of the minimum wage, will result in costs not offset by population growth.

The Assistance Benefits to the elderly and disabled could play an important role in this demographic transition, rescuing a large number of people from extreme poverty, increasing household consumption, enabling economic growth and the generation of new working posts.

The complexity of Social Security policies and the difficulties in their implementation across the country led to its division into three branches in order to obtain better results in the handling of the growing needs of citizens regarding Healthcare,

Social Security in the strict sense, and Social Assistance. Under the Constitution, the State provides assistance to citizens in various ways, such as legal assistance (Constitution, Article 5, Item LXXIV) and assistance to the family (Constitution, Article 226, Paragraph 8), among others. The assistance to the needy was inserted in Chapter II, which deals with social rights, along with the rights to education, health, food, work, housing, leisure, security, motherhood and childhood protection, and social security. Assistance is also due by the collectivity itself, as in the case of the assistance provided by employers to the children of their workers (Constitution, Article 6, Item XXV).

It also falls under the competence of the Union, States, Federal District, and municipalities the provision of general assistance to people with disabilities as well as combating the causes of poverty and marginalization, promoting the social integration of disadvantaged sectors (Constitution, Article 23). As for the elderly, it is the duty of their own family, as well as the State and the society as a whole, to provide for them, ensuring their dignity, well-being, and their right to life (Constitution, Article 230).

Social Assistance, as part of the Social Security, will be provided to those who need it, regardless of the payment of taxes, fees, or any other form of compensation whatsoever. Among its objectives are the protection of the family, maternity, childhood, adolescence, people with disabilities and the elderly (Constitution, Article 203). All of the Social Assistance policies shall be borne by the Social Security budget (Constitution, Article 204; Article 195, Paragraph 2).

Among the main measures introduced by the Constitution to give effect to the right to Social Security, the monthly payment of a minimum wage (guaranteed to the handicapped and the elderly who prove not to have means to provide for their own maintenance or having it provided by their family, according to the law—Constitution, Article 203, Item V) stands out as subject of this study. This benefit, known as Continued Payment Benefit (CPB), Assistance Aid, Assistance Benefit or by the acronym LOAS (a reference to the Organic Law of Social Assistance, which regulates the granting), is considered the most important cash benefit of the Social Assistance (de Moraes 2010; Cardoso and da Silva Júnior 2013).

12.2 The Continued Payment Benefit Regulation

The assistance benefit is an ongoing monthly cash provision from Social Assistance amounting to a minimum wage. It does not give right to the 13th salary because of the lack of any legal provisions regarding it. It is granted without any final term, but is subject to review by the Brazilian Social Security Administration (INSS) every 2 years in order to evaluate the continuity of the conditions that gave rise to them (Law 8742/1993, Article 21). Despite being a benefit provided in the Constitution, it was not specifically regulated until the passing of the Law 8742/1993, which defined Social Assistance, in Article 1, as a "non-contributory social security policy, providing minimum social grants, carried out through an integrated set of public and society initiatives, to ensure fulfillment of the basic needs of the population." The grant of the benefit, however, began only from January 1, 1996 (Decree 1744/1995, Article 40), which shows a considerable delay in the realization of this fundamental right.

This definition is relevant when seeking to identify the doctrinal concept of existential minimum, which refers to the set of minimum conditions of dignified human existence, which in addition to not being subject to restrictions by the State, requires positive benefits for its effectiveness. In this sense, the social minimum benefits would be needed to guarantee a dignity floor to the so-called existential minimum.

Several aspects of the regulation of the CPB have been considerably discussed in doctrine and jurisprudence, including the minimum age for access to the benefit, the concept of family and the setting of an objective criterion to measure poverty and exclusion of the minimum wage for fixing the income parameter.

12.2.1 Concept of Elderly

Law 8742/1993 initially provided for the grant of assistance benefit for people aged more than 70 years (Article 20, "caput"). Decree 1744/1995 (after repealed by Decree 6214/2007) reduced the age requirement to 67 years from January 1, 1998, and for 65 years from January 1, 2000 (Decree 1744/1995, Article 42). The Elderly Statute (Law 10741/2003) reaffirmed the minimum age for granting the benefit at 65 years (Article 34).

The latest redaction of Article 20 of Law 8742/1993, introduced by Law 12435/2011, kept the minimum age of 65 years. The age reduction of 70–65 extended the benefit to a greater number of elderly people, especially when considering the increase in life expectancy that has been achieved in recent years. Up to a certain extent, this increase is due to public health policies and Social Assistance, among them the granting of welfare benefits to the elderly. Hence already can be noted its extreme relevance for aging with dignity guaranteed.

The Elderly Statute (Law 10741/2003) ensures rights to people aged more than 60 years old (Article 1). Nevertheless, the age for granting assistance benefit should be maintained at 65 due to the increase in life expectancy, either because the decrease in age could mean a stimulus for workers who receive minimum wage or close to the minimum to abandon the labor market in order to obtain a benefit from Social Assistance.

It should be noted also that Social Assistance does not bring different age criteria for men and women and this is a measure of realization of the constitutional principle of gender equality as well as an improvement for the Social Assistance in comparison to the Social Security, which still has great difficulty in achieving the effectiveness of this principle.

12.2.2 Concept of Disabled

In the original redaction of Article 20, Paragraph 2, of Law 8742/1993, regulated by Article 4, Paragraph 2, of Decree 6214/2007, also in its original wording, for purposes of the granting of the continued payment benefit, the disabled person was considered "incapacitated for independent living and working." The disability required went beyond of mere incapacity for work (mere incapacity for work is a prerequisite to the granting of some Social Security benefits) and also should not be confused with civil incapacity (Decree 6214/2007, Article 18).

In Brazil, the Convention on the Rights of Persons with Disabilities (New York Convention) was ratified by Legislative Decree 186/2008 and promulgated by Decree 6949/2009. Ratification occurred according to the procedure under Article 5, Paragraph 3, of the Federal Constitution and so the rights and guarantees provided under the Convention now have the status of constitutional amendment with immediate applicability (Constitution, Article 5, Paragraph 1). Therefore, the Social Assistance legislation provisions that were contrary to the Convention succumbed before its normative force. The requirement for granting the CPB is no longer the inability for independent life and work and we have started to demand a broader concept of disability based on "the existence of long-term impediments of physical, mental, intellectual or sensory nature, which, in interaction with various barriers, obstruct their full and effective participation in society on an equal basis with others [...]" (Decree 6214/2007, Article 9, Item I, amended by Decree 7617/2011). Disability is no longer just a clinical concept and has become a situation resulting from a set of factors that relate to citizen interaction with the environment.

One of the consequences of adapting the concept to the ratified convention rule is the need for medical and social assessment to verify the existence of disability and the degree of impairment in interaction with various barriers that obstruct the full and effective participation of citizens in society in equal conditions with others (Law 8742/1993, Article 20, paragraph 6). This assessment should be made by medical experts and social workers from the Social Security Administration (INSS). Article 15 of Decree 6214/2007 explains better the evaluation, which should be based on the principles of the International Classification of Functioning, Disability and Health—CIF, established by resolution of the World Health Organization. The social assessment should consider environmental factors, social and personal; the medical evaluation will consider the deficiencies in the functions and structures in the body; both will consider, moreover, the limitations in the performance of activities and the restriction of social participation, according to their specificities (Law 8742/1993, Article 20, paragraph 2).

Thus, there is an evolution of the concept of disability, much more suited to the constitutional design of public policies to support people with disabilities, which sought from the beginning the integration of those people into society and was reinforced by the ratification of the New York Convention.

12.2.3 Concept of Family

Continued payment benefit is granted to elderly or disabled that prove not to have means to provide for their own maintenance or to have it provided by his family (Law 8742/1993, Article 20). It becomes important to analyze the concept of family because of its direct influence in the calculation of the monthly family income. Pereira (2011) states that "Continued Payment Benefit regulation has also appeared restrictive since its origin, due to the access to the benefit being strongly linked to family and not the elderly and people with disabilities as individual holders of a fundamental right."

However, Social Assistance is part of Social Security and its maintenance is the responsibility of public authorities, society, and family (Constitution, Articles 194, 203, Item V, 227, 299 and 230). In this sense, the constitutional delimitation itself of Social Assistance provides for the granting of the CPB to the disabled and the elderly who prove not to have the means to provide for their own maintenance "or have it provided by their family" (Constitution, Article 203, Item V). Therefore, the performance of public programs of Social Assistance is subsidiary and only takes place when the family cannot provide for the subsistence of the elderly or disabled.

Although the Constitution refers to the concept of family, leading to the conclusion that it is necessary to sue the family according to the civil law, before seeking the State's help, the Social Assistance law has set other rules in this regard. Law 8742/1993 understood the family as "the mononuclear unit, living under the same roof, whose economy is maintained by the contribution of its members" (Article 20, Paragraph 1). This concept was completely detached from the biological relationships or civil kinship.

Law 9720/1998 changed the concept of family, which began to be understood as "the set of persons listed in Article 16 of Law 8213/1991, provided that they live under the same roof." Thus, there was adopted the understanding laid down in the legislation of the Social Security, which was narrower than the previous law. Moreover, the son or brother with more than 21 years, and also others like the stepfather, stepmother, uncles, grandchildren, etc. began to be excluded from the calculation of the "per capita" family income, which eventually led to increasing the chances of obtain the CPB.

One of the recent changes introduced by Law 12435/2011 resulted in major modifications in the concept of family, which came to be understood as "made by the postulant [to obtain the benefit], spouse or partner, parents and, in the absence of one, the stepmother or stepfather, unmarried siblings, unmarried children and stepchildren and minors under tutelage, on condition that they live under the same roof" (Law 8742/1993, Article 20, paragraph 1). Thus, there were set specific criteria, more suitable for the calculation of family income. In the absence of the parents, stepfather and stepmother were included and, in addition, the unmarried sister of 21 years was included, as well as unmarried stepchildren and minors under tutelage. Nevertheless, the establishment of a comprehensive concept of family unit can be subject to criticism (Pereira 2011), because it cannot reflect the reality of the modern notion of family that deserves state protection.

On the other hand, if there are persons living under the same roof with the financial capacity to promote the maintenance of the elderly or disabled person, it is necessary to delimit those whose income will be included in calculation of the "per capita" monthly family income. In this sense, the legal criteria chose to disregard the descendants and married brothers and those who do not live under the same roof. As observed Cardoso and da Silva Júnior (2013), "anyone who does not fit the legal list of the Article 20, Paragraph 1, of Law 8742/1993, should be excluded from the family group concept the LOAS, although it has kinship or provide economic assistance to the claimant of the continued payment benefit."

Therefore, changes in the Law 8742/1993 have enlarged the possibilities of granting the CPB, because they restricted the concept of family. Descendants who do not live under the same roof, although having the liability for the support of parents, will not have their income computed to analyze the granting of the benefit.

12.2.4 Need for an Objective Criterion for Establishing the Misery

The assistance CPB has a subsidiary character in relation to Social Security. Nevertheless, it must be recognized the limitations of State resources in relation to the need to guarantee the well-being of citizens. In other words, it is necessary to choose which group of people will benefit from the resources available.

The constitutional function of the benefit is to provide Social Assistance to the elderly and disabled people who need it, preventing them from remaining in poverty and guaranteeing them a minimum of dignity. The identification of the persons who can be elected as beneficiaries shall be made by objective criteria, even to prevent personal favoritism or discrimination at the time of implementation of public policies for Social Assistance.

Law 8742/1993 (LOAS) has delimited 1/4 of the national minimum wage as objective criterion for establishing the concept of economically dispossessed. The family whose "per capita" monthly income is less than this limit is considered incapable of providing the maintenance of disabled or elderly (Law 8742/1993, Article 20, Paragraph 3).

Some authors (Moro 2003; Pereira 2011; Moreno Filho 2013) affirm the difficulty of realization of CPB, especially given to the restrictive legislative regulation and the "literal interpretation of legal provisions" practiced by the INSS (Pereira 2011), the agency responsible for granting and maintenance of the benefit. Nevertheless, it is needed to keep in mind that the INSS has operations throughout all the country and looks after the maintenance of more than 30 million benefits. Therefore, the performance of the INSS should be uniform and objective, avoiding margin of interpretation that can lead to personal favoritism in certain locations. The existence of fraud is common news in the media. Therefore, the judgment of the administrative authority should be restricted to the analysis of the personal circumstances, only according to objective criteria established by law, and should also strive for obedience to the principle of legality.

Moreover, the judiciary activity allows for the correction of any claim for unduly denied Social Assistance benefit. In last years, jurisprudence has enlarged the initially restrictive rules of Continued Payment Benefit.

The Supreme Federal Court (STF), on 27/08/1998, in the Direct Unconstitutional Action (ADI) 1232/DF, dismissed the claim of unconstitutionality statement of Article 20, paragraph 3 of Law 8742/1993. Since that decision, understandings like Precedent 11 of National Standardization Court of Special Courts Federal (TNU), that allowed the proof of misery by other means and also a subjective analysis for granting the benefit, became overcome and said precedent was canceled.

Nevertheless, many courts and TNU itself began to understand that an income less than 1/4 of the minimum wage as the only valid criterion could not exclude other evidence if the family income "per capita" surpasses this level, although able to presume absolutely the claimant's misery when proven. (STJ, REsp 464.774/SC, REsp 756.119/MS, REsp 1.025.181/RS, REsp Repetitivo 1112557/MG; TRF3, AC 00045614920034036109, Rel. Batista Pereira, e-DJF3 17/11/2011, AC 00412225020104039999, Rel. Therezinha Cazerta, e-DJF3 10/09/2012; TRF4 AC 200504010277442, Rel. Fernando Quadros da Silva, D.E. 09/12/2009, TNU, PEDILEF 200643009017410, Rel. Élio Wanderley de Siqueira Filho, DJU 22/01/2008, PEDILEF 200584015002615, Rel. Maria Divina Vitória, DJU 21/12/2007).

According to the jurisprudence, the legal rules that fix this limit (1/4 of the minimum wage) does not prevent the analysis of other constituent elements of the specific economic situation of the family. It has been admitted, therefore, the recognition of the economic insufficiency by other evidence. The repeated decisions of the lower courts to the effect that the criterion of Article 20, Paragraph 3 of Law 8742/1993, though constitutional, is not the only evidence of the misery carried the matter to the analysis of the Supreme Court again.

In Supreme Court itself, several decisions of ministers had pointed out the unconstitutionality of the process of legal criterion in face of factual and legal changes (STF, Recl 4374/PE). On February 1, 2007, in the Complaint 4374/PE, Judge Gilmar Mendes dismissed the injunctive claim of the INSS, keeping the first instance decision that had granted CPB in situations of social misery, although the family income "per capita" exceed the legal limit. On February 9, 2008, the Supreme Court recognized the general repercussion of the issue, signaling the possibility of change of position by the court (RE 567985/MT).

On April 18, 2013, in the judgment of Extraordinary Appeals (RE) 580963/PR, 567985/MT and Complaint 4374/PE, the Supreme Court pronounced the partial unconstitutionality without nullity pronunciation of Article 20, Paragraph 3, of Law 8742/1993, as a result of subsequent factual transformations that changed the rules reality, making unconstitutional the norm previously considered legitimate.

The reasons for the decision were based on the change in the economic development stage of the country and in the emergence of laws that brought more elastic criteria for the granting of other welfare benefits. These laws increased the limit of "per capita" income to half the minimum wage and instituted programs such as Bolsa Família (Law 10836/2004), the Food Access National Program (Law 10689/2003), Bolsa Escola (Law 10219/2001), and other actions of income transferences of the Federal Government. In the decision, it weighed the need for the legislature to treat the matter in a systematic way, avoiding inconsistencies in the granting of benefits. Such a solution stating that there is a supervening unconstitutionality, based on the 1/2 minimum wage criterion set in subsequent welfare policies, had already been proposed by the doctrine and jurisprudence (Moro 2003).

However, the Supreme Court decision is not free of criticism. To establish the legal criterion on half the minimum wage "can also be criticized for lack of better evidence base," although it cannot "be accused of being overly restrictive as the previous" criterion (Moro 2003). In this regard, Cardoso and da Silva Júnior (2013) opine that "the Supreme Court decision has gaps that, on the contrary, will expand the discussions around such a sensitive issue, especially in the legislative framework, increasing the pressure over the Legislative Power to redefine the criteria previously employed." After the decision of the Supreme Court, the legislation has been changed, in order to adapt it to the jurisprudence. Law 13.146/2015, known as Statute of Person with Disabilities, modified the redaction of Article 20, Paragraph 11, of Law 8.472/1993 to set that for granting the CPB, may be used "other evidence of misery condition" of the familiar group and the situation of vulnerability, according to regulation, yet to be performed.

The absence of an objective criterion affects the administrative analysis of the CPB. The constitutional definition, by a limited efficacy rule (Constitution, Article 203, Item V), allowed the ordinary legislator to establish the group of people who would be eligible to the benefit. Thus, the criterion would be unconstitutional only if it would not provide the granting of a reasonable number of benefits, according to the possibilities of the budget.

The fixation of an objective criterion is necessary for the legal certainty of the administrative process, besides allowing the uniformity of administrative decisions and the avoidance of personal favoritism or discrimination. Fixing a fluid criterion certainly entail a reevaluation by the judiciary of all cases in which the benefit was denied, generating divergent decisions and therefore not necessarily being fairer than administrative decisions.

12.2.5 Amounts Excluded from the Concept of Income

Law 8742/1993 has set the family monthly income "per capita" of less than 1/4 (one fourth) of the minimum wage as the objective criterion for the CPB granting (Law 8742/1991, Article 20, Paragraph 3). Law 12435/2011 amended the wording of said provision, replacing the adjective "carrier" (of deficiency) by the conjunction "with" (disabilities), which did not alter its content.

The use of this criterion makes arise questions related to the concept of income. Some authors state that in the absence of a concept of "income" by welfare law, it must be borrowed the definition given by Article 43, Item I of Law 5172/1966, which established the National Tax Code (Moreno Filho 2013). The mentioned command establishes that income is the "capital of the product, work or a combination of both." This definition is given by the CTN to the purposes of income tax and earnings of any nature. According to this understanding, as the amounts received by way of CPB for other family members are not coming from capital or labor, it is not possible that these people make part of the composition of household income. However, we cannot agree with the use of the concept of the income tax law, because the benefits of Social Assistance will be provided regardless of contribution payments to Social Security (Constitution, Article 203). In the field of Social Assistance, the concept of family monthly gross income is well established by Decree 6214/2007:

> VI – family gross monthly income: the sum of the monthly gross income earned by family members composed of wages, salaries, pensions, alimony, benefits of public or private pension, unemployment insurance, commissions, pro-labor, other labor income self-employed, informal or autonomous market income, incomes from the patrimony, Lifetime Monthly Income and Continued Payment Benefit, except as provided in the sole Paragraph of Article 19. (Wording given by Decree 7617/2011.)

In addition, the exclusion of any value of the concept of income for assistance purposes depends on legislative provision. Understanding otherwise would be disregard the provisions of Article 34, sole Paragraph, of the Statute for the Elderly, since this rule excludes from the calculation of family income the CPB already given to any family member. If it is necessary a rule to assert that specific gain does not comprise the concept of income it is because the others certainly are part of it.

Thus, the best foundation for the exclusion of any minimum wage benefit (be it from Social Security or from Social Assistance) of the income calculation is the solution given by the jurisprudence, according to which the literal restricted possibility of Article 34, sole Paragraph, of the Statute for the Elderly violates the equality.

Article 4, Paragraph 2, of Decree 6214/2007 states that the following will not be counted as family gross monthly income:

> I – benefits and welfare aid and events of a temporary nature; (Included by Decree 7617/2011)
> II – values such as social cash transfer programs; (Included by Decree 7617/2011)
> III – traineeship exchanges; (Included by Decree 7617/2011)
> IV – special pension compensatory nature and healthcare, as provided for in Article 5; (Included by Decree 7617/2011)
> V – eventual income or seasonal nature, to be regulated in a joint act of the Ministry of Social Development and Hunger Alleviation and Social Security; and (Included by Decree 7617/2011)
> VI – payment to the person with disabilities as apprentices. (Included by Decree 7617/2011)

In that way, amounts related to other social programs to transfer income such as Bolsa Família, and other benefits and welfare aid and events of a temporary nature and other income from any or seasonal nature are also excluded from the concept of income.

An innovation that came at a good time was the forecast of Paragraph 9 of Article 20 of Law 8742/1993, which ensures the exclusion of the concept of income the remuneration of persons with disabilities in apprentice status, limited this concurrent receipt to a period of 2 years (Law 8742/1993, Article 21-A, Paragraph 2). The Paragraph 9 of Article 20, included by Law 12470/2011, enables the integration of disabled people into the labor market.

In the same spirit, Article 21-A was introduced, which now only provides for the suspension of the benefit when the disabled person's engaging in remunerated activity, including the individual microenterprise condition. Once terminated the employment relationship or entrepreneurial activity, it may be required to continue the payment of the suspended benefit (Law 8742/1993, Article 21-A, Paragraph 1).

12.2.6 Cumulation Possibility

The CPB cannot be cumulated by the recipient with other Social Security benefits or benefits from other system, unless Healthcare and special pension compensatory nature (Law 8742/1993, Article 20, Paragraph 4).

Under Article 19 of Decree 6214/2007, it is possible grant the CPB to more than one family member, providing that the family "per capita" income is not equal nor more than 1/4 of minimum.

It is worth mentioning the possibility of granting the CPB even if another family member receives any benefit from Social Security or Social Assistance. If all members of the family group are elderly, receipt of CPB by one of them will not prevent others from accessing the same benefit (Law 10741/2003, Article 34, sole Paragraph; Decree 6214/2007, Article 19, sole Paragraph). As the mentioned rule is present in the Statute for the Elderly and provides for the exclusion only of CPB already given to other elderly in the family, there is a current that interpret such rule restrictively, in such a way that receipt of any other benefits shall be considered in the calculation of the family income. In this sense, the Regional Federal Court (TRF) of the 3rd Region already decided:

> Article 34, sole Paragraph, of Law 10741/03: the benefit granted in accordance with the "caput" of this article is not to be counted for purpose of determining the amount of the "per capita" family income. In contrary sense, all receipts, unless social protection, described in command in use must necessarily be computed for the measurement proposed. (TRF3, EI 00395669720064039999, 3ª Seção, Rel. Vera Jucovsky, e-DJF3 30/11/2011. See also: TRF3, AC 00137856820094039999, Rel. Marisa Santos, e-DJF3 21/09/2011, p. 547).

Although this rule is provided only for the elderly, there is another current in jurisprudence that extends it to the disabled member already receives or will receive the benefit (TRF3, APELREEX 00349951520084039999, Rel. Fausto de Sanctis, e-DJF3 18/11/2011; AC 00513884920074039999, Rel. Leide Polo, e-DJF3 29/09/2011, p. 1453; TRF4, APELREEX 200571000452570, Rel. Guilherme Pinho Machado, D.E. 10/08/2009).

If the new benefit has nature of Social Security, there is also jurisprudence stating that this benefit can be cumulated without changing the conditions for granting the previous CPB, for the purpose of biennial review (in this position, beyond the above-mentioned judgments, see the Precedent 20 of the Federal Appeals Group of Santa Catarina and also: STJ, Pet 7203/PE; AgRg no REsp 1351525/SP; TRF4 AC 200471150007060, Rel. João Batista Lazzari, D.E. 10/08/2009; TNU, PEDILEF 200543009000310, Rel. Élio Wanderley de Siqueira Filho, DJU 31/01/2008).

Moreover, there is no impediment to receive amounts from other social programs of income transference, such as Bolsa Família.

The receipt of CPB can also be cumulated for a period of up to 2 years, with the remuneration of the disabled person as an apprentice (Law 8742/1993, Article 20, Paragraph 9 and Article 21-A, Paragraph 2).

12.3 Continued Payment Benefit *versus* Social Security Benefits

In Brazil, Social Security encompasses three branches: Healthcare, Social Security in the strict sense, and Social Assistance as complementary policies with different objectives. As stated by de Moraes (2010), "the distinction made by Federal Constitution between Social Security in the strict sense and Social Assistance is a fact which results that the legislature or the interpreter cannot treat them interchangeably."

Within the constitutional framework, there are unforeseen situations or even expected that give rise to social protection. Those described in Article 201 give the insured or their dependents a certain pension coverage, such as disability, maternity, involuntary unemployment, and death. There are other situations that could lead to the granting of a benefit of the Social Security in the strict sense or Social Assistance, as in the case of old age, which could be able to provide to the elderly an age retirement or a CPB.

Although described in Article 201, Item I of the Constitution, the "Disease Benefit" is more connected to the provision of Healthcare. The Social Security risk covered by the benefit entitled Disease Benefit (but it should be better called Temporary Incapacity Benefit) is not the existence of the disease itself, but the inability resulting therefrom.

Social Security refers to policies directed at persons performing paid work, emphasizing therefore the primacy of work as one of the pillars which support the social order (Constitution, Article 193). In addition, the valuing of the work is one of the foundations of the constitutional economic order (Constitution, Article 170).

12.3.1 Membership

The first difference between benefits of Social Security in the strict sense and benefits of Social Assistance is relative to the form of membership. The complementarity between the Social Security in the strict sense and Social Assistance is evident when we see that the affiliation to Social Security is compulsory for workers in gainful activity (Constitution, Article 201, "caput", Law 8213/1991, Article 11). People who qualify for insurance and have already paid the minimum number of contributions required or otherwise have the right to some Social Security benefit (Law 10666/2003) and also disabled persons who are in a period in which, by law, they are eligible to some benefit of Social Security in the strict sense, even without payment of taxes, may not receive the CPB provided for in Article 203, Item V, of the Constitution.

Thus, the CPB will be due only if there is not a case of concession of retirement payment benefits. In this sense, says de Moraes (2010) that "the continued payment benefit is aimed, by exclusion, to those who cannot join the Social Security precisely for being unable to work, being concrete (people with deficiency) or fictitious (elderly) such disability."

12.3.2 Covered Events

Another difference between the systems under discussion is related to the constitutional provision about the events to be covered. While the benefits of Social Security in the strict sense cover events such as disability and old age of the insured, the benefit of the Social Assistance is provided in situations where elderly and disabled person have no means to provide for their own maintenance or to have it provided by their family. Thus, Social Assistance considers personal and socioeconomic aspects.

Harmonizing the principles of universality of coverage and of selectivity and distributivity in the provision of benefits and services (Balera 2014) (Constitution, Article 194, Items I and III) with the principle of financial and actuarial balance (Constitution, Article 201) (this one specific to the Social Security in the strict sense), it is concluded that there is the need for extension of the fundamental right to Social Security to a greater number of workers. The result of the combination of these constitutional commandments is the adoption of differentiated contributions for workers considered low-income or with insufficient resources to pay the tax in equal basis with other persons without risk to their livelihood and their family (Martinez 2001).

Thus, to a certain extent, the Social Security in the strict sense starts to have outlines that approach Social Assistance, although this one is seen as complementary to that. The function of Social Security in the strict sense in the (re)distribution of income arises from its inclusion in the scope of Social Security in a broad sense, no longer a mere private insurance. This role now evolved to reach a greater number of citizens, especially given the economic and social situation of Brazil and the need for social inclusion of a large number of informal workers. An example is the differential contribution for individual micro-entrepreneurs (MEI) (Constitution, Article 201, Paragraph 12; LC 128/2001) and for the optional insured without their own income devoted exclusively to domestic work within his residence (Law 12470/2011), which can contribute a 5 % rate on the minimum wage, getting access to the main Social Security benefits, which demonstrates how tenuous is currently the distinction between Assistance and the Social Security in the strict sense, which has become increasingly social.

12.3.3 Old-Age Retirement Versus CPB

The differences between the CPB granted to the elderly and the old-age retirement is related to subjective and objective aspects. As to the subjective aspect, for granting the CPB is required the minimum age of 65 for men and women, whereas to be eligible to retirement, the minimum age required is 65 years for men and 60 for woman, reduced in 5 years for rural workers. With regard to the condition of insured and minimum number of monthly paid taxes (admitted for rural workers the proof of monthly rural work activity), both these exigencies are also elementary for the granting of old-age retirement.

The relevance of CPB has shown how much we need to develop a more inclusive and efficient Social Security system. In most situations, especially in rural areas, after decades of work, the insured cannot get access to retirement benefit in value above the minimum. In January 2014, the average value of the benefits of the General Regime (RGPS) paid to urban people (18 million members) was R$ 1,112.83, while for rural workers (8.9 million beneficiaries) was R$ 647,35 (Ministry of Social Security 2014). Moreover, 51.90 % of 377,155 pension benefits granted in January 2014 had value equal to or less than the minimum wage (Ibidem). Analyzing the consequences of reducing the minimum age to get CPB at 60 age years, it would not make sense ensuring the CPB of one minimum wage to a 60-year-old man who did not contribute to the pension plan and to grant monthly benefit of equal amount to the insured that has the same age and effectively contributed to the pension plan during the period required. People whose economic insurance is insufficient and who, when calculating the income of their future retirement benefit, found that their income would be close to the minimum wage would not wait for the age of 65 years. It would be sufficient at the age of 60 years to make an application for the CPB. Therefore, the supplementary character of Social Assistance justifies the requirement of a superior age for granting the CPB than the age fixed to retirement, because of the factual situation of having a large number of beneficiaries receiving retirement equivalent or close to the minimum value.

Social Assistance fulfills its constitutional role and the failures of the Social Security cannot be attributed to it, but to the inefficient and poorly inclusive Social Security in the strict sense, unable to do more for its beneficiaries than the Assistance does to people who receive CPB. In this sense, the Social Security in the strict sense perform nothing more than a function near to assistance, namely, a function as a barrier against misery.

12.3.4 Disability Benefits Versus Continued Payment Benefit

The greater proximity between an event covered by Social Assistance and for Social Security is the relationship between the disability retirement and the CPB granted to the disability people. It is necessary to establish the difference between disability and impairment.

In the case of disability retirement, disability is the key requirement, as well as the status of insured and the minimum number of contribution (Constitution, Article 203, Item I). Under the law, disability is understood as the situation of the insured "considered unable and ineligible for rehabilitation for the exercise of any activity which guarantees his/her subsistence [...]" (Law 8213/1991, Article 42).

As for the CPB, will be due to the handicapped person who "has no means to provide for their own support or having it provided by his/her family," according to the law (Constitution, Article 203, Item V). The previous wording of the Law 8742/1993 considered person with a disability that "incapacitated for independent life and work" (Law 8742/1993, Article 20, Paragraph 2).

Social Assistance has a supplementary character, in that, with capacity for work, the disabled will be referred to Social Security, be as compulsory insured or as optional insured. In this regard, measures have been created for the inclusion of disabled people in the labor market, both in the private sector (Law 8.213/1991, art.93) and in the public sector (Constitution, Article 37, Item VIII) with reserve places for persons with disabilities.

Laws 12435/2011 and 12470/2011 successively altered the wording of Paragraph 2 of Article 20 of Law 8742/1993, to adapt the concept of disability to international standards and to public policies to support people with disabilities established in the Brazilian Constitution. Deficiency has been a situation due to number of factors that relate to citizen interaction with the environment. However, the legal definition is very generic and is not free of criticism. In any case, it is clear that disability concerns the impossibility of full and effective participation in society on an equal basis with others because of long-term physical, mental, intellectual, or sensory impairments.

This participation in society referred in law regards to integration into the labor market, because the social value of work is one of the foundations of the Republic (Constitution, Article 1, Item IV), of the economic order (Constitution, Article 170, "caput"), and of the social order (Constitution, Article 193), in addition to being one of the goals of Social Assistance (Constitution, Article 203, Item III).

The disabled cannot be simply equated to the taxpayer of Social Security in the strict sense or to the person temporarily unable to work. The temporarily incapacitated taxpayer was or is still (actually or potentially) integrated into the labor market and therefore should contribute as compulsory insured or optional insured to be eligible to Social Security benefits. However, the disabled do not have conditions to participate in the labor aspect of life in society on an equal footing with others.

On the other hand, to the CPB grant purposes, the disabled should be characterized by a relevant impediment to participate in the labor market (on equal terms with others). The disabled with conditions to be integrated into the labor market (public or private) in reserved places regime should also be considered (compulsory or optional) insured, being applicable in this case the qualification and professional rehabilitation (Law 8742/1993, Article 2, Item I, Points c and d). As clarify Cardoso and da Silva Júnior (2013)

> the barriers that arise to the disabled are due to work environment, not yet fully adapted to the disabled's condition (sociological aspects, in coordination with the biological, namely the long-term physical, intellectual and sensory) and such deficiency is no longer considered as such as soon the government and others responsible for their reintegration are fulfilling their purposes.

Therefore, the existence of inability to provide for their own support or having it provided by their family is relevant to characterize the right to benefit from continued provision. That is because if there are long-term impediments that obstruct their full and effective participation in society on an equal basis with others, but if the person still has capacity for their own maintenance, there will be no right to CPB.

Incapacity for work and disability for independent life are no longer criteria for the classification of disability. Nevertheless, once verified the deficiency to the CPB grant purposes, the conclusion is that there will also be inability to work and independent living.

The current concept of disability is quite broad and refers to the need of individualization of legislative provision to the case, which will be done by means of medical and social assistance evaluation (Law 8742/1993, Article 20, Paragraph 6). It depends, moreover, to the social context in which the deficient is.

12.3.5 Handicapped Retirement versus Continued Payment Benefit

Complementary Law 142/2013 regulated the Paragraph 1 of Article 201 of the Brazilian Constitution with regard to the retirement of handicapped person insured by the General Regime (RGPS). This law established different criteria for old-age retirement and contribution-time retirement of the person with disabilities (de Freitas 2012). It has not been instituted two new types of retirement, but only different conditions for access to such benefits.

For old-age retirement, the handicapped must prove: (a) the deficiency in the day of the application entry, except in case of acquired right; (b) the minimum age of 60 years if men and 55 for women; (c) the minimum number of contributions correspondent of 15 years of monthly contributions; (d) the existence of a handicap during the same period.

In the case of time-contribution retirement for handicapped person, such benefit is assured:

(a) after 25 years of contribution as handicapped if man and 20 years for women in the case of insured with severe disabilities;
(b) after 29 years of contribution as handicapped if man and 24 years for women, if handled with moderate disabilities;
(c) after 33 years of contribution as handicapped if man and 28 years for women in the case of insured with mild disabilities.

The required contribution period varies according to the deficiency is severe, moderate, or mild. For getting the benefit is necessary to prove: (a) the deficiency in the day of application entry, except in case of acquired right; and (b) the minimum number of 180 contributions, pursuant to Article 25, Item II, of Law 8213/1991.

The differentiated form of counting work time for handicapped person is admitted, even for the period prior to the effective date of the Complementary Law 142/2013. The existence of deficiency previous to the time of the validity of that law must be certified, including regarding their level, at the first expert examination.

The analysis of these newly regulated benefits in Social Security legislation is relevant, mainly due to the concept of disability laid down in Article 2 of Complementary Law 142/2013, identical to that set out in Article 20, Paragraph 2 of Law 8742/1993, as amended by Law 12470/2011. Both are in accordance to the requirements of the International Convention on the Rights of Persons with Disabilities, which has Constitutional Amendment force in Brazilian law since it was adopted in accordance with paragraph 3 of Article 5 of the Constitution.

The basic difference between the CPB and Social Security benefits granted to handicapped person lies in the fact that there are no fundamental elements of the Social Security relationship in the CPB, namely: membership, condition of insured, and minimum number of contributions required.

Incapacity for acts of daily life was a criterion that in revoked legislation did not allow a clear verification of the existence of a disability. Complementary Law 142/2013 has brought parameters for the evaluation of disabilities, including saying it will be "medical and functional, in accordance with Regulation" (Article 4). The (administrative or judicial) evaluation to grant any benefit (of Social Security or of Social Assistance) to the disabled cannot be limited only to the aspect of the (in) ability of the labor. The jurisprudence should help to establish the goals that differentiate disability to the incapacity to work, this one a requirement present in Social Security benefits given due to disability (sickness allowance, accident, and disability retirement).

12.3.6 Survivors Benefits Versus Continued Payment Benefits

It is also possible to identify some relations of approaching between the CPB and the survivors benefit. In not rare cases, the citizen seeks the INSS to obtain a benefit of Social Security in the strict sense, but for lack of information, insufficient documentation and even due to the restrictive administrative interpretation, ends up getting the CPB.

In other cases the recipient was eligible to retirement (after working in urban or rural activities), but went on to receive the benefit of Life Monthly Income (Law 6179/1974, Article 2, Item I), which, because it did not generate benefit to survivors (Article 7, Paragraph 2), was considered by the INSS as a Social Assistance benefit, despite having features in common with Social Security, since it required that for certain period there was the exercise of activity referred in the then current law Social Security (INPS or Funrural).

If it is noted that CPB was granted in place of a Social Security benefit, it is possible the application for undoing the concession and granting the most appropriate benefit, which eventually will bring other advantages to the recipient, as the 13th salary payment and the right to a survivor's benefit for their dependents.

The dependents of the deceased beneficiary who received monthly income for life or CPB also may require the survivor's benefit. If it is proven that the deceased beneficiary had the right to retirement, but instead started receiving another benefit that does not generate survivor's rights, this situation should be corrected by the approval of a survivor's benefit to their dependents (STJ, REsp 196.946/SP, REsp 210.862/SP, TRF3, AR 00199652220124030000, Rel. Sergio Nascimento, 3ª Seção, e-DJF3 09/10/2013; TRF4, AC 200972990030414, Rel. Eduardo Vandré Oliveira Lema Garcia, D.E. 05/02/2010).

12.4 Final Considerations

In order to meet the objectives of the Brazilian Republic, especially the construction of a free, just and solidary society, eradicating poverty, and reducing social and regional inequalities, the role of the CPB is crucial. Twenty years after its regulation, this mechanism is also essential for achieving the goals initially sought of social transformation, as evidenced by the existence in January 2014, of 4.1 million CPB maintained by the INSS (Ministry of Social Security, 2014).

Law 8742/1993 represented a step forward in reaffirming the character of public policy Social Assistance, carried out by an integrated set of actions initiated by society and the State. The changes introduced by Laws 12435/20011 and 12470/2011 will enable the expansion of the granting of CPB to a greater number of elderly and disabled.

The recent change in the jurisprudence of the Supreme Court will also enable the expansion of the granting of CPB, especially the possibility of consideration of other factors that may identify the applicant when in economic disadvantage. However, the absence of an objective criterion will bring difficulties for administrative granting of the benefit, further increasing judicial demand for this assistance provision vital for the guarantee of human dignity.

The possibility of differentiated contributions for some categories and the existence of a great number of benefits in the minimum wage demonstrate the close relationship between Social Assistance and Social Security in the strict sense. Despite the need for expansion of Social Security coverage to underserved populations, the CPB still plays an important complementary role. Hence, the importance of analyzing the close relationship between the Social Assistance and Social Security benefits, especially in view of the similarity of the events covered by these two subsystems that make up the tripod of Social Security in Brazil.

References

Balera W (2014) Sistema de seguridade social, 7. ed. LTr, São Paulo.

Botelho MC (2010) A pessoa com deficiência no ordenamento jurídico brasileiro. Revista da Advocacia-Geral da União, Brasília, DF 9(26):251–272, out./dez.

Cardoso OV, da Silva Júnior AJ (2013) O benefício de prestação continuada da assistência social e a nova definição de miserabilidade pelo Supremo Tribunal Federal. Revista de Previdência Social, São Paulo 37(393):669–677, ago.

Ministry of Social Security (2014) Boletim estatístico da Previdência Social. Brasília, DF, v. 19, 1, jan. Disponível em: <www.previdencia.gov.br>. Acesso em: 25 fev. 2014.

de Freitas FS (2012) O benefício de prestação continuada devido à pessoa portadora de deficiência física e a inclusão social. Revista de Previdência Social, São Paulo, 36(375):143–152, fev.

de Moraes RQ (2010) O benefício assistencial à luz da estrutura constitucional da seguridade social. Revista da Advocacia-Geral da União, Brasília, DF 9(23):277–294, jan./mar.

de Oliveira EL, Givisiez GHN (2011) La transition démographique au Brésil. Agir. Paris 47:143–155, set.

Martinez WN (2001) Princípios de direito previdenciário, 4. ed. LTr, São Paulo.

Moreno Filho IdS (2013) Loas: a possibilidade do múltiplo recebimento familiar. Revista de Previdência Social, São Paulo 37(397):1044–1059, dez.

Moro SF (2003) Questões controvertidas sobre o benefício da assistência social. In: da Rocha DM (Org.) Temas atuais de direito previdenciário e assistência social. Livraria do Advogado, Porto Alegre, pp 143–160.

Pereira LM (2011) A concretização dos direitos fundamentais do idoso no ambiente do neoconstitucionalismo: uma análise do benefício de prestação continuada. Revista Direitos e Garantias Fundamentais, Vitória 10:31–100, jul./dez.

Serau Junior MA (2009) Seguridade social como direito fundamental material. Juruá, Curitiba

Chapter 13
Immigrants' Right to Continued Benefit Payments: A Citizenship Question

Camila Bibiana Freitas Baraldi, Táli Pires de Almeida, and Tatiana Chang Waldman

Abstract The 20 years of the Organic Law on Social Assistance is an interesting moment to approach current increasingly important subjects in Brazilian society—as the international migrations and immigrants' rights—and its relation with this important document of guarantee of rights. In the social assistance benefits field, a subject that stands out in contemporary debates is the concession of Continued Benefit Payments (BPC) to the resident immigrant population in Brazil. The constant violations of this social right, illustrated by the request denials on the concession of social assistance benefit motivated by the solicitant nationality, despite the fulfillment of the legal requirements, will be the central concern of this article.

Keywords Brazil • Continued benefit payments • International migrations • Social assistance benefits • Social rights

13.1 Introduction

The 20 years of the Organic Law on Social Assistance is an interesting moment to approach current increasingly important subjects in Brazilian society—as the international migrations—and its relation with this important document of guarantee of rights. In the social assistance benefits field, a subject that stands out in contemporary debates is the concession of Continued Payment Benefit (CPB) to the resident immigrant population in Brazil. The constant violations of this social right, illustrated by the request denials on the concession of social assistance benefit motivated by the solicitant nationality, despite the fulfilment of the legal requirements, will be the central concern of this article.

The presence of immigrants in Brazil is historically a constituent part of Brazilian economic growth and social life. Today's newspapers highlight Latin American

C.B.F. Baraldi • T.P. de Almeida • T.C. Waldman (✉)
São Paulo, Brazil
e-mail: baraldi.camila@gmail.com; tali81pa@gmail.com; tatiana.waldman@gmail.com

M.A. Serau Junior, J.R. Caetano Costa (eds.), *Assistance Benefits in Brazil*,
DOI 10.1007/978-3-319-27046-3_13

immigrants working in conditions analogous to slavery, and the fact that many companies advocate a more flexible legislation to facilitate the entry of high-skilled workers arriving especially from Europe. Since the arrival of the Portuguese in our territory, the forced arrival of black Africans and the incentive policies to Europeans and Japanese immigrants in the nineteenth and twentieth centuries, thousands of immigrants marked our history and forged our social identity, our history, and our economic trajectory.

Most studies dealing with the issue of international migration observe the historical and structural factors related to the phenomenon. In general, countries that receive immigrants witness a period of expansion and economic growth followed by a need for manual labor, whether qualified or not. While that, most of the immigrants' countries of origin go through situations of economic crisis and unemployment. This scenario, in spite of that, is more complex and diverse. Contemporary international migration mobilize only 3 % of humanity, a rate that has remained stable over the last 50 years, even though it is a topic that increasingly gained attention from society and governments (CSA 2008; PNUD 2009). According to the Human Development Report (PNUD 2009), there are more than 200 million international migrants in the world and most of them moved between countries with similar levels of development.[1]

When observing the recent data regarding the number of foreigners in Brazil, as well as their trajectories, we will realize a more complex and diverse scenario than in the past: there are immigrants from the five continents and migration conditions are very diverse. There are people who seek refuge in Brazil due to political and religious persecution, and there are those who come in search of better conditions of life and work.[2]

Although immigrants suffer from stigmatization associated with poverty and vulnerability and are discriminated in public life, their main concern refers to the difficulties to ensure migratory regularization, which often affects their economic situation. The link between migration and poverty is not always accurate because looking for new possibilities of life requires an initial financial investment, besides a contact with migratory networks that passes through kinship relations and/or professional and academic experience (Grimson 2011). The poorest and most vulnerable groups do not always have such dynamism.

It is important to take into account the economic and social asymmetry between countries when analyzing the phenomenon of international migration. However,

[1] "Only 37 % of migration around the world is from developing to developed countries. Most migration occurs between countries with the same level of development: about 60 % of migrant move between developing countries or between developed countries (the remaining 3 % refer to traveling from developed to developing countries)" (PNUD 2009, p. 21). The large part of people's displacement, however, does not occur from one country to another, but within countries. The estimative is that the number of internal migrants is four times greater than the international migration (PNUD 2009).

[2] The social and economic conditions by which immigrants live in their home countries give us elements to affirm that migration is not always an option held in a context of total freedom, but the only possible alternative at some point in their lives.

recent studies (Grimson 2011; Portes 2011; Truzzi 2008) point out that more and more people migrate within networks. That is, although individual choices and economic aspects are important, international migration is a social process that involves multiple relationships.

When analyzing a migratory flow between countries, it is possible to find situations of migration by employment agencies recruiting workers willing to fill vacant jobs in recipient countries, or even bilateral or regional agreements between countries seeking to promote the circulation of workers and people in general. From a country that sent migrant workers abroad during the 1980s and 1990s, Brazil reversed this position and today is a country that receives immigrants.

Currently Brazil is experiencing a period of economic expansion capable of generating a high demand for workers with high qualification and expertise in areas such as engineering (civil, naval, transport) and oil extraction and refining, for example. Likewise, the country has offered jobs that Brazilian population has increasingly avoided, as sewing in the textile industry (mostly occupied by Bolivians, Paraguayans, and Peruvians immigrants) and professions linked to the sector services such as domestic employment, leisure, and tourism (stewards and waiters).

It is important to describe this scenario: if it is true that migration is a complex social process involving various social relationships and decisions, it is also clear that migration is deeply related to work—individuals wishing to sell their labor power in areas willing to receive—as well as the economic and social role that these actors, the immigrants, play.

In addition to all this, it is relevant to Latin Americans migrants' situation the integration context in South America through the Southern Common Market (MERCOSUL)[3] and the Union of South American Nations (UNASUL).[4] Human Development Report estimated that half of international migrants move within the same region of origin and around 40 % move to neighboring countries (PNUD 2009). The international migration of Latin American workers towards the metropolitan areas of Brazil, such as São Paulo and Rio de Janeiro, is indeed a growing phenomenon (Baeninger 2012). However, the irregular migration status of many people—despite the possibility opened by the Mercosul regulation—complicates the task of measuring the number of immigrants due to the lack of this flow documentation and registration.

[3] There are agreements on the issue of migration signed within Mercosul: the *Agreements on Residence for Nationals of Member States of Mercosul, Bolivia, Chile, Peru, Colombia and Ecuador*, in effect since 2009 and promulgated in Brazil through Decrees No. 6,964/2009 and 6,975/2009. These agreements favor the immigrants from signatory countries to regularize their immigration status in a simple manner, without employment contract requirements or qualifications.

[4] The Constitutive Treaty of Unasul, signed in Brasilia on May 23, in 2008, and promulgated by Decree No. 7,667/2012, in its Article 3 refers to the construction of a South American citizenship as one of its specific objectives: "i) to consolidate South American identity recognizing the rights of nationals of a member State resident in any other member State, with the aim of attaining a South American citizenship."

Even regarding registered immigrants in Brazil, it is difficult to find data on their number and their profile. The main sources of information on the number of foreign residents in Brazil are the Federal Police and the Department of Foreigners/SNJ, linked to the Ministry of Justice.[5] The major newspapers—which obtain information directly from government authorities[6]—and the web page of the Ministry of Justice[7] published the latest figures about the immigrant presence in Brazil. According to these data, the number of foreign residents regularly in Brazil is about one million and 500 thousand, which represents less than 1 % of the population.

The migration of Latin Americans, however, is already somewhat consolidated (Silva 1995; de Freitas 2010). The flow of Bolivians to the city of São Paulo, for example, dates back to the 1950s. The novelty in this arrival of Bolivians, Paraguayans, and Peruvians in Brazil is their large number and the niche of the labor market opened to them: the clothing and household employment industry.[8]

The changes that occurred in the textile industry in Brazil since the late 1980s are the result of an intense process of productive restructuration. The attempt to streamline the costs related to labor payment in the sewing sector led to the choice of outsourcing production and the flexibilization of labor relations. Many small factories with poor working conditions and security have been holding sewing as a job step.

Job search and desire for social mobility permeate the entry of Latin American immigrants in the textile industry. In turn, the solidarity networks are essential for the establishment of immigrants in the destination country, since they are the alternatives able to offer the necessary acceptance and immediate work. In many cases, immigrants start as tailors, collect money and after that buy their first sewing machine looking forward to have their own workshop and employees. Examples like these make immigrants support more than 10 h of daily work (Silva 1995; Almeida 2013).

Ethnographic researches (Silva 1995, 2008; Almeida 2013) reveal that, in the destination country, despite reported bureaucratic difficulties, the immigrant seeks its migratory regularization and compliance with local legislation. As well, the immigrants work to ensure sufficient economic gains to pay their taxes and still hope for a prosperous future.

[5] The data, whose source is the Department of Foreigners of the Ministry of Justice, are administrative records. The purpose of this compilation is to control residence permits and the compliance of legal provisions at national level. These records do not provide information to enable analysis of the entire population present in the territory, especially on those in irregular migratory situation. In addition, the limitation of access to this information only allowed finding numbers for certain countries in South America.

[6] For example: O Globo. O sonho brasileiro. 30 out 2011, Caderno de Economia, p. 35; and Folha De São Paulo. Brasil recebe 57 % mais mão de obra estrangeira. 05 fev 2012. Available in: http://www1.folha.uol.com.br/mercado/1044123-brasil-recebe-57-mais-mao-de-obra-estrangeira.shtm

[7] See: http://portal.mj.gov.br/main.asp?View={A5F550A5-5425-49CE-8E88-E104614AB866}&BrowserType=NN&LangID=pt-br&params=itemID%3D{BA915BD3-AC38-4F6C-81A1-AC4AF88BE2D0}%3B&UIPartUID={2218FAF9-5230-431C-A9E3-E780D3E67DFE}.

[8] In February 2013, the number of South American foreigners who had temporary stay or permanent residency amounted to: 48,252 Argentines, 76,460 Bolivians, 27,904 Chileans, 9661 Colombians, 21,189 Paraguayans, 21,493 Peruvians, and 32,359 Uruguayans. Source: National System of Foreigners Registration—SINCRE, Department of Foreign Affairs—Ministry of Justice.

State actors involved in the international migration process are plural: countries of origin, transit, and destination. Therefore, the actors share the responsibility and there are multiple dimensions in terms of policy: access to the labor market, education, health, social security, and human rights. Given the centrality of work for immigrants, policies of access to work, employment, and income are critical in the design of migration policies that seek to ensure decent conditions of life and work for immigrants, in full respect for human rights.

Against reducing the immigrants to a workforce, and recognizing them as a human being who possesses identity and culture, we must reaffirm that even when they are in an irregular migration status, or in a work situation that does not involve legal labor claims, they still workers (Ferreira 2011). According to Sayad:

> The authorized stay of immigrants is entirely subject to work, the only reason of being that is recognized [...] It was the work that made "born" the immigrant, that made he exists, and when work ends, so "die" the immigrant. Work decrees the immigrant denial and turns him into a non-being. This work, which affects the whole life of an immigrant, is not any work, is not anywhere; it is the work that the "labor market for immigrants" assign to the immigrant as well as the place assigned to him: work for immigrants who require immigrants; immigrant to work that become thus work for immigrants (Sayad 1998).

Either in search of refuge, of work or of better living conditions, through established migratory networks or not, international migration is a fact and its subjects, men and women, require that their demands and rights are respected and guaranteed regardless of the place on the planet where they are and regardless of their authorization to exist.

13.2 The Continued Payment Benefit (CPB) and Its Granted to Immigrants

Brazilian Federal Constitution (CF) of 1988, which is still in effect today, declared the Continued Benefit Payments (BPC) an individual benefit, not lifetime and non-transferable:

> Article 203: *Social assistance shall be rendered to whomever may need it,* regardless of contribution to social security and shall have as objectives:
>
> *V - The guarantee of a monthly benefit of one minimum salary to disabled person and to the elderly who prove their incapability of providing for their own support or having it provided for by their families, as set forth by law* [emphasis added].

The Organic Law of Social Assistance (LOAS), Law No. 8,742, of 7 December, 1993, in its Chapter IV (Benefits, Services, Programs and Projects of Social Assistance), Section I (Continued Benefit Payments), established[9]:

> Article 20. *The Continued Benefit Payments is the guarantee of one minimum monthly salary to the person with disability or elderly with 65 (sixty-five) years or more, proving to have no means to provide it for their own support or to have it provided by their family*

[9] The LOAS has changed in some devices by Law No. 9,720/1998, Law No. 12,435/2011 and Law No. 12,470/2011.

§ 1. For the purposes of the provisions in the caput, family is the applicant, the spouse or partner, parents and, in the absence of one, the stepmother or stepfather, unmarried siblings, unmarried children and stepchildren and minors protected, provided living under the same roof.
§ 2. For the purpose of granting this benefit, disabled person is considered one that has long-term physical, mental, intellectual or sensory impairments which in interaction with various barriers may hinder their full and effective participation in society on an equal basis with others.
§ 3. It is considered incapable of providing the maintenance of a person with disability or an elderly, a family whose monthly income per capita is less than ¼ (one quarter) of the minimum salary.
§ 4. The benefit that this article refers to may not be accumulated by the beneficiary with any other benefit from the social security field or from any other regimen, except for those of medical assistance and special indemnities allowance.
§ 5. The situation of being confined in long-term institutions does not prejudice the right of an elderly or a person with disability to the benefit.
§ 6. The benefit concession shall be subject to the assessment of disability and to the degree of impediment mentioned in § 2. Medical experts and social workers of the National Institute of Social Security – INSS – shall carry out medical and social assessment.
§ 7. In case no services exist in the municipality where the beneficiary has his residence, it is assured, as provided in regulations, his referral to the next county having such services.
§ 8. The monthly family income referred to in § 3 shall be declared by the applicant or his legal representative, being subject to the other procedures on the regulation for the request approval.
§ 9. The remuneration of the disabled person as an apprentice will not be considered for purposes of the calculation referred to in § 3 of this article.
§ 10. It is considered long-term impediment for the purposes of § 2 of this article, the one that takes effect for a minimum period of two (2) years.

The benefit was also regulated by Decree No. 6,214 of September 26, 2007,[10] which in its Article 7 brings, inappropriately, as a requirement to grant the benefit to have Brazilian nationality (born or naturalized), excluding all immigrants from the list of potential beneficiaries. Such a device was the main agent of the debate we want to achieve through this article:

Article 7: *Brazilian natural-born or naturalized will receive the Continued Benefit Payments*, provided domicile and residence in Brazil and all the other criteria set out in this Regulation [emphasis added].

Governed by the principle of "equal rights to access to care without discrimination of any kind" (Article 4, IV, LOAS), one of the objectives of social assistance is therefore to ensure the BPC (Article 2, I, "e" LOAS). As already mentioned, the BPC will be granted to whomever may need it, without any discrimination on constitutional and infra-constitutional legal text between nationals and foreigners (Article 203, V, CF; Article 20, LOAS.).

If in certain devices LOAS alludes to citizen expression—as "Social assistance, citizen's right and duty of the State […]." (Article 1, LOAS), or with respect to the principles governing the social assistance—as "respect for the dignity of the citizen,

[10] Decree No. 6,214/2007 revoked the former Decree 1,744/1995 and has undergone some changes from Decree No. 6,564/2008 and No. 7,617/2011.

his autonomy and his right to benefits and quality services, as well as family and community, forbidden any vexatious evidence of necessity" (Article 4, III, LOAS.), it does not exclude foreign citizenship. In other words, it does not distinguish between national citizen and immigrant citizen, as we will see throughout this article.[11]

The Federal Constitution itself included social security, and therefore health, welfare, and social assistance in the title VIII (Social Order), which aims the welfare and social justice (Article 193, CF). Moreover, it is incumbent upon the Government to organize social security taking as a guideline the universality of coverage and service (Article 194, sole paragraph, I, CF).

The universality of coverage and service is one of the so-called constitutional principles of social security, which indicates that social protection should achieve all events to which the repair is imperative to bring livelihood for those who need it (de Castro and Lazzari 2008). In this sense, we emphasize, once again, the Federal Constitution does not provide a distinction between nationals and foreigners.

The Federal Public Prosecution has already presented in court this understanding[12] when pointed a question about "how to ensure the principle of universality excluding foreign resident in the country to social assistance right?". Moreover: "what would be the reason for the Defendants [Union and INSS] to depart their national from the misery situation and do not guarantee the same right to foreign resident in the country?". "Do the Defendants perceive the right to social assistance as a privilege and not a State duty for all individuals residing in it?".

There is no support or plausible justification to give the benefit solely to nationals, as did the Decree 6,214/2007 (Article 7). As shown, the exclusion of immigrants from a fundamental human right is inconsistent with national law. Could a decree regulating the benefit lower its potential beneficiaries constitutionally established by nationality discrimination criteria?

Some people say so. For example, this is the position taken by the Ministry of Social Development and Fight against Hunger (MDS). The MDS is competent to implement, coordinate, regulate, finance, monitor, and evaluate the provision of the benefit, conducted through the National Secretariat of Social Assistance (SNAS), and the National Institute of Social Security (INSS), which is responsible for MDS operation.

The Ministry of Social Development and Fight against Hunger, in the Circular Letter No. 02/2014—SENARC/MDS and SNAS/MDS, 11 of February, 2014, brings clarification on the issue of the inclusion of foreigners in the Single Registry of Social Benefits and in the access to *Bolsa Família* Program. The same Circular

[11] On the other hand, Marques (2012, p. 10) advocates that "just assuming that assistance was only 'citizens' right' [Article 1, LOAS], and citizen is a born or naturalized Brazilian, Decree no. 1,744/95 explicit left the impossibility of the foreigner who was not naturalized get the benefit [BPC]. In this direction, accordingly to the Article 4 of the mentioned Decree [...] this same provision remains in the existing Decree that regulates the LOAS (Decree No. 6,214/07)." Such an interpretation, in our view, implies detract from the essence of the right at issue.

[12] Civil Action No. 0021229-88.2004.4.03.6100 dealing with the BPC for foreigners not naturalized and resident in Brazil.

Letter mentions the BPC and clarifies that this is a right expressly reserved to Brazilian citizens based on Article 7 of Decree No. 6,214/2007. With regard to *Bolsa Família* Program access, the same office states that there would be no impediment due to foreign nationality, observed the legal criteria.

Beyond this, the National Institute of Social Security through the INSS Resolution/PR No. 435, 18 of March, 1997 (Official Federal Gazette of 04/04/97),[13] established standards and procedures for BPC operation, and likewise adopted limited access to BPC to native and naturalized Brazilians.

Faced with a scenario where the Ministry of Social Development and Fight against Hunger and the National Institute of Social Security deny access to immigrants to the BPC, the debate on this right went to court.

The Federal Public Prosecution, through the Regional Attorney for Citizens' Rights, filed a civil action (No. 0021229-88.2004.4.03.6100) with a request for preliminary injunction against the Federal Government and the National Institute of Social Security. It attempted to recognize the right to BPC referred to in section V of the Federal Constitution, Article 203, for foreigners not naturalized residents in Brazil.

According to the Federal Public Prosecution, the INSS argued[14] that requests made by foreigners should fill beyond the ordinary requirements for granting the BPC, presenting extraordinary requirements, namely: be naturalized and resident in Brazil and not be supported by the social security system of their country of origin. Such a requirement brought by Decree No. 1,744/95, and today by Decree No. 6,214/2007, violates the Federal Constitution, which delegates to the ordinary legislator the regulation of Article 203, section V, who must comply constitutional limits and purposes, as did the aforementioned decrees. Furthermore, the Federal Public Prosecution reminds us in the petition that the decrees are normative instruments by which executive power issue to enforce compliance with the law.

Finally, Public Civil Action purpose is to protect all the immigrants who have the *animus* to stay in the country, having joined regularly in Brazil or, even those who have settled without documents and have regularized their situation, including here all foreigners who grant permanent residency in Brazil, as well as refugees. Federal Public Prosecution also questions "why we should demand from foreign residents in the country the duties to which we subject our nationals, denying them, on the other hand, the minimum rights guaranteed by the Constitution?". The public civil action is pending decision by the TRF/3rd Region.

Therefore, on granting the BPC to a more specific group, the refugees, the Federal Public Prosecution, through the Regional Attorney for Citizens' Rights,

---

[13] Resolution INSS/PR No. 435, of March 18, 1997, revoked the INSS Resolution/PR No. 324 of December 15, 1995.

[14] Federal Public Prosecution heard the INSS—Administrative Procedure No 1.34.001.000473/2003-14-, in order to ascertain federal government's conduct, through the INSS, in the BPC appreciation of application when formulated by foreigners—reaping manifestation from the General Coordination of Benefits and its executive management in São Paulo (Center, East, West, South, and North) to request information about the requirements for granting the assistance benefit.

filed a Public Civil Action No. 0023528-28.2010.4.03.6100, against the National Social Security Institute. Its object was to impose the obligation to pay the BPC to elderly Palestinian refugees in São Paulo. The action went extinct without resolution of merit, understanding the prosecutor's illegitimacy to defend the individual interests in discussion.

In addition to the Public Civil Actions, there are also a significant number of individual actions, and it seems the case law has been favorable to the possibility of granting the benefit to immigrants, provided the legal requirements are met:

> ASSISTANCIAL AND CONSTITUTIONAL. TORT LEGAL. ARTICLE 557, § 1 OF THE CPC. SOCIAL ASSISTANCE BENEFIT. ARTICLE 203, V, OF THE CF. FOREIGN RESIDENT IN THE COUNTRY. CONDITIONS OF EQUALITY. ARTICLE 5 OF THE FEDERAL CONSTITUTION. POSSIBILITY. LE GAL REQUIREMENTS FULFILLED. 1. The following requirements are necessary for the granting of social assistance benefits (LOAS): 1) to have disabilities or to be elderly with 65 (sixty-five) years or more (Article 34 of the Elderly Statute. - Law No 10,741 of 01.10.2003); 2) to have no means of subsistence or have it provided by the family, whose per capita monthly income is less than ¼ of the minimum wage (Article 203, V, of the Federal Constitution. Article 20, § 3, and Article 38 of Law No. 8,742 of 07.12.1993). 2. *Foreigners should not have any obstacle to enjoy the benefits provided by social security, fulfilling of the legal requirements.* The caput of Article 5 of the Federal Constitution ensures foreign resident in the country the enjoyment of individual rights and guarantees, on equal terms with the national. 3. Social care is a fundamental right therefore foreigners residing in the country and fulfilling the requirements should also be supported by social assistance benefit due to the universality of this right. 4. Meeting the legal requirements for the grant of the benefit. 5. Legal tort denying the appeal. (AC 00120721920134039999, FEDERAL CHIEF JUDGE FAUSTO DE SANCTIS, TRF3 - SEVENTH CLASS, e-DJF3 Judicial 1 DATE: 18/09/2013, REPUBLICATION) [emphasis added].

> SOCIAL SECURITY. TORT. SOCIAL ASSISTANCE. FOREIGN RESIDENT IN THE COUNTRY. POSSIBILITY. CONDITIONS OF EQUALITY AS PROVIDED FOR IN ARTICLE 5 OF THE FEDERAL CONSTITUTION. PERSON WITH LOW INSTRUCTION OR HYPOSUFFICIENT. OLD AGE. IMPLEMENTATION OF THE REQUIREMENTS. I - Social assistance is paid to children with disabilities and the elderly with 65 (sixty-five) years or more that prove to not have means to provide their own subsistence or having it provided by their family (Federal Constitution, Article 203, V, Law No. 8,742 / 93, Law No. 9,720 / 98 and Law No. 10,741/03, art. 34). II - *The fact that the plaintiff party has a foreign condition does not constitute obstacle for granting the benefit, fulfilling the legal requirements, since the Federal Constitution does not promote the distinction between foreign resident in the country and Brazilians. Continued Benefit Payments are granted "to those who need it," there is no restriction on the concession to foreign resident in the country.* III - In addition, Article 5 of the Federal Constitution guarantees to foreign resident in the country the enjoyment of individual rights and guarantees on equal condition with the national. IV - *It should be noted that, although the general repercussion is recognized and the issue is still under review in the Supreme Court (RE 587,970), it is a dominant position in this Court granting the benefit to foreigners, being fully applicable the authorized rule of Article 557 of the Civil Procedure Code.* V - Legal tort denying the appeal. (AC 00002189220074036004, FEDERAL CHIEF JUDGE WALTER DO AMARAL, TRF3 - TENTH CLASS, e-DJF3 Judicial 1 DATE: 10/10/2012, REPUBLICATION) [emphasis added].

One of these individual actions of social benefit perception gave rise to the extraordinary appeal No. 587,970. This appeal deals with the possibility of granting assistance benefit to the immigrant domiciled in Brazil, provided in Article 203, section V, and had its general repercussion recognized by the Supreme Court:

> SOCIAL ASSISTANCE - MINIMUM WAGE GUARANTEE – FOREIGN RESIDENT IN THE COUNTRY – RECOGNIZED RIGHT – It has general repercussion the controversy over the possibility of granting foreign residents in the country the social benefit provided for in Article 203, section V of the Federal Constitution. (RE 587,970 RG, Reporter: Minister MARCO AURÉLIO, judged on 25/06/2009, DJE-186 DIVULGED 01-10-2009 PUBLISHED 02-10-2009 EMENTE VOL-02376-04 PP-00 742).

Supreme Court did not give yet the final word about the Extraordinary Appeal No. 587,970, but the general repercussion of the controversy debated now indicates the importance of the issue and generates expectations.

We understand that the criteria of nationality cannot be an excluding factor when it comes to social rights such as "assistance to the destitute" as stated by Federal Constitution of 1988 (Article 6, CF). According to da Silva (2004), the fundamental principle is that foreign residents in the country are entitled to the same rights and have the same duties of Brazilians, and the only accepted limitations are the ones expressly established in the Federal Constitution:

> The Constitution guarantees to foreign residents in the country inviolable right to life, liberty, equality, security and property as far as the Brazilians (Article 5, caput, CF). It does not say here that it ensures social rights, but in fact, it does not restrict the enjoyment of these only to Brazilian [...] in this way, Article 5 is not good, because it covers less than the Federal Constitution gives (Silva 2004).

Even the Statute of Foreigner (Law No. 6,815/1980) states in Article 95 that foreign resident in the country is the holder of all rights acknowledge to Brazilians, under the Constitution and laws.

Therefore, this discussion points out that understanding the concept of citizenship is a central issue. Miserability and the lack of a threshold necessary for dignified survival and its consequences are not exclusive to national or foreign resident in a State. Similarly, social benefits that aim to mitigate such a state of deprivation cannot adopt discriminatory criteria of nationality.

13.3 Citizenship and International Migration

The modern international system appropriated national discourse to create the necessary legitimacy to the governments of the States outlined at the end of the eighteenth century. Since the Peace of Westphalia in 1648, a system of sovereign and independent States was established, but nationalism was the social amalgam to legitimize areas of political unity, which, in fact, did not have emotional historical tightened links, as the modern history wanted us to believe.

This homogenization process led to the emergence of nations and allowed the creation of a people who would compose the theoretical elements of the State: defined territory, people, and self-government. Sovereignty planted its roots in this scenario and developed itself during the modern period. Basic corollaries of sovereignty concept were, externally, independence in the presence of its peers and, internally, self-government over its territory.

For many years, this autonomy presented itself as an unlimited power of the rulers over the lives of their subjects. Only from liberal revolutions, this state of affairs has changed, and the ruled succeeded in establishing limits to the exercise of government. This route corresponds to the affirmation of human rights in the domestic sphere (Bobbio 2004). The dualism between rulers and ruled, defining the concrete contours of power, is therefore central to discuss citizenship. The modern sense of citizenship as ownership of subjective rights has the State and the legal centralization as assumptions. The national State assumes the prerogative of granting such legal position.

Among all the problems posed by this new political form, the modern State, one of the major was the identification of citizens to the State and the ruling system. In the Middle Ages, intermediate bodies such as religion, social hierarchy, and corporations ensured this identification (Hobsbawn 1990).

The original revolutionary–popular idea of patriotism, according to Hobsbawn (1990), was state-based rather than a nationalist idea. Nationalism rarely reflects a long-term tradition or a coherent way of life. Nor is it necessarily founded on a common language or ethnicity. All these are more often the result of sovereignty than its reason: they are social artifacts. French Revolution appealed to this identity between the State and the people, asserting popular sovereignty as the principle of the State's legitimacy. Thus, the State confronted nationalism as a political force separated from it. Nevertheless, at some point, nationalism was appropriated as a useful tool in the search for social cohesion, creating strategies for an imaginary community by building symbols and common myths.

Hobsbawn (1990) makes a distinction between state patriotism and nationalism proper. The state patriotism had an inclusive trend—the citizen was the one who decided to adopt the homeland—while nationalism had an excluding trend, based on language, ethnicity, among other criteria. The risk of excluding part of the population did not cause immediate problems since the very process of modernization encouraged homogenization and assimilation of minority groups, particularly the establishment of a national language.

The linkage of citizenship to nationality determined that only individuals belonging to the nation, this "imagined community" (Anderson 2008), would be the holders of the rights that were being progressively incorporated as citizenship rights.

However, this is clearly only the modern conception of citizenship:

> Such simplification by which citizenship is nothing but the legal status of whoever is part of a State is meaningless. Sovereignty can only be understood as indivisible in the fullness of absolute State […] (Quaglioni 2004, p. 83).

Migration is a constitutive part of human experience as well as part of this formation process of most political communities we now call State (Moulin 2011). From a conceptual point of view, international migration is inexorably linked to the idea of nation States, materialized through crossing the political State borders. For this reason, the cultural, economic, political, and legal perception, as well as the objective conditions of mobility, have undergone great changes over time, particularly from the late twentieth century. The political history of migration—as well as the political history of citizenship—is a series of discontinuous emergencies: it is a history of struggles for recognition (Boubeker 2007), which continues to be told.

The classic Marshall's theory of citizenship describes a logical order of expansion to those rights, which historically occurred in England, the country where he lived: civil, political, and social rights. In Brazil, however, it was another story. Since independence, in 1822, free men with certain income became political rights holders (de Carvalho 2011). Many Brazilians, at the same time, still did not have the guarantee of their civil rights: the slaves, for example, only acquired civil rights after the slavery abolition in 1888. Moreover, women were granted the right to vote only in 1932.[15] Labor and social rights, in turn, go back to 1930s, but more than the result of citizen demands—political rights holders, these rights emerged as State benefits. Gradually, Brazilian constitutions and national legal system incorporated the principle of equal rights as a whole. In this process, the Federal Constitution of 1988 consecrated this principle, including foreigners, as provided for in Article 5, but the struggle for its realization is permanent.

Interestingly, human rights affirmation is placed against all forms of discrimination that may reduce the rights. The differentiation between nationals and foreigners, however, still endures, despite the new interpretations of citizenship concept that gained space in reality and literature. What migrations bring up is exactly the exclusive nature that is at the origin of modern citizenship concept.

Given there is no justifiable reason for this differentiation, some theorists argue that the residence is the most appropriate criteria for ownership of citizenship rights. Still others go further and say that citizenship is beyond the legal limits established for it. Thus, the legal systems do not recognize the resident immigrants, but they practice daily acts of citizenship, in other words, resident immigrants act as citizens.

Therefore, it is important to rescue the earlier discussion about the context in which migratory movements occur. The labor movement is central to the capitalist system in general, and especially to its most recent presentation, neoliberalism (Mezzadra 2006), which relies on migrant labor.

The dynamics of neoliberal capitalism structure the displacement of people by transforming production means and capital accumulation, and creating global capital markets, commodities and precarious work (subject to control) that meets the demands of flexibility and cost reduction (Glick-Schiller 2009; Hewinson and Kallerberg 2012).

[15] Decree No. 21,076 of 02/24/1932, signed by President Getúlio Vargas.

The behavior and the struggles of immigrants, however, the subjective side of migration, are concrete demands of the right to mobility that force the boundaries of citizenship (Mezzadra 2006). Mobility is a key factor in the development of work, citizenship and forms of life today. Migration is a movement of people, a social movement, which is autonomous in relation to the migration policies built exclusively from the interests of States and their labor markets.

In this sense, citizenship is a site of struggle. Migration is a concrete search, an exercise of freedom, with all the difficulties and ambiguities of economic, political, legal, and social origin, which a fight presupposes. Immigrants' social behaviors expressed themselves as rights claims that often exceed structurally the grammar and the language of law. The law and the structural design of citizenship may recognize more or less the immigrants, but immigrants always propose to renew the concepts of freedom and equality (Mezzadra 2006).

Solidarity is one of the guiding principles of social security and to invoke it is necessary to remember that the economic, social, and political structure that compels immigrants to make the decision to immigrate is international. Globalization intensifies the relations between nation-States making them all "united" in the construction of this scenario, in the production of wealth and world poverty, by the division of land in areas of interest and exploration, by the co-presence of openness and economic protectionism, etc. (Mezzadra 2006).

To escape from local conditions that hinder the development of life is a political gesture, although it is not a completely conscious gesture. This gesture questions the limits of the legal division of the world into nation-States and national citizenship imposed on people. It questions the consolidated configurations borders not only in economic and political terms but also in terms of identity and daily life (Mezzadra 2006).

It is commonplace to say that the free movement of goods and especially capital gained strength with globalization while the movement of people is increasingly restricted. The factual description is correct, but it only illustrates the contradictions and the selectivity in the process of globalization, besides the already mentioned fact that migration and citizenship are areas of struggle for freedom. The unpredictability, due to the subjectivity that characterizes these movements today, is what bothers States and market because they would like to keep control on the labor movement (Mezzadra 2006).

Mobility and porous borders result from the ability of migratory movements to produce their own spaces (transnational), these movements are not limited to accept the political geography built around the sovereign rule of the nation-States (Mezzadra 2006). To recognize the transnational nature of migration does not mean to deny the significant role of national States, but to realize its transformation (Vertovec 2004). National States policies and laws are what guarantee rights and distribute benefits in a predominant way nowadays (Glick-Schiller 2009). The problem is in the disparity of logical migration policies, which follow a national logic, and the forces that determine and shape the transnational movements (Castles 2004). Thus, if guided by a methodological nationalism, politics disregard what happens in the transnational system in which nation-States are not only included but also helped to shape it (Glick-Schiller 2009).

Several sociological studies have already documented the growing transnationalism in the sense that immigrants live their lives in and across multiple nation States borders (Glick-Schiller 2009). Politically, however, the continuity of a methodological nationalism which assigns State borders as social boundaries (Vertovec 2004), continues to treat the immigrant as a threat. Furthermore, it ignores the social and cultural divisions that exist between own nationals within its borders (Glick-Schiller 2009).

Immigrant movements are not mere responses to social and economic problems of immigrants, but a creative force within the social, economic, and cultural structures (Mezzadra 2013). Continuing Marshall's theory of citizenship, and briefly, citizenship is dynamic:

> Citizenship sets its perspective as one space at the same time objective (institutional and sovereign) and subjective (with movement and action), where politics finds each time, at historically certain circumstances, the very unstable set of its representation (Mezzadra 2006, p. 22).

Citizenship is in crisis and it is not because of migration, but because work and social protection net attached to it are in crisis (in Brazil the welfare state was never reached). Migration only fit into this scenario and bring light to the problem (Mezzadra 2006).

The growing labor precariousness and the dispossession of rights are realities for everyone. Putting the discussion as it was a problem of immigrants serves only to those who want to put a veil over these processes, allowing them to move more easily. While all argue that the problem is the presence of immigrants and that the solution would be to bar them or to remove them, the exploitation and the deregulation of labor are developed for immigrants—who will continue to enter in the country—and Brazilians. All of these with the encouragement of our labor market and the connivance of our legal system.

To implement administrative logic in constitutional matters, or rights, which is widely accepted when referred to foreigners, legally sanction the breaking of citizenship universalism. It only strengthens the deterioration of rights inclusive among the nationals. Immigrant exclusion, therefore, sanctions the end of the whole historical cycle of expansion of modern citizenship (Mezzadra 2006).

This view justifies restrictive policies and selective policies that create different categories of immigrants.[16] To enforce the admission criteria, this selectivity is usually related to a strong securitization of borders. There are countries, like the USA, that invest hard in this area, but with low efficacy in preventing the entry of immigrants outside the established schemes. The most visible result of these differentiation mechanisms is the violation of immigrants' human rights. A recent report about the deaths at the border between Mexico and the USA demonstrates that they increased significantly with the securitization of borders since 1990 (The Binational Migration Institute 2013).

---

[16] The idea of closed borders, fortresses, does not serve to explain much of the current migration policies, because for some the borders are open and there are incentives (even though there are a number of conditions that must be met and respected), for others not. In many of these differentiations reproduce racial and colonial hierarchies, see (Rigo 2011).

Another result from the creation of many categories of immigrants and the creation of a hierarchy between ideals and unwanted immigrants is the irregularity, since it is impossible to prevent completely the displacement. Irregular immigrants are among the most exploited workers in the labor market because of their vulnerability not only economic but also social and legal.

Admission rules vary considerably depending on the economic and political developments. Thus, irregularity is not a condition linked to a substantive immigrant situation. This condition results, rather, from the technical and political States' decisions that consider the immigrants only as objects of their policies, labor for their market and not as subjects with wishes and rights.

In this sense, all residents need an equal treatment. Democracy cannot tolerate part of its population deprived of rights. As we have seen, the bonds between individuals and States are not exclusive. Therefore, there is no need to talk about reciprocity since immigrants also have links with their country of destination, links built from their residence in that territory. It is not justifiable to apply administrative differences (regular or irregular entry) to constitutional issues as the fundamental rights.

13.4 Final Considerations

Social assistance, unlike social security, is not contributory. The immigrants living in the country are part of Brazilian society, they pay their taxes and develop their daily life in the country. Therefore, we must understand that immigrants establishes ties also of solidarity with Brazilian society, underlying the granting of welfare benefits.

In this sense, there is no need to talk about reciprocity and subsidiarity in relation to the country of origin. Transnationalism characterizes the reality of these people and results in a mosaic of links that cannot be hierarchical. Migration policies that consider only the interests of States and the reciprocity between countries for granting welfare benefits are challenged by the transnational migration and the respect of immigrants' choices.

It is misleading to invoke bilateral and multilateral social security agreements as examples of reciprocal practice since these agreements point to regulate the co-financing of contributory social security benefits when these contributions are made to more than one country. Another totally different situation are the social benefits not based on contributions, as is the case of BPC.

With respect to other social rights, the interpretation shows up today in favor for their guarantee to all foreigners in the country, even if sometimes there are still some violations in their daily exercise, what make us reaffirm that the struggle for the realization of these rights is permanent. Health, for example, as well as social assistance, is included in social security and is expressly declared a universal right and duty of the State, with the guideline of an universal and equal access to actions and services for its promotion, protection, and recovery (Article 196, CF). Today in Brazil, both Brazilian and foreigner—in regular or irregular immigration status—have this guaranteed access.[17]

[17] About migratory movements under the perspective of the right to health, see Waldman (2011).

Regarding the right to education, although widely guaranteed in our legal system and now understood as a right which guarantee must necessarily be universal, it has suffered serious violations. These violations were due to devices with limitations not received by the Federal Constitution of 1988 (Articles 48 and 97 of the Foreigner Statute—Law No. 6,815/80),[18] similar by its consequences and restrictions to the device now debated (Article 7, Decree No. 6,214/2007).

Finally, we note the great contribution and the relevance of the debate on the BPC. In other words, its enforcement to domestic and foreign residents in Brazil and the forthcoming decision by the Supreme Court on the issue, with repercussions overall, for the provision of decent living conditions for immigrants in the State that welcomed them.

References

Almeida TP (2013) As imigrantes sul-americanas em São Paulo: o trabalho feminino na construção de trajetórias transnacionais. Dissertação de Mestrado, PROLAM-USP

Anderson B (2008) Comunidades Imaginadas. Reflexões sobre a origem e a difusão do nacionalismo (trans: Bottman D). Companhia das Letras, São Paulo

Baeninger R (2012) O Brasil na rota das migrações latino-americanas. In: Baeninger R (ed) Imigração Boliviana no Brasil. Núcleo de Estudos de População—NEPO/Unicamp; FAPESP; CNPQ; UNFPA, Campinas, pp 9–18

Bobbio N (2004). A era dos direitos (trans: Carlos Nelson Coutinho). Nova ed. Elsevier, Rio de Janeiro

Boubeker A (2007). L'héritage de l'immigration postcoloniale comme expérience vécue. Amnis (online) – Revue de civilisation contemporaine Europes/Amériques, 7

Castles S (2004) Why migration policies fail. Ethnic Racial Studies 27(2):205–227

Confederación Sindical de Trabajadores/as de las Americas (CSA) (2008) Las Migraciones Internacionales en las Américas. Confederación Sindical de Trabajadores y Trabajadoras de las Américas, São Paulo

da Silva JA (2004) Curso de Direito Constitucional Positivo, 23rd edn. Malheiros, São Paulo

de Carvalho JM (2011) Cidadania no Brasil: o longo caminho, 14ª Ed. Civilização brasileira, Rio de Janeiro

de Castro CAP, Lazzari JB (2008) Manual de Direito Previdenciário. Conceito Editorial, Florianópolis

de Freitas PT (2010) Imigração e Trabalho: Determinantes históricas da formação de um circuito de subcontratação de imigrantes bolivianos para o trabalho em oficinas de costura na cidade de São Paulo. Trabalho apresentando no XVII Encontro Nacional de Estudos Populacionais, ABEP

Ferreira CER (2011) O imigrante como um subversivo prático-político, possibilidade de um "novo mundo" – o projeto universal-cosmopolita dos Direitos Humanos em contraposição à Soberania territorial. Revista Emancipação, Ponta Grossa 11(2):253–266

Glick-Schiller N (2009) A global perspective on transnational migration: theorizing migration without methodological nationalism. In: COMPAS Working paper series no 67, University of Oxford

Grimson A (2011) Doce equívocos sobre las migraciones. In Latinoamericanos en tránsito: Migración, mitos y fronteras. Revista Nueva Sociedad 233:34–43

[18] On the question of the fight for the education access to immigrants in the State of São Paulo, see Waldman (2012).

Hewinson K, Kallerberg AL (2012) Precarious work and flexibilization in south and Southeast Asia. Am Behav Sci 57(4):507–530

Hobsbawn EJ (1990) Nações e nacionalismo desde 1780. Programa, mito e realidade. 1990. Paz e Terra, Rio de Janeiro

Marques CGM (2012) O Direito do estrangeiro residente no país ao Benefício Assistencial de Prestação Continuada. Revista Internacional de Direito e Cidadania 12:09–18

Mezzadra S (2006) *Diritto di Fuga*. Migrazioni, cittadinanza, globalizzazione. Ombre Corte, Verona

Mezzadra S (2013) *Movimenti indisciplinati*. Migrazioni, migranti e discipline scientifiche. Ombre Corte, Verona

Moulin C (2011) Eppur si muove: mobilidade humana, cidadania e globalização. Contexto Internacional 33(1): 9–17

Portes A (2011) Migración y desarrollo: un intento de conciliar perspectivas opuestas. In Latinoamericanos en tránsito: Migración, mitos y fronteras. Revista Nueva Sociedad 233:44–67

Programa das Nações Unidas para o Desenvolvimento (PNUD) (2009) Relatório Humano de Desenvolvimento Humano 2009, Ultrapassar Barreiras: Mobilidade e desenvolvimento humanos. Programa das Nações Unidas para o Desenvolvimento, New York

Quaglioni D (2004) La sovranità. Laterza, Bari

Rigo E (2011) Citizens despite borders: challenges to the territorial order of Europe. In: Squire V (ed) *The contested politics of mobility*: border zones and irregularity. Routledge, Abingdon

Sayad A (1998) A imigração ou os paradoxos da alteridade. Editora da Universidade de São Paulo, São Paulo

Silva SA (1995) Costurando Sonhos: Etnografia de um grupo de imigrantes bolivianos que trabalham no ramo da costura em São Paulo. Dissertação de Mestrado, PROLAM—USP

Silva CF (2008) Trabalho Informal e Redes de Subcontratação: Dinâmicas Urbanas da Indústria de Confecções em São Paulo. Mestrado em Sociologia, Universidade de São Paulo

The Binational Migration Institute (2013) A continued humanitarian crisis at the border. Undocumented border crosser deaths recorded by the Pima County Office of the Medical Examiner, 1990–2012, The University of Arizona, June

Truzzi O (2008) Redes em processos migratórios. Tempo Social, Revista de Sociologia da USP 20(1):199–218

Vertovec S (2004) Migrant transnationalism and modes of transformation. Int Migr Rev 38(3):970–1001

Waldman TC (2011) Movimentos migratórios sob a perspectiva do direito à saúde: Imigrantes bolivianas em São Paulo. Revista de Direito Sanitário, São Paulo 12(1):90–114

Waldman TC (2012) O acesso à educação escolar de imigrantes em São Paulo: a trajetória de um direito. 2012. 236f. Dissertação (Mestrado) – Faculdade de Direito, Universidade de São Paulo, São Paulo

The manufacturer's authorised representative in the EU is Springer Nature Customer Service Centre GmbH, Europaplatz 3, 69115 Heidelberg, Germany. If you have any concerns regarding our products, please contact ProductSafety@springernature.com

Printed and bound by CPI Group (UK) Ltd, Croydon, CR0 4YY
30/09/2026
02225229-0001